"ONE PERCENTER... IT ONLY MEANS THAT WE'RE THE BEST OF THE BEST—NOT ANYTHING ELSE.
THERE'S ALL KINDS OF MAGAZINE ARTICLES AND POLICE AGENCIES AND EVERYTHING
THAT TRY TO SAY THAT IT MEANS SOMETHING ELSE,
BUT ALL IT MEANS IS THAT WE'RE THE BEST OF THE BEST."
—J.W. ROCK, BANDIDOS MC

"THEY ARE THE ONE PERCENT OF SOCIETY THAT DOESN'T CONFORM;
THAT'S WHY THEY LIVE BY THEIR OWN RULES."
—SGT. STEVE TRETHEWY, ARIZONA DEPARTMENT OF PUBLIC SAFETY

"I'M ROYALLY PISSED THAT THE 1% SIGN IS ABUSED BY A LOT OF PEOPLE.
MANY OF THESE GUYS HAVE NO CLUE ABOUT THE SIGNIFICANCE AND THE VALUE OF THIS PATCH
AND THEY SHOULD NOT WEAR IT.
WOMEN SHOULD NOT WEAR IT. PULL IT OFF!"
—LOMMEL 1%, BORN TO BE WILD MC, GERMANY

THIS BOOK IS DEDICATED TO THE POSITIVE ENERGY AND POWER
OF THE MOTORCYCLE CLUB COMMUNITY.

The
ONE PERCENTER ENCYCLOPEDIA

THE WORLD OF OUTLAW MOTORCYCLE CLUBS FROM ABYSS GHOSTS TO ZOMBIES ELITE

BILL HAYES

First published in 2011 by Motorbooks, an imprint of
MBI Publishing Company, 400 First Avenue North,
Suite 300, Minneapolis, MN 55401 USA

Motorbooks titles are also available at discounts in
bulk quantity for industrial or sales-promotional use.
For details write to Special Sales Manager at MBI
Publishing Company, 400 First Avenue North, Suite
300, Minneapolis, MN 55401 USA.

To find out more about our books, visit us online at
www.motorbooks.com.

ISBN-13: 978-0-7603-4110-0

Library of Congress Cataloging-in-Publication Data

Hayes, Bill, 1950-
 The one percenter encyclopedia : from Abyss Ghosts
to Zombies Elite / Bill Hayes.
     p. cm.
 Summary: "Ever wonder how the Hells Angels got
their name? Ever wonder about that little demonic crit-
ter on the Pagan's patch? Ever wonder about the local
one-percenter motorcycle club that hangs out at the
corner bar? The One-Percenter Encyclopedia answers
these questions and many more. Featuring concise
entries that include information on founding chapters, founding dates, number of chapters, number of
members, and club biography, this book covers all the
major clubs--Hells Angels, Outlaws, Pagans, Mongols,
Vagos--as well as lesser-known clubs from around the
world."-- Provided by publisher.
 Includes bibliographical references.
 ISBN 978-0-7603-4110-0 (flexibound)
 1. Motorcycle gangs--Encyclopedias. 2. Motorcycle
clubs--Encyclopedias. I. Title.
 HV6486.H39 2011
 364.106'603--dc23

                          2011034845

Editors: Darwin Holmstrom and Steve Casper
Design Manager: Kou Lor
Designer: John Barnett, 4Eyes Design

On the back cover: © 2011 Mark Shubin

Club cut photos © 2011 Mark Shubin: pages 9, 12, 13,
23, 50, 63, 67, 70, 97, 113, 114, 117, 124, 131, 139, 149,
155, 164, 173, 185, 189, 192, 213, 214, 217, 225, and 252.

Page 256: Lindsey Robinson

Printed in China

10 9 8 7 6 5 4 3 2 1

CONTENTS

INTRODUCTION

THIS BOOK ISN'T AN EXPOSÉ; it's an *education*. It's an education that gives the devil—*and* his death's head—his due. It gives respect and recognition to the righteous god who placed the tattooed flesh and the crossed bones into the body of modern biker culture.

This "encyclopedia" is a look into that *creator*. It's an examination of the origins, histories, legends, and current keepers of the "one percenter" lineage; the powerful brotherhoods that are the outlaw motorcycle clubs.

The truth is that the clubs—especially the one percenters (a term with a colorful and subjective patchwork of definitions)—have carved a deep and open legacy into the entirety of this lifestyle and beyond; from the machines to the mystique to mainstream entertainment.

The influence on the machines is more than apparent as each new model year's factory bikes are rolled out. The showroom bobbers, choppers, and retro-rods are assembly-line mirrors of what club brothers were hammering together in beer- and oil-slick garages in the 1940s, 1950s, and 1960s.

The mystique is *the image*. Whether that means tattoos needled into non-members with deliberate familiar club-style letterings and images; or embossed dealer club-like leathers and "cuts"; or generic skull back patches with perfectly placed rockers that read everything from "Independent" to "Old School" to "John 3:16"—they are *all* essentially fast facsimiles and bolt-on forgeries of the hard patch "signatures" of the MCs.

And how much pop culture deals with the clubs? *Sons of Anarchy* and *Gangland* and all the other "daring documentaries" don't sell their high-dollar commercials and attract millions of viewers because they deal with riding clubs or H.O.G. chapters.

But along with all of this seductive love and interest, there is the fear. It's one thing to look at the big cats in the zoo; it's quite another to open the cage doors.

And the locks on those doors are getting stronger.

The signs are increasing: "NO COLORS ALLOWED"—in towns from Daytona, Florida; to Prescott, Arizona; to Alberta, Canada, at event after event, even in the once-holy sanctity of Sturgis.

But just as the *real* patches are being shut out more and more, their influence is being *enjoyed and displayed* more and more—but at an increasingly safe level. Establishments, venues, and runs openly expose some particularly icy consciences as they hawk their "officially licensed" garb that's designed to emulate the very three-piece patches they exclude and ban.

Get your thrills *looking* at those beasts but, damn it, keep those cages closed!

But in the *real* world—in the wild, natural environment where the clawing, fanged creatures are born and habitate among their own—there *are* no cages.

And that's where we're going to travel.

This book faces down confinement and chains, ripping away those NO COLORS ALLOWED decrees to allow a *genuine* look inside.

Along with this book's encyclopedic "introductions" to the worldwide population of one percenter clubs, we include sit-downs and face-to-face talks with members and associates who help make these MCs tick—*and* roar.

The clubs on the list are not only the clubs that wear the diamond 1% patch. And they're not necessarily the clubs that embrace either the one percenter file heading or the outlaw persona. But they are indeed a part of it.

There are truly legendary clubs like the Hessians with their "100% Hessians" patch.

There are the "pioneer" clubs that never considered themselves to be one percenters in the modern—especially in law enforcement's—sense of the word. But they were the ones who rutted those trails into the promised land of MCs that now cover the globe and color the daydreams and fast-fantasies of millions.

There are the three-piece-patch, hard-riding, non-AMA, non-H.O.G. clubs that just may be on that thick-skinned bubble—that bubble of public recognition that has any three-piece-patch-wearing (or any "outlaw-looking") club doing what the media says they all do. Maybe an "introduction" will educate.

There are the extinct clubs and the slightly extreme. There are the Big Five and the ones close in line.

All these clubs have a place in the one percenter outlaw world, through their individual shades of the colors in this entire lifestyle.

There are *no* law enforcement clubs on The List, nor Christian clubs, clean and sober clubs, nor any other clubs formed for any specific group-help "along life's sometimes difficult paths." These clubs certainly serve a purpose in many lives, of course. But they are not for this list.

Of all the stretching that has been done to the one percenter definition, we have at least tried to be purists in looking at what drove the pioneers to do what they did—ride motorcycles and raise a bit of good-natured hell. That was *their* group-help. From all the "old guys" that I've sat and talked and drank with down through the years, that was pretty much it—*and damn that other 99% who just don't get it!*

And, as has been mentioned, not *every* club is here on The List. Just as not every warm body is counted in the census, some holes are bound to be left here as well—though none on purpose.

No one with a clipboard and a plastic ID-on-a-lanyard went door-to-door to get this information. Most of these stats and details came from the streets—from people involved in this lifestyle all over the world. Knowing things, remembering things, knowing *someone* who knows *so-and-so* who remembers this and that. This kind of straight-up, five-card no-draw info, coupled with newspaper reports; Internet investigations; your basic forty-five years of personal on-the-road osmosis; and a lot more in-the-trenches research has gone into this List—the essentials in the one percenter encyclopedia—and well beyond.

FOREWORD

by Dr. Stephen "Skinz" Kinzey, Devils Disciples Motorcycle Club

FOR THE PAST FIFTEEN YEARS, I've been wearing a motorcycle club patch. To the average outsider, this may seem more like a badge of dishonor than one of honor.

Because of my choice to wear this *badge*, I have endured prejudice on many levels. Integrating this choice into my daily life—including my position as a university professor—presents great challenges. However, the relationships among brothers, solidified by bonds based upon honesty, commitment, pride, and a passion for motorcycling, are what make my motorcycle club—and every motorcycle club—special.

And worth it.

Bill Hayes and I have been friends for ten years. In his prior works dealing with the subject, Bill has done a wonderful job chronicling the mindset of those choosing to join a motorcycle club. In this book, Bill provides a tremendous amount of information based upon *real* knowledge. He has assimilated interviews, factual research, and his own personal experiences as a member of a motorcycle club, dealing with clubs literally from A to Z.

Without a doubt, this work will not be totally inclusive of all motorcycle clubs. The sheer number makes that impossible. And the fact that so many clubs exist should be no surprise; man has been tribal since the beginning of time.

Tribes of men, including motorcycle clubs, do their best to become totally self-reliant. They have their own rules. They enforce those rules with their own punishments. They require members to make contributions on emotional, physical, and financial levels. This requires members to have complete trust and commitment to the organization.

Commitment like this can be very demanding for all members, including the leaders. Leaders in the motorcycle club community are devoted, trustworthy, passionate, and sympathetic.

They have to be.

The best clubs are the ones that are wise enough to accentuate each member's positive strengths and overcome his weaknesses through the strengths of others. The club is an incredible model of valuable teamwork.

I hope that after reading this book, people outside the motorcycle club culture will realize that the scary part about motorcycle clubs is that they're an in-your-face representation of characteristics that everybody talks about but that no one else lives up to. Because when you are a member of an outlaw motorcycle club—whether you call yourself an outlaw, or a one percenter, or just a member—you are a living, breathing embodiment of those values.

CHAPTER 1

13 Rebels-Bunker

13 Rebels

- ♦ **ESTABLISHED:** 1937
- ♦ **PLACE OF ORIGIN:** Southern California
- ♦ **FOUNDER(S):** Ernest "Tex" Bryant and the other twelve top-seeded AMA motorcycle racers in Southern California
- ♦ **CHAPTER LOCATIONS:** Various U.S. states
- ♦ **CENTER PATCH:** Black Cat
- ♦ **MOTTO:** *Not to bully the weak. Not to fear the powerful.*
- ♦ **CLAIM TO FAME:** One of the oldest clubs in existence

13 REBELS - Yes, most alphabetic lists begin with the "numbers"—we'll do the same, just to keep things honest. And it makes the start of this encyclopedia just that much better because we are fittingly kicking things off with one of our "pioneer" clubs—a club that may not have exactly been "one percenters" by today's definitions and standards, but a club that laid the foundation for this entire lifestyle. The 13 Rebels definitely helped lay that biker base. Established in 1937, they were there when the AMA made its "statement." They were there when Hollister started the "outlaw" smoke that would flame into an eternal blaze. The 13 Rebels were one of those rebel-yell California, post–WWII clubs. They even once had "Wino Willie" Forkner among their membership. Willie went on to found the iconic club the Boozefighters and was actually kicked out of the 13 Rebels for drinking a bit too much, *even for them.*

13TH CHAPTER - Established in 1991 in Thailand. Well, we've gotten into the international clubs pretty damn fast! This Asian motorcycle club has a purpose, which is also their motto: *"To have fun, do lots of riding around Thailand and neighbouring countries, and to support each other as needed."*

✠

69ERS - A three-piece-patch, 1% motorcycle club out of New York: Brooklyn, Staten Island, and the legendary city of Troy. And this entry represents the first of another heavy denim thread that will weave and fray its way through this entire encyclopedia. That thread is the noting (or maybe even celebrating, in some circles) of the clubs in America that made it onto the 2010 edition of the "U.S. Outlaw Motorcycle Gangs" multicolored map! This map is co-sponsored and constructed by the IOMGIA (International Outlaw Motorcycle Gang Investigators Association, founded in 1974), the Rocky Mountain Information Network, the Bureau of Justice Assistance, and RISS (Regional Information Sharing Systems). Each state is filled with a neatly distributed itemization of MC names that these agencies have deemed to be Outlaw Motorcycle Gangs (OMGs)! And we'll fill you in on each and every one!

✠

888 - Established on 8/8/2008, these are the "triple-eighters" out of Malta. Besides their founding date, "888" stands for HHH, which equals "Hell, Havoc, and Hellions." Their motto: *"We are not a Sunday socializing club, Boy Scouts, or choirboys, we are straight-up bikers, riding our bikes on a daily basis. Biking for us is a daily ritual!"*

✠

ABYSS GHOSTS - A three-piece-patch club out of Tel Aviv, the first motorcycle club in Israel. Motto: *"Founded according to the heritage and customs of our ancestor bikers!"* Oy!

ACES AND EIGHTS, ACES & EIGHTS - This brings us to another of the twists in this list that will continue throughout: the "multiple clubs with the same name" slant.

One Aces and Eights apparently existed in the Riverside, New Jersey, area until they were reportedly absorbed into The Breed MC in the early 1980s. In 2007, one of the club's vintage cuts was offered on eBay (final selling price unknown).

In 2009, members of another Aces and Eights MC in Texas (reported to be a Bandidos support club) were arrested in Texas on drug sales charges that alleged an operation extending from Texas on into Arizona and California. Ironically, also in that year, members of the club were given a proclamation by Mayor C. L. Brown of Corsicana, Texas, for their work in the Texas Confederation of Clubs' (COC) "Ride Safe in Texas" program. There is an Aces & Eights MCC (a *front*-patch club) in Ireland that features the infamous poker hand on their patch, and there's another Aces & Eights MC in Canada that features a cow skull for their center patch.

AK-81 - Established in 2007 in Denmark. "AK" stands for *"Altid Klar,"* which is Danish for "Always Ready." The lowdown on this club is that they are a support club for the Red and White, but they are not *really* an MC as such—not being required to own bikes. However, they are always mentioned heavily in media discussions of MC occurrences in Scandinavia.

And the media has discussed MC occurrences in great detail over the years. From 1994 until 1997, the so-called "Great Nordic Biker Wars" created headlines and heat as club feuds and disputes—mainly between the Angels and the Bandidos—drew eyes and attention.

It was four years of chaos and crackdowns, attacks and arrests, which apparently had an auspicious origin that went back much further:

The war has its roots back in the 1970s, when Denmark's Hell's [sic] Angels, formed in the image of their idols in Oakland, California, were threatened by a rival biker gang known as Bullshit. Eleven died in that conflict before the Angels emerged victorious, keeping the peace on the streets of Denmark until 1993, when the Bandidos, an offshoot of another American gang, were first formed.
       —*The Independent* [UK], May 12, 1996

But on September 25, 1997, it was all officially over as the Red and White and the Red and Gold declared an end to "the war." Less than a month later, members of both clubs were "formally" photographed together in front of the Finnish Parliament in Helsinki. The following year, when the Bandidos' club secretary died from illness, both clubs rode in the funeral—with many having been members of the Overkill MC together years before.

✠

ALABAMA RIDERS - This motorcycle club made it onto the law enforcement map in, yes, Sweet Home Alabama!

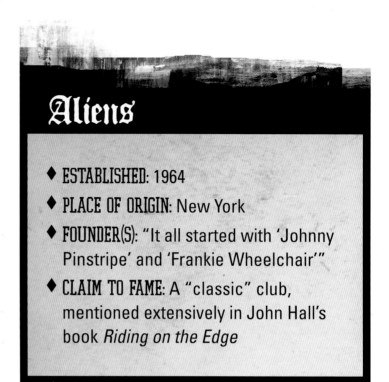

Aliens

- ♦ **ESTABLISHED:** 1964
- ♦ **PLACE OF ORIGIN:** New York
- ♦ **FOUNDER(S):** "It all started with 'Johnny Pinstripe' and 'Frankie Wheelchair'"
- ♦ **CLAIM TO FAME:** A "classic" club, mentioned extensively in John Hall's book *Riding on the Edge*

✠

ALIENS - Established in 1964 in New York. This entry represents yet another *designation* that we're going to bestow on certain clubs: that of a "classic" club—one that may not have been around as early as the "pioneer" clubs, but one that was riding and partying during one of the seminal eras of the biker culture, like the 1960s. The Aliens fit that "classic" brand. A perfect example of the Aliens' "classic" status can be seen in a passage from John Hall's vintage-loving book about the early days of the Pagans MC, *Riding on the Edge: A Motorcycle Outlaw's Tale*:

The Brooklyn Aliens were the most colorful club, and that's where it all started with Johnny Pinstripe and Frankie Wheelchair. Pinstripe owned a shop in Bay Ridge, where he did the best custom paint jobs in New York. That was back in the days when it was all done with a brush by hand, so that's how he got his name... The Bronx was the biggest Alien club, and it was also the baddest. The guys had been together for 20 years...The street gang became a car club, and the final incarnation was the Bronx Aliens Outlaw Motorcycle Gang. Now some bikers are offended by the word gang. *They prefer* club *instead. To us, back in those days, a club was always a place where rich bastards went to play golf or bridge. But a gang, now that was a bunch of blue-collar guys hanging out drinking beer in a garage with a dirt floor.*

Today, an Aliens MC exists in Helsinki, Finland, with a very traditional "Grey" for a center patch.

☩

ALII'S - The Alii MC was one of just eleven motor-cycle clubs (an "Ocean's Eleven" of sorts) to make the law enforcement map in the Hawaiian Islands! They make the news now and then, but a while back they were actually the subject of a newspaper retraction during the somber time of the death of their "P":

The Alii's of Hawaii, Maui Chapter, would like to correct and clarify the photo caption in the Dec. 11 issue of The Maui News. *Maui Chapter President Nelson Sakamoto of the Alii's of Hawaii was not in a casket in the hearse, but in an urn on one of his motorcycles.*

☩

ALKY-HAULERS - Established in 1989 in San Mateo, California. They specifically note that they are *"a club, not a gang"* and are built on *"brotherhood and loyalty."*

☩

AMERICAN IRON - Established in 2002 in Denver, Colorado. They are considered the "first support

club for the Sons of Silence." (This is our first mention of one of the clubs in the Big Five. In alphabetic order: Bandidos, Hells Angels, Outlaws, Pagans, Sons of Silence.)

☩

American Steel

- ◆ **ESTABLISHED:** 1983
- ◆ **PLACE OF ORIGIN:** Okinawa, Japan
- ◆ **FOUNDER(S):** U.S. military and government civilians stationed in Japan
- ◆ **CHAPTER LOCATIONS:** Japan, Philippines, United States
- ◆ **CLAIM TO FAME:** A club that expanded from East to West

AMERICAN STEEL - Established in 1983 on the island of Okinawa, Japan. The original members were U.S. government civilians and active-duty military riding U.S.-made bikes. Their official history states, *"As the years passed, these ASMC Brothers moved to other assignments in different continents and different countries. This was the seed from which American Steel MC has grown, expanded, and spread throughout the world."* This is our first club, alphabetically, to expand from East to West, now with chapters in the U.S., Japan, and the Philippines.

☩

AMIGOS - This friendly Texas-based Bandidos support club made it onto the law enforcement map— in *El Estado de la Estrella Solitaria*, of course. An Amigos MC also made the map in California.

⊹

AMONS - This motorcycle club out of Contra Costa in Northern California also made the law enforcement map out in the Golden State!

⊹

ANARCHY BIKERS - This is our first motorcycle club (alphabetically) from Canada. Again, we have the beginnings of some continuing "threads." We will be mentioning a *lot* of Canuck motorcycle clubs. The country of Canada and its provinces is right up there with the Australia, New Zealand, and "Great Nordic" areas in having a ton of clubs and a ton of activity and interaction among them. Indicative of that is this club's—Anarchy Bikers—mention on one of the strangest (and never-ending) "anti-gang" websites in the universe, as an associate club of the HAMC (Hells Angels Motorcycle Club) in Canada. (I'm not going to divulge the site—it's easy enough to find, but I really don't want to give it much love. It even includes Ollie North as being tied into things, in some way or another. It's a lot of Area-51-aluminum-foil-hat kind of stuff, but it does catalog many of the motorcycle clubs of the north that were involved in one form or another with Canada's motorcycle organization conflicts.)

⊹

ANATOLIAN TIGERS - A diamond-patch 1% club out of Turkey. And their center patch isn't a regular ol' tiger—it's a saber-toothed.

ANCIENT IRON - The originator of the West Coast "Bike Blessing," the Ancient Iron Motorcycle Club is based in Santa Clara County, California. They're not one percenters in the purest sense, but true preservers of an important part of the lifestyle's history: ancient iron.

⊹

APOCALYPSE - Established in 2004 in Sonderborg, Denmark. While they say they are not "an outlaw club," Apocalypse adheres to standard guest-hangaround-prospect-member protocol, as well as no women members. Motto: *"The brotherhood of Apocalypse MC values their brothers more than the bikes."*

⊹

APOSTLE OF NIGHT - Our first Ruski riders, a three-piece-patch-wearing, Outlaws MC support club.

⊹

ARA TOA WHANAU - One more first—again, at least alphabetically—signifying the beginning of a long list of strong and prominent motorcycle clubs Down Under. The Australian/New Zealand motorcycle club culture is potent down there, to say the least! Ara Toa Whanau MC is the first of many. And, like the "U.S. Outlaw Motorcycle Gangs" map listing, the Aussie authorities and media have put together their own lists of the "most dangerous motorcycle gangs" in Australia and New Zealand. Ara Toa Whanau, based in Palmerston North, Horowhenua, and Heretaunga, has made those lists—and they also make the news. In November 2010, *The Marlborough Express* reported:
Ara Toa Whanau MC gang members were stopped by police in a routine check as they left

the Interislander ferry on their motorcycles in Picton yesterday.

Senior Sergeant Peter Payne, of Picton, said police were tipped off about the arrival by the gang members, who hail from Palmerston North, Horowhenua and Heretaunga, in Picton. Licenses, registrations and warrants of fitness were checked.

There were no arrests, Mr. Payne said.

It was normal procedure to stop gang members coming off the ferry, he said.

Constable Michelle Stagg, of Blenheim, said more checks were likely this week as gang members travelled to the Burt Munro Challenge motorcycle event being held in Southland from November 24 to 28.

Some of the motorcyclists took photos of their friends being spoken to by police, and joked and laughed with the police as the checks were made.

⊹

Heavy Duty is the perfect name for Australia's most popular Harley-Davidson magazine—a thick, 150-page bimonthly Aussie organ of biker culture. Everything about the motorcycle lifestyle is heavy duty down under. Say "G'day" to the magazine's associate and technical editor, Doc Robinson, as he explains about outlaws in the outback:

THE ONE PERCENTER DOWN UNDER
By Doc Robinson

Australia has a land mass comparable to the lower forty-eight states of the United States, with year around riding made enjoyable by mild weather conditions. The main city of Sydney has a climate similar to Los Angeles. While the north of the country is tropical, even the southernmost section almost never experiences snow except in the mountains, so motorcycling has always been popular down under, virtually from day one, with both Harley-Davidsons and Indians being imported in relatively large numbers.

Australian culture has always been influenced by a combination of its British heritage and the influence of American movies, television shows, and pop songs. Movies from *The Wild One* to *Easy Rider* to *Wild Hogs* have all contributed to the psyche of Australian motorcyclists.

For quite some years, however, the Australian outlaw culture was distinctive, with movies like the Australian-produced *Stone* (1974) being a more or less true-to-life portrayal of the scene in the late 1960s and early 1970s, when the bikes of choice rarely included Harley-Davidsons, but rather Kawasakis and Hondas.

The last forty years have seen a change in the makeup of clubs from less formal hangaround types of associations to the adoption of formal one-percenter rules and regulations. This is particularly so with international clubs, many of whom are now represented in greater or lesser numbers across the country. In that time, many of the dozens of clubs that were unique to Australia have patched over to some of the larger international clubs—the Darwin-based Blonks MC becoming Hells Angels, for example. Australian crime intelligence recently floated an estimate that from a total population of just under twenty-four million citizens, there are probably around 3,500 fully-patched motorcycle club members representing some thirty-nine clubs.

As in other parts of the world, an ongoing battle is fought between the one-percenter clubs—whose members are referred to as "bikies"—and the forces of law and order, especially around election time. South Australian Premier Mike Rann, who was then Opposition leader, introduced a

macho law-and-order campaign by the Labor party in the lead-up to the 2002 election and pledged to bulldoze the outlaw club fortresses, saying, "We are not just dealing with meatheads on motorbikes; we are dealing with basically the foot soldiers of organized crime." It is now three election victories later, and not a single fortress has been demolished under Rann's leadership. At least eight major complexes still stand in South Australia, including those of the Hells Angels, Descendants, Finks, Gypsy Jokers, and Rebels. And there are no current plans to bulldoze any.

However, Rann's legislation in South Australia was touted to be "the world's toughest laws to combat criminal motorcycle gangs." This landmark Serious and Organised Crime legislation is designed to "disrupt and dismantle criminal bikie gangs and prevent them from carrying out their illegal activities in South Australia." Unfortunately for the government, it has not withstood legal challenges by the clubs at this time. In a big "me too" rush, other states pushed through anti-bikie legislation, which has also stalled because of legal challenges.

Unfortunately, at times, one-percenter clubs can be their own worst enemies, such as with the much publicized Milperra Massacre, a firearm battle between rival motorcycle club members on September 2 (Father's Day), 1984, in Milperra, a southwestern suburb of Sydney. Seven people were killed: six motorcycle club members and a fourteen-year old female bystander. And more recently, the bashing death at Sydney airport in early 2009 involving two one-percenter clubs. These and a number of other incidents across the country have resulted in somewhat of a swing in public sympathy away from the clubs.

Yet despite this, the "anti-bikie" legislation is widely seen as extremely flawed, with opposition coming from many sources including the ultra-conservative Law Society presidents of several states and even the South Australian police commissioner, Mal Hyde, who said earlier this year that "Bikies have cultivated an image of committing more crime than they actually do, and there is a great deal of public concern that may not necessarily match the serious crime that they are committing."

How the anti-bikie legislation pans out in the long run is yet to be determined. But it would be a brave person to predict the demise of the one-percenter clubs down under. Australia began as a convict colony and an anti-establishment, anti-authority streak has always been a part of the Aussie society. This is not going to go away any time soon. Club members with whom I spoke recently say there has been an increase, not a reduction, in prospective members across the country. Don't wave goodbye to

ARAWYNS - This club out of Louisiana made some news of their own in 2010. In April of that year, the Associated Press ran this report:

BATON ROUGE, La. (AP) — A decorated soldier responsible for anti-terrorism efforts of the Louisiana Army National Guard is on trial in federal court for allegedly making false statements to a federal agent investigating the Bandidos motorcycle gang.

New Orleans attorney Ralph S. Whalen Jr., who is representing First Sgt. William B. "Benny" Creel, of Franklinton, told jurors Monday that his client made statements that "were not correct" but added that "this is not a common street criminal."

Assistant U.S. Attorney Joseph E. Blackwell says Creel is a member of the Arawyns Motorcycle Club, made up of law enforcement officers and military members. He says federal and state investigators are trying to identify people who are exposing law enforcement sources to the Bandidos.

The Bandidos, the LA Riders and the Arawyns are under investigation by the U.S. Bureau of Alcohol, Tobacco, Firearms and Explosives and Louisiana State Police for narcotics and firearms trafficking.

Raymond Tullier, a former Bandidos gang member, testified that Creel deliberately warned the gang that federal investigators would be present at a November bike rally in Bogalusa.

The trial is before U.S. District Judge Frank Polozola. Jurors were expected to begin deliberations on Tuesday.

ASA

- ♦ **ESTABLISHED:** Unknown
- ♦ **PLACE OF ORIGIN:** Scandinavia
- ♦ **FOUNDER(S):** Unknown
- ♦ **CHAPTER LOCATIONS:** Outside the prison walls
- ♦ **CLAIM TO FAME:** Joined with Brotherhood MC members released from prison and became part of the Great Nordic Biker Wars

ASA - The ASA was right there in the middle of the "Great Nordic" activity. In 1995 they allegedly joined up with Brotherhood MC members who had been released from prison. The Brotherhood had been a group inside, and now the first Brotherhood chapter was founded outside. At that point, a very strange chapter of the Great Nordic Biker Wars rapidly opened. Now that there was a Brotherhood outside the prison walls, Brotherhood members still inside began to use the name "Wolfpack."

According to authorities, "during the period from 1996 to 1998 several Brotherhood members in Stockholm were arrested and convicted for various crimes such as extortion, illegal possession of firearms, and abduction."

In January 1998, Brotherhood founder Danny Fitzpatrick was released from Hall prison. Again, according to authorities: "During his celebration party a defector from the club was shot in the leg and another man received an axe blow to the head."

Asgard

- ◆ **ESTABLISHED:** 1979
- ◆ **PLACE OF ORIGIN:** Biloxi, Mississippi
- ◆ **FOUNDER(S):** Unknown
- ◆ **CHAPTER LOCATIONS:** 8 chapters in Mississippi
- ◆ **CENTER PATCH:** A Viking with snakes
- ◆ **MOTTO:** *My Word, My Honor*

ASGARD - Established in 1979 in Biloxi, Mississippi. And they made the law enforcement map in the Magnolia State. They're Southern boys with a Norse influence (their patch has a Viking and snakes), with a motto: *"My Word, My Honor."* They look at the biker lifestyle as having a lot in common with the Vikings—much like Dave Nichols did in his book *One Percenter: The Legend of the Outlaw Biker*—with the Norse influence representing "the sense of adventure, freedom, and enjoyment of life that all the Vikings displayed and the close brotherhood they shared."

✠

AVENGERS - The Avengers name and the span of the club is easily one of those "classic" cases in the motorcycle club world. The club made the law enforcement map in Ohio and next door in West Virginia. But much of the history stems from Michigan; an obituary circulated in 2007 for Ron "Big Ron" Swalwell from Michigan, crediting him for being one of the "founding members of the Avengers Motorcycle Club."

And in 2010, the *Examiner* (in Washington, D.C.) relived an anniversary of sorts—a little Avengers "history" that occurred many years ago on the East Coast. The newspaper piece includes some of that hype that was thrown around a lot back in the day. Was this little mix-up *really* up there with the Civil War?

On this day, June 14, in 1966, a motorcycle gang shoot out between the Maryland-based Pagans and the local Avengers rocked a shopping center in Arlington [Virginia], in what police then called the worst violence in the county since the Civil War.

The Avengers resented the Pagans, a jacket-wearing motorcycle gang that was trying to become an East Coast model of the Hell's [sic] Angels. The outfit was started in Prince George's County by Lou Dobkins, a biochemist at the National Institute of Health, who was into British Triumph bikes.

The Pagans wore denim vests depicting the Norse fire-giant Surt wielding a flaming sword. The Avengers' colors featured a big Maltese cross and a skull.

At a parking lot at Lee Highway and Harrison, the Pagans ambushed the Avengers, who returned fire. Some 100 shots rang out.

Only one youth was injured. Sixteen were arrested and a cache of bolt-action single shot weapons and pistols were confiscated.

Arlington County Police Chief William G. Fawver said it was "the most serious single outbreak of mass violence this county has ever seen."

✠

AVIATORS - Established in 1988. A three-piece-patch club out of South County, Norway.

✠

Bacchus

- ◆ **ESTABLISHED:** Unknown
- ◆ **PLACE OF ORIGIN:** Nova Scotia
- ◆ **FOUNDER(S):** Unknown
- ◆ **CHAPTER LOCATIONS:** Nova Scotia
- ◆ **CENTER PATCH:** Skull-headed depiction of Bacchus, the god of wine and intoxication
- ◆ **CLAIM TO FAME:** Allegedly introduced 1%ers back into Nova Scotia
- ◆ **CLUB ASSOCIATIONS:** Associate club of the Hells Angels

BACCHUS - Another of the Canadian clubs included on that site we described on page 16 as one of the "strangest (and never-ending) 'anti-gang' websites in the universe," as an "associate club of the HAMC" in Canada. But beyond that little distinction, the MC really has been a major player in much of that activity in the Great North.

And it has made the news. In January 2010, the CBC reported in a frenzy of one percent and outlaw oratory:

Eight members of the East Coast Riders were "patched over" by the Bacchus motorcycle club Saturday night at the Bacchus main clubhouse in Albert County, N.B.

The new "1%" crest hasn't been seen in Nova Scotia since the Hells Angels chapter folded in 2003 after a series of police raids that put most of its members in prison.

Insp. Greg Laturnus, with the RCMP Intelligence Unit, said the 1% designation is an open claim of outlaw status among bike gangs.

"We have a national strategy to combat outlaw motorcycle gangs, and certainly the Bacchus motorcycle club is considered an outlaw motorcycle gang," Laturnus told CBC News.

But Paul Fowler, a new Bacchus Nova Scotia club member, disputes that, saying members have families and jobs.

"We are far from organized. And we're not a crime group neither," said Fowler.

"In our mind, the true meaning of the 1% is that we are the one per cent that doesn't fit in with the other 99 per cent of society, for whatever reason. You know, we like to do things our own way. We like to hang out together, ride motorcycles and party."

Canadaeast news service had a bit to add:

...One per cent clubs and their members are at the top of the outlaw biker hierarchy and are linked to organized crime.

They can be identified by a diamond patch with "1 per cent" embroidered on it.

The Canadian Security Intelligence Service (CSIS) flags the group [Bacchus MC] as an "Outlaw Motorcycle Club" listed among far more notorious gangs such as the Hells Angels, The Bandidos, The Pagans and The Outlaws.

"Any time that any organization expands and takes on greater jurisdiction or territory they become a more complicated group for us to monitor," Noble said. "And there is then the propensity that they become more organized in any criminal activity they could be involved in.

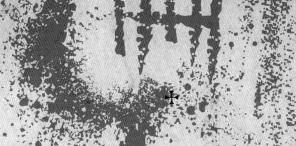

"Traditionally the Bacchus has been a one chapter club until recently, but from intelligence and information we have received they are also courting other groups around the Maritimes to join in as chapters of the Bacchus."

Noble said New Brunswick RCMP officers are working closely with provincial law enforcement partners to ensure the gang is closely monitored.

"We will investigate if we notice any criminality," he said.

MacQueen said the potential for gang violence is greater in what is uncharted Nova Scotia territory.

"The fact that the Bacchus are now moving in to say 'this is our area, we are not going to give it up easily and don't bother coming to take it from us' causes concern," MacQueen said. "Because if a rival group does come in here I think the Bacchus Nova Scotia is going to have to take a stand they didn't have to before.

"By changing their patch and putting 'Nova Scotia' they now have to back it up."

MacQueen said police are intensely watching the developments.

"We got rid of the Hells Angels in 2003 and we have been successful in keeping rival groups out of here up until this point," he said. "We consider the Bacchus a criminal group—their members have been involved in drug trafficking, weapons and violent offences for a long time.

"We want to let them know that we're not welcoming them here, we consider them a criminal group and we are going to make it uncomfortable for them to exist."

BAD ATTITUDE CREW - A Bandidos support club out of Finland with chapters in Lohja and Helsinki.

✜

BAD SEVEN - A heavy-duty club in Germany and throughout Europe. This is another of our firsts: a support club for one of the big-league motorcycle clubs in Europe. Bad Seven is "The official support club for Gremium MC world." As we will see later, Gremium is indeed one of the Euro behemoths.

✜

BALTIMORE RAMBLERS - Another of our "pioneer" clubs. The Baltimore Ramblers Motorcycle Club is one of the oldest American Motorcyclist Association clubs, having become a Charter Member in 1929.

✜

BANDALEROS - A couple of motorcycle clubs with this name: One, a Bandidos support club in the Southwest, U.S. A second is a 1%, three-piece patch motorcycle club in Spain.

✜

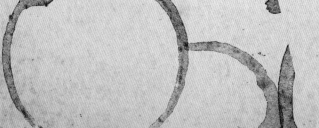

Bandidos

- ♦ **ESTABLISHED:** 1966
- ♦ **PLACE OF ORIGIN:** Texas
- ♦ **FOUNDER(S):** Marine Vietnam vet Don Chambers
- ♦ **CHAPTER LOCATIONS:** Worldwide
- ♦ **CLUB COLORS:** Red & Gold
- ♦ **CENTER PATCH:** The "Fat Mexican"
- ♦ **CLAIM TO FAME:** One of the Big Five
- ♦ **CLUB ASSOCIATIONS:** Has support clubs worldwide

BANDIDOS - Our *alphabetic* first of the "Big Five." The mark of the Big Five beast is meted out in a few different ways—with law enforcement being the first to begin this kind of penal pigeonholing. Their "leader board" was based on a lot of factors: club size, international influence, law enforcement's carefully analyzed potential for mayhem and public carnage, longevity, and probably several other types of crime-criteria that are known only to those with badges and four-door Ford Crown Victorias.

But common bikerdom also caught on to looking at a "list" of the most powerful, most popular, and most likely to succeed; and the leader board idea stuck. Evidently, everyone loves "ratings"—from VH1's "Worst 100 One-Hit Wonders" to college football's always-argued-about BCS.

The Big Five list began—and remained for many years—as the *Big Four*. Again, in alphabetic order, the Big Four were the Bandidos, the Hells Angels, the Outlaws, and the Pagans. With growth and other factors in motion, the Sons of Silence has rounded out the fab five over the last several years.

As we look at each, we're going to try to not get mired in redundancy. A lot of stuff has been written and produced about these motorcycle clubs. There are library shelves of books that cover many different shades of Red and White throughout the world, and the Red and Gold are becoming frequent literary subjects as well. For a variety of reasons the Outlaws and Pagans have not been subject to as much media madness—but it's there. And I'm sure it's only a matter of time before pages will turn up about the Sons as well. *Gangland* and other cable empires have given a large share of TV time to *probing* these clubs.

So what we are going to do is give you the obligatory nuts and bolts of these clubs, applying a few chrome billet washers here and there, dressing things up in a way becoming of these chart-toppers.

Established on March 4, 1966, the Bandidos were founded by Marine Vietnam vet Don Chambers (hence the red and gold colors). Texas was home, but the exact city of origin ranges from San Leon to Houston to Galveston to San Antonio, depending on the source.

Chambers was convicted of murder in Texas in 1972. He was given a life sentence, but was paroled in 1983. He remained in Texas after his release, but in a non-club life. He died on July 18, 1999.

The biker world is not without its own urban legends and it seems that the theory that the Bandidos center patch was patterned after the "Frito Bandito" was a bit of a motorcycle misnomer—the corn-chip cartoon didn't hit the commercial airwaves until 1968. It appears that Chambers' "Fat Mexican" creation pulled out his machete first.

Like most of the Big Five, the Bandidos are worldwide. And that global reach has been celebrated—or at least dissected—in a few books over recent years. Authors Edward Winterhalder and Alex Caine have plunged their hands deep into the exposé pot. But on the positive side of things, *The Story of Bandidos Motorcycle Club Europe*—"how it all started in 1989 in Marseille"—is an hour-plus

DVD of the club's everyday activities in Europe as told by the members themselves.

And support clubs for the Bandidos are *numeroso*, *numbreux*, und *zahlreich* in the EU.

One branch of the Bandidos that proves that motorcycle clubs are still primarily formed around the concept of actually riding a motorcycle is their drag racing team. It's a serious competitive force that makes the racing rounds. Even their support clubs, like the Amigos MC, are into the racing end of motorcycle club life.

The crusade for bikers' rights has also come to the Bandidos in the person of Texas Bandido Gimmy Jimmy. Jimmy has become a powerful and tireless national voice of activism. He has spearheaded the Defenders political action organization, a high-caliber weapon in the constant fight to keep this lifestyle truly free.

BANSHEES - The Banshees M.C.N.O.L.A. was established in New Orleans in 1966, earning it that "classic" title. They have a pretty straight-ahead motto: *We kiss no ass!*

Okay! And they made the law enforcement map in Louisiana. They expanded into Fürth, Germany, in 1989.

✠

BARBARIAN - An HAMC Support Club out of the Ukraine. One of the *"official support clubs of the 81 world"*—many of which we will see on our list.

✠

BARBARIAN STORMTROOPER - Another of the motorcycle clubs that make all "the lists" in New Zealand.

✠

BARBARIANS - It may be slightly barbaric, but several clubs have chewed off a piece of this name:

One is a full one percent motorcycle club out of Britain (not to be confused with Pennsylvania's Barbarians MC, *"the oldest sport bike club in Philly!"*) Barbarians in West Virginia made it onto the law enforcement map in the Mountain State and they also made it into the West Virginia Drug Threat Assessment report for 2003:

> *Outlaw motorcycle gangs (OMGs) such as Barbarians and Pagans also transport and distribute illicit drugs throughout the state. Out-of-state African-American, Jamaican, and Mexican criminal groups, among others, as well as street gangs such as Bloods also transport and distribute drugs in the state, although to a lesser extent.*

The Canadian Barbarians MC was started in Calgary, Alberta, Canada in 1973. They describe themselves as an *"old skool, no bullshit club."*

There is *yet another* three-piece-patch Barbarians in Austria.

Barhoppers

- **ESTABLISHED:** 1962
- **PLACE OF ORIGIN:** Merced, California
- **FOUNDER(S):** Manuel Victor
- **CHAPTER LOCATIONS:** California
- **CLAIM TO FAME:** Mentioned by the History Channel as one of the "gangs" in Merced County, to which two out of every hundred people in the county belong.
- **CLUB ASSOCIATIONS:** There is a now a Manuel Victor Memorial MC

Sundowners and Barons are the notable OMGs in Utah. Both are linked to the production and distribution of methamphetamine as well as the distribution of other drugs, but to a lesser extent. Law enforcement also has linked the OMGs to credit card fraud, gambling, vehicle theft, prostitution operations, and assault. A truce between the two gangs has been in effect for at least 4 years. Barons are closely affiliated with the Brothers Speed OMG in Idaho, and Sundowners are linked to Hells Angels.

But the Barons Motorcycle Club was also a motorcycle club born in St. Cloud, Minnesota, "sometime in the mid-1950s" as an AMA-sanctioned club. After what the club calls a "difference of opinion," the club turned "outlaw." With some of the original members entering the military, the Barons were soon spread around the world. Their Korean chapter is very much still alive and well!

✠

BARHOPPERS - The Barhoppers were mentioned by the History Channel in a very mathematically stimulating statistic: *"Two out of every one hundred people in Merced County are gang members."* And, yep, they list the Barhoppers as a "motorcycle gang" there (although the club didn't make the 2010 law enforcement map!). The founding of the Barhoppers is credited to the late Manuel Victor—1928–1982. Victor is said to have begun the club in 1962.

✠

BARONS - The Barons made the law enforcement map in Utah and their origin has also been listed as Utah by the media in the Beehive State.

The Barons have also attracted the attention of the International Outlaw Motorcycle Gang Investigators Association (the clever cartographers behind that colorful law enforcement map):

BASTARDS - A trio of Bastards here:

One, established in 2002, in Germany: *"We wear red and black and support no one."*

There's an HAMC support club in Bakersfield, California.

There are also Bastards in Sweden.

✠

BATS - Established in 1982, a diamond-patch MC hanging around in Austria.

✠

✛

BAY RIDERS - This San Francisco Bay–area HAMC supporter club made it onto the law enforcement map in Cali. They've also made it into a couple of somewhat harsh news reports up in the Bay Area's *SF Weekly*:

Three supposed members of the Bay Riders, a motorcycle club that police say is an affiliate of the Hells Angels, have been charged with assault and gang enhancements after one allegedly stabbed a victim during a brawl on Broadway Street in December.

This is the first San Francisco case to bring gang charges against members of the Bay Riders, a self-proclaimed club of "motorcycle enthusiasts" which formed after the shooting death of Mark "Papa" Guardado, the president of the Hells Angels San Francisco chapter in September 2008. Police say the Riders claim at least 30 members in the city, North Bay and the Peninsula, while keeping a clubhouse on 10th Street in SoMa. One of the late Guardado's sons, Dominic, told SF Weekly *both he and his brother are Riders members in November, yet wouldn't talk about any affiliation with the Hells Angels. "We're all about the community," he said. "We're not around to intimidate people. We're motorcycle enthusiasts."*

That was in 2010. They also had more than fifteen minutes of fame in 2009:

On any Thursday night, dozens of dudes on Harleys descend on a 10th Street SOMA clubhouse painted red and black. Their leather vests and jackets are emblazoned with diabolic skulls in fedoras and the words "Bay Riders." The club is a registered nonprofit, and was recently on the TV news for donating $1,000 to foster kids. But police don't buy the philanthropic Santa on wheels bit. They say the Riders have many characteristics of an outlaw motorcycle gang, and operate under the control of the Hells Angels.

Silver says there are at least 30 Bay Riders members in San Francisco, the North Bay, and the Peninsula. They dock their bikes at hangouts in the Excelsior, SOMA, Dogpatch, and the Embarcadero, and have been advertising their first anniversary motorcycle run on Nov. 8. "To keep the Mongols out of the city, the Bay Riders appeared like wildfire," he says. "A huge new group was formed to increase the number of allied personnel."

The Riders first appeared on the cops' radar at their "Break Out Party" one year ago at Jelly's club on Pier 50, which ended in gunfire. The club's manager said he heard a car had driven up to the club, "ghost ridding [sic], wilding out, driving out of control," according to the police report. Someone opened fire on the vehicle and hit the woman passenger in the shoulder. She survived, and police have made no arrests in the case.

✛

BEDOUINS - A three-piece-patch club out of St. Petersburg, Russia. The informal hymn of Bedouins is the Guns N' Roses epic, "Riad N' the Bedouins."

✛

BIKERS BROTHERHOOD - A straight-ahead 1% diamond-patch club out of Indonesia.

✛

BIKER SNAKES - Established in 1999, this motorcycle club (with an incredibly cool name) slithered out of Denmark.

✠

BLACK BARONS - A motorcycle club out of South Africa. Founded by what they call their "first 5."

✠

BLACK CATTLE - Established in 1995, in Turnov, Czech Republic. HAMC supporters.

✠

Black Devils

- ◆ **ESTABLISHED:** 1969
- ◆ **PLACE OF ORIGIN:** Wiesbaden, Germany
- ◆ **FOUNDER(S):** Native Germans (not U.S. expats!)
- ◆ **CHAPTER LOCATIONS:** Germany, Italy
- ◆ **CENTER PATCH:** Varies by chapter; all variations of devil heads, horns, and skulls

BLACK DEVILS - Established in 1969 in Wiesbaden, Germany, in 1969. "Unlike a lot of other MCs which were founded by NATO soldiers in the old continent," the club says of their history, "the Black Devils MC had a typically German identity and only after some years the family was joined by foreign members among which were American soldiers…the Club has changed and grown having, nowadays, several chapters in Italian regions like Emilia Romagna, Marche, Abruzzo, Trentino, and Puglia. On the contrary, what has never changed for more than forty years are the original ideals such as brotherhood, sincerity, reciprocal trust and deep bond of friendship among the Club members, ideals which still lead the philosophy and all the activities of the club."

✠

BLACK DRAGONS - Established in 2001 as the Outcast MC. In 2004, they became the Desperados. In 2007, they became Black Dragons. In 2010, they absorbed The Savages. This is a busy club!

BLACK HAWKS - Established in 1938. A "pioneer" club, but this time out of Canada. The club discusses some of its history:

The club became well known for our charitable nature with such events as Toy runs, Food drives and the famous "Blood Run", the first of its kind that also un-nerved the community until they learned that it was our Club Members donating blood to the Red Cross. In 1939 and 1940 our members were actively sought out by Military recruiters for their expertise on motorcycles to be used as couriers and dispatch riders during the Second World War…With the strong resurgence in the sport of motorcycling in recent years, we feel it is our responsibility to pass on the experience and knowledge that has been accumulated by our older members through the years. This guidance will provide the newer members with a safe, organized and exciting riding experience, allowing them to enjoy to the fullest, the greatest sport of them all—Motorcycling.

There is also a Black Hawks MC in Belgium, established in 1987.

BLACKHEADS - Established in 1991 in Helsinki, Finland, by seven former Overkill MC members. In 1999, the Frogs MC joined. Members from other clubs followed—clubs like Götti MC, Perkele MC, Mosa's, Tonocks MC, Wääkcystrasen's. And they've got a great (and very practical) motto: *"Party Hard, but do not spill around!"*

BLACK IRON - A full-on 1% diamond-patch club out of Brazil.

BLACK JOKERS - A three-piece-patch Outlaws MC "affiliate" MC out of Belgium.

Black Pistons

- ♦ ESTABLISHED: 2002
- ♦ PLACE OF ORIGIN: Germany
- ♦ CHAPTER LOCATIONS: Europe, U.S., Japan, Philippines, Australia
- ♦ CLUB COLORS: Black and White
- ♦ CENTER PATCH: Crossed pistons
- ♦ CLUB ASSOCIATIONS: The main support club for the Outlaws MC

BLACK PISTONS - Established in 2002, interestingly enough in Germany. While considered to be the main support club for the Outlaws MC, the Black Pistons have become a huge club on their own, with chapters in the U.S., throughout Europe, and reportedly in Japan, the Philippines, and Australia. And, oh yes, they've made pretty much all of the "maps" and "lists" that the OMC has made as well!

✠

BLACK POWER - Now we go back Down Under. Black Power makes all those lists in New Zealand. According to the New Zealand Police: "There are numerous gangs in New Zealand, of varying criminality, organisation and ethnicity. The three most prominent New Zealand gangs are Black Power (not related to the African-American movement); the Mongrel Mob, and the Nomads."

And according to the book *Gangs* by Ross Kemp, New Zealand has more gangs per head than any other country in the world, with about seventy major gangs and over 4,000 patched members in a population of about 4,000,000 people.

✠

BLACK RAIN - A Bandidos support club out of Germany.

✠

BLACK RAVEN CREW - From Norway, this is another of the "Black 7" support clubs—backers of the giant Gremium MC in Germany: "We don't support other MCs but we respect other MCs that give us the same respect!"

✠

BLACK RHINOS - A Scandinavian Bandidos support club.

✠

BLACK ROSES - Established in 1986, a three-piece-patch motorcycle club in Germany.

✠

BLACK SHADOWS - A three-piece-patch club out of the Czech Republic. HAMC supporters.

✠

✠

BLACK SHEEP - There are a couple of Black Sheep roaming around:

One is out of Canton, Texas, famous for their "Shitcrew"—a crew/patch that recognizes members who have shown "extra effort and involvement."

Another is a pretty big Christian club with chapters throughout America. (My guess is that *they* don't have a "shitcrew"!)

Then there's a "small private motorcycle riding club based out of Hamilton, Ontario, founded in June of 2005 with members in England, the United States, and Canada…We are not a 1%-er club nor do we want to be one but we respect all clubs. We aren't exactly a nice family-oriented bunch either. We're a little 'in yer face' with a bit of attitude and don't take any shit! We don't always ride within the posted speed limits! We like to get where we're going quick!"

And in Pattaya, Thailand, there is a Black Sheep MC, established in 2009 by "Hellboy" and "Frog" with a clubhouse called "Titty Twister" on the "dark side of Pattaya."

There are Black Sheep in three-piece patches in the Netherlands, established in 2008, and Black Sheep grazing in Australia and Brazil.

✠

BLACK UHLANS - Another from Down Under. The Black Uhlans make all the lists. In 2002 they were involved in a very strange lawsuit, attempting to retain ownership of their clubhouse. Aussie reporter, Neil Mercer explained—sort of:

The Equity division of the NSW Supreme Court is not usually where you hear evidence about a bloke called Knuckles.

Equity, after all, is a gentlemanly precinct—some might even say dull.

Not this week, or at least not in court 8B, where bearded, ponytailed and tattooed members of the Black Uhlans motorcycle club—police would say "gang"—were filing in and out of the witness box.

There was the president of the Sydney chapter, Mark Florence, and a former president, Steven Gioffre. Present—sadly in name only—was John "Knuckles" Damoulakis.

In an unusual action, Black Uhlans Incorporated is suing the NSW Crime Commission and the State of NSW in a bid to gain ownership of the Peakhurst clubhouse where members have been gathering every Wednesday night since 1984.

The proceedings date back to the 1993 arrest on drug charges of Black Uhlans member Alan Reardon, better known to his mates as Jack Wilson.

At the time he was pinched, the clubhouse and two other factory units in Stanley Street, Peakhurst, were in his name.

Justice Joseph Campbell heard that Mr. Reardon had bought the property in 1991 for $400,000 after obtaining a $227,500 mortgage from Citibank.

When Mr. Reardon was jailed in 1996 for manufacturing large commercial quantities of amphetamines, the Crime Commission pounced and the property was forfeited to the Crown under the Criminal Assets Recovery Act.

But Julian Sexton, SC, for the Black Uhlans, told the court that Mr. Reardon was in fact a nominee and held the premises in trust for the club. His name was on the title because, at the time, he was the only person who owned property and held down a job, and thus had a chance of obtaining a loan.

Mr. Sexton said there was objective evidence from bank accounts that the Black Uhlans had put forward "substantial funds" for the purchase as well as stamp duty and fees.

Mr. Florence said a special $1000 levy had been paid by members when "it became apparent we didn't have enough money to purchase the property." Mr. Gioffre said he had arranged meetings with solicitor Justin Hill to discuss the purchase.

Other members, including "Knuckles" Damoulakis, had also attended and all up between $80,000 and $90,000 in cash had been handed over to Mr. Hill, who arranged finance via Citibank.

Asked during cross-examination if he was being frank about some of his evidence, Mr. Gioffre replied: "No, I am not being frank, I am telling the truth."

Giving evidence, Mr. Hill confirmed the Black Uhlans had wanted to buy the clubhouse.

Under cross-examination by Ian Temby, QC, for the NSW Crime Commission, he admitted he had been struck off after being sent to jail for eight years for being involved in the production of amphetamines.

One of the key witnesses for the Black Uhlans, Mr. Reardon, said he had never wanted the property put in his name but he was the only member who would succeed in getting a loan. "I was not buying it for myself," he said.

Mr. Reardon cheerfully admitted to his drug conviction and agreed with Mr. Temby he would support the Black Uhlans and its members in all circumstances.

"I suppose you could say that, yeah...if they wanted me to shoot someone down the road, that might be a different story, I wouldn't be doing that," he said.

Justice Campbell reserved his decision.

✠

BLOODY DEVILS - Established in 1984 in Germany. Another of the support clubs for a Euro power-house, Germany's Rolling Wheels.

✠

Blue Angels

- ♦ **ESTABLISHED:** 1963
- ♦ **PLACE OF ORIGIN:** Glasgow, Scotland
- ♦ **FOUNDER(S):** Allen Morrison, Lenny Reynolds, Tommy Howells
- ♦ **CHAPTER LOCATIONS:** U.K.
- ♦ **CENTER PATCH:** A winged skull with a German army helmet
- ♦ **MOTTO:** *BLUE = Bastards, Lunatics, Undesirables, and Eccentrics*
- ♦ **CLAIM TO FAME:** Oldest MC in Europe, and one of the largest clubs in the U.K.

BLUE ANGELS - Established in 1963 in Glasgow, Scotland. A true "classic" club. "BLUE" is an acronym for "Bastards, Lunatics, Undesirables, and Eccentrics" but, according to the club, "the name also came from other sources—blue is the main colour of the Scotland flag."

The Blue Angels are one of the largest motorcycle clubs in the United Kingdom, just behind the Outlaws, Hells Angels, and Satans Slaves—and reportedly the Slaves and the Blue Angels are the only one percent clubs to have chapters and wear "colours" in Scotland. The Blue Angels are also reportedly the oldest motorcycle club in Europe, with chapters throughout Scotland, and in Leeds. Their "classic" status is even more enhanced by the fact that they came together in a 1960s-type coffee/jazz joint called the Papingo, "which appealed to the beatniks, artists, and rockers who populated the Hillhead districts."

There's also a Blue Angels MC in Detroit.

BOANERGES - A North Carolina three-piece-patch club that made it onto the law enforcement map in the Old North State with their brother Tar Heels.

BOND SLAVES - Established "in the early 2000s" in Princeton, Minnesota. Well, this may have something to do with religious oppression, but this Christian "motorcycle ministry" made the map in Minnesota and Iowa.

BONES - Established in 1968, a Euro "classic" club out of Mannheim, Germany, that had their full history featured in a monster article in *Bikers News* in 1999, before merging with the Hells Angels soon after. They leave behind a tribute club, Old Bone MC.

They also left behind a relic that turned up on eBay:

BONES MC Germany Shirt biker Club/gang 1% very rare!

Original BONES MC Germany ALL CHAPTERS Shirt. This Shirt is an Original and was only available to Club Members. This Club was Respected all over Germany and far beyond. It ruled from the late 60s all the way to the late 90s with an Iron Fist. It merged after that to the biggest MC in the World SUPPORT 81.

This is an Original and should be the RAREST Biker Item you ever find on eBay. SEE PHOTOS. Good Luck and bid High

Boozefighters

- **ESTABLISHED:** 1946
- **PLACE OF ORIGIN:** Los Angeles, California
- **FOUNDER(S):** "Wino Willie" Forkner
- **CHAPTER LOCATIONS:** North America, Europe, Asia
- **CLUB COLORS:** Green and White
- **CENTER PATCH:** Booze bottle with three stars on it
- **MOTTO:** *A drinking club with a motorcycle problem*
- **CLAIM TO FAME:** The "original wild ones," upon whom Stanley Kramer's seminal film *The Wild One* was based

BOOZEFIGHTERS - In 1946 in Los Angeles, California, at the All American Café (bar!) by "Wino Willie" Forkner and a pack of WWII vets. The club was at the "wild" epicenter of the "Hollister incident" in 1947 and that whole tire-spinning shebang became the "birth of the American biker" and put Hollister on the biker mayhem map. It also led to Stanley Kramer's monster motion picture *The Wild One*, released in late 1953, after which this lifestyle has never been the same. The BFMC is still "wild" and rolling, featured in countless newspaper and magazine articles, books, and television shows—and there is even a legitimate drama being written around the club. And they even made it onto the law enforcement map in Connecticut, Rhode Island, Ohio, Missouri, Indiana, Florida, Mississippi, Arkansas, Texas, New Mexico, Kansas, and California.

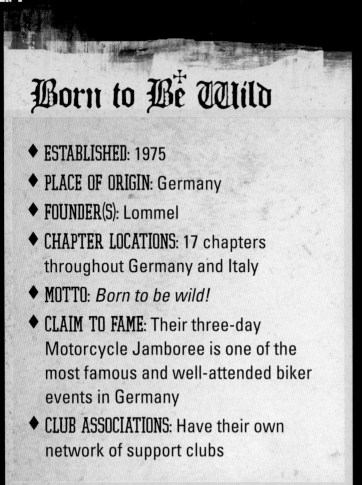

Born to Be Wild

- ◆ **ESTABLISHED:** 1975
- ◆ **PLACE OF ORIGIN:** Germany
- ◆ **FOUNDER(S):** Lommel
- ◆ **CHAPTER LOCATIONS:** 17 chapters throughout Germany and Italy
- ◆ **MOTTO:** *Born to be wild!*
- ◆ **CLAIM TO FAME:** Their three-day Motorcycle Jamboree is one of the most famous and well-attended biker events in Germany
- ◆ **CLUB ASSOCIATIONS:** Have their own network of support clubs

BORN TO BE WILD - Established in 1975 in Germany. BTBW is a bona fide heavyweight. The motorcycle club's founder, Lommel, has very strong feelings about the one percent world, his club, and what this lifestyle means to him:

BORN TO BE WILD MC GERMANY
by Lommel, BTBW MC

More than thirty-five years ago, in 1975, I started the motorcycle club Born to Be Wild Germany (BTBW MC). Contrary to many other German MCs, BTBW was not founded by American GIs.

In the subsequent years, four other presidents and I evolved the six-member group into a stable and well-organized motorcycle club. Today, the Born to be Wild MC is one of the largest and most respected 1% MCs in Germany. We have eleven chapters throughout Germany, with Berlin as the mother chapter, and six chapters in Italy. Our traditional three-day party, known as the Motorcycle Jamboree, is one the most famous and well-attended biker events in Germany.

Getting to be sixty years old and still being an active biker and BTBW member, I made the decision to publish a book about my life and the history of the Born to Be Wild MC. The postface of my book contains my personal opinion about today's 1% scene in Germany as follows:

I'm royally pissed that the 1% sign is abused by a lot of people. Many of these guys have no clue about the significance and the value of this patch and they should not wear it. Women should not wear it. Pull it off!

As a member of a 1% motorcycle club, I went through a lot of shit, but I am proud being a 1%er. As the time goes by, a lot of former values went down the toilet. Today, there are guys hiding themselves behind a motorcycle club, many of them have never ridden a motorcycle. What is that all about? It's bullshit! Don't they have another home or family to go to? I don't understand that and I am really concerned about the outcome and the increasing downturn of our values. Being not able to stop that shit, all I can do is to set my hope on our young offspring.

It is my personal opinion that the freedom of the biker lifestyle, the freedom of the road, was much more uncomplicated in the past. Today, we are over-regulated, over-controlled, chained and gagged by laws and rules, such as the helmet law or ridiculous technical inspections like the German TÜV.

Nowadays, you can't even give someone a one-finger salute without the risk of getting a penalty. What will be the outcome in twenty years?

However, I am far away from being a sour old man. I am satisfied with what I have done in my life right now. I was and still am an active player in the creation and preservation of Germany's 1% family.

I am proud of my brothers. I can count on them all the time. This was true in the past and will be true in the future. I am sure that they will never desert me. Our honor is called loyalty! Show us respect and you will get it back. I am convinced that respect is the only way to get along.

—Lommel 1%
From *Lommel, eine Rockerlegende aus Berlin*

Lommel (Seated). *Courtesy of Lommel and Born to Be Wild MC*

All photos courtesy of Lommel and Born to Be Wild MC

BPM - "BPM" may just mean "booze, pussy, motorcycles," and they may just have made the law enforcement map in Minnesota. In 2007 they were involved in a lawsuit that may just have changed the meaning of BPM to "Bad Police in Minnesota." The Associated Press reported:

ST. CLOUD, Minn. (AP) Two St. Cloud–area judges have dismissed a dozen court complaints filed by bikers who were stopped in July 2007 during a run near St. Joseph.

The 12 bikers sued the Central Minnesota Drug and Gang Task Force, which was one agency represented among the nearly 20 officers that stopped the bikers.

District Judge Michael Jesse dismissed six conciliation court cases Monday. Stearns County District Court Judge Elizabeth Hayden dismissed six on Friday.

The conflict comes from a run of more than 70 bikers, which included some recreational riders and some members of the BPM Motorcycle Club.

Minnesota Gang Strike Force Commander Ron Ryan has said the club fits the criteria of a criminal gang as established by the Legislature. Club members deny wrongdoing.

The bikers alleged civil rights and due process violations, but didn't offer any evidence to justify the financial reimbursement they sought.

Authorities say officers responded to complaints that previous runs had clogged traffic. The bikers say the gang task force was looking for drugs and weapons, and finding only a few violations issued tickets for running stop signs instead.

Bikers' rights organizations were, of course, solidly behind the BPM's suit. They described the results as:

Basically, the judges ruled that the bikers did not deserve to be compensated for their time, embarrassment and inconvenience. The police have nothing to lose by violating the Constitution.

✠

BRANDED MC - A club that appeared to exist in the 1980s in the New Jersey area, and was reportedly absorbed into The Breed MC in 1986.

✠

Branded Few

- ◆ **ESTABLISHED:** 1969
- ◆ **PLACE OF ORIGIN:** Northern Nevada
- ◆ **FOUNDER(S):** An original 7 members
- ◆ **CHAPTER LOCATIONS:** Northern Nevada
- ◆ **CENTER PATCH:** Contains a controversial swastika
- ◆ **CLAIM TO FAME:** Oldest existing club in Northern Nevada

BRANDED FEW - Established "in the late summer of 1969," the Branded Few MC is the oldest club in Northern Nevada today. And they made the law enforcement map in the Silver State. Their center patch has also generated some controversy—at least the *swastika* part. They go to great lengths to explain the full lineage of the ancient symbol, beyond the Hitler/Nazi taint.

✠

BRANDED ONES - Established in 1967, solidly settling into Connecticut in 1970, and having a "resurrection" in August of 1994. They made it onto the law enforcement map in the Constitution State. And at this point, we have to mention a little something about Connecticut. This relatively diminutive state is like Australia, New Zealand, Germany, Finland, certain parts of Canada, and those other cartels of superdense motorcycle club populations. The law enforcement map has the vast majority of the club list for Connecticut neatly arranged out in the Atlantic—nowhere near enough space in the tiny blue swatch of real estate to list all of the many "OMGs" roaring through Hartford, New Haven, and the suburbs.

☩

BRAVADOS - The Bravados made the law enforcement map in California, and they were involved in a 1997 landmark court case that really was one of the first stands against the discrimination of club members. A Confederation of Clubs press release described the "fight":

BIKERS WIN LEGAL CHALLENGES OVER "CLUB COLORS"

November 18, 1997—Two recent legal actions have favored the right of motorcycle clubs to wear "colors," as guaranteed under the U S Constitution First Amendment freedom of speech protections.

In early August, the County of Santa Barbara and the Santa Barbara County Sheriff's Department agreed to settle a lawsuit brought by the Bravados Motorcycle Club, based upon actions by about a dozen Sheriffs deputies to refuse club members entry into the Santa Barbara County Fair on April 29, 1995, because they found their club "colors," or back patch, to be "gang attire."

Police Officers offered to let the Bravados enter without their vests, but the club decided instead to file suit against the county and the Sheriff's Department. "It is our right to wear our vests," said David Cordero, treasurer for the club that has been in Santa Barbara for more than 30 years. "We are proud to be Bravados." The club members claimed their First Amendment rights were violated by a dress code that discriminated against their style of clothing.

The lawsuit was pursued by the Southern California Confederation of Clubs, of which the Bravados MC is a member club, and the Sheriff's Department and county eventually agreed to settle for $10,000 in damages and about $15,000 in legal fees. In addition, the Bravados also won the right to attend the fair in full club regalia.

"This was a great victory for the Bravados MC and the Confederation of Clubs," said Richard M. Lester, founder of Aid to Injured Motorcyclists and legal counsel for all Confederations of Clubs throughout North America. "It validates our position that bikers should not be discriminated against based solely on their style of dress or mode of transportation."

☩

Breed

- ◆ **ESTABLISHED:** 1965
- ◆ **PLACE OF ORIGIN:** Asbury Park, New Jersey
- ◆ **FOUNDER(S):** Unknown
- ◆ **CHAPTER LOCATIONS:** New Jersey, Pennsylvania
- ◆ **CLAIM TO FAME:** 1971 "large-scale" brawl with the HAMC in Cleveland, Ohio, leaving four Breed members dead and one Hells Angel

BREED - Established in 1965 in Asbury Park, New Jersey. The Breed made it onto the law enforcement map in Jersey *and* Pennsylvania. Like we mentioned earlier, they reportedly absorbed members of the Aces and Eights Motorcycle Club, based in Riverside, New Jersey, in the early 1980s. In 1986, the Branded Motorcycle Club was also reportedly absorbed into the Breed. A little after that, the Breed also made it into a bit of a damning dossier by Jersey authorities. It may be ancient history now, but it does show the consistencies of law enforcement:

Outlaw Motorcycle Gangs –
State of New Jersey Commission
of Investigation 1989 Report

THE BREED—The most prolific and fastest growing outlaw motorcycle gang in New Jersey, the Breed's origins go back to the mid-1960's.

Significant recruitment activity occurred in 1983 when attempts were made to absorb members of the Aces and Eights Motorcycle Club based in Riverside, New Jersey. Almost simultaneous with this effort was the assimilation of members of the Branded Motorcycle Club into the Breed. More recently, during 1986–1987, the Breed reportedly was negotiating to merge with the Bandana Motorcycle Club, with the Breed retaining organizational control. The Breed, with a membership of about 60, has three chapters in New Jersey—the Jersey Chapter, which is the founding or "Mother" chapter, operating out of Middlesex County, the South Jersey Chapter operating out of Riverside in Burlington County, and the Trenton-Bucks Chapter operating in the state capital and in Bucks County, Pennsylvania.

There is a growing concern that Breed members in the Trenton-Bucks Chapter are exerting considerable influence in the drug market. Authorities estimate a local presence of 30 members or significant associates and indicate that this group has a substantial distribution network in place. The location and range of activities of this chapter suggests that state boundaries mean little in defining this organization's jurisdiction. All indications are that this chapter operates freely between the two states.

Similar to other outlaw motorcycle gangs, the Breed is adopting a lower public profile. Observations in the Mercer County area support their presence there, but more conventional behavior, dress and mode of transportation make them less noticeable.

The Breed uses violence to settle disputes and enforce policy. Instances of intergang rivalry have been well documented, particularly with the Pagans. In 1987 and more recently in 1989, gang members were involved.

✛

BRIDGE RUNNERS - Established in 1992, an old-school diamond-patch-wearing motorcycle club out of Brooklyn. They made it onto the law enforcement map in the Empire State but they also made it into a blog in 2007 by a guy named Danny. Danny's words bring home the feel of a true "old school" club:

I wasn't born and raised in Brooklyn, but it's my proud home. I have so much love for Brooklyn that I've stopped telling people to move here. "Moving to New York? Great, you should check out Queens!"

My block was a piece of garbage five years before I showed up, and now there's many like me, boppin' around the newly cleaned up part of town, jackin' up the rent, and drawing in Starbucks and organic food markets. Change is afoot and has been; I know I'm part of the change.

There are swanky restaurants and nicely restored Sesame Street brownstones, but there's still an underbelly that hangs on the edge, that goes beyond shady dollar stores and an occasional storefront church. The Gowanus Canal, Red Hook, and beyond, there's still some serious Brooklyn grit to be had.

I've seen lots of it vanish even in my short stay here: a massive block of shipyard buildings razed for a coming IKEA, a huge abandoned sugar mill bulldozed for condos, land prospecting for condo developments along a literally toxic body of water.

But…last night we stumbled onto a biker clubhouse. Tucked in between the projects, some old industrial buildings and the fetid canal was a brightly lit windowless building with a stenciled sign that read: Bridgerunners MC. A huge row of motorcycles and a sole beefy doorman stood out front. I could actually hear the radio DJ from The Warriors broadcasting inside my head:

"Hey young boppers… it looks like the Warriors ran into a little trouble with the Brooklyn Bridge Runners and got off clean…this one goes out to you…" (cue "Nowhere to Run To")

I don't know what these cats are about; maybe they're really nice guys who just like to ride. Or maybe they'd love to run their motorcycles over my head just for living. Either way, I was happy they were there. If for no other reason than to represent the rugged and mysterious elements of Brooklyn that seem to be fading all around me. I may very well represent what they hate most about the new Brooklyn. But still, I wanna tip my hat to the old guard and the hard old history that gives my home its flavor. They don't know it, but I've added their link to our Friends section. Bridge Runners, much respect.

⛨

Brödraskapet

- **ESTABLISHED:** 1995
- **PLACE OF ORIGIN:** Inside the maximum security prison in Kumla, Sweden
- **FOUNDER(S):** Danny "The Hood" Fitzpatrick
- **CHAPTER LOCATIONS:** Sweden
- **MOTTO:** Brödraskapet is Swedish for *The Brotherhood*
- **CLAIM TO FAME:** *Very* integral to the "Great Nordic Biker Wars"

BRODRASKAPET - "Brödraskapet" is Swedish for *The Brotherhood*. Shortened to BSK, *this* Brotherhood is a Swedish prison gang that was founded on May 27, 1995, by inmates inside the maximum security prison in Kumla, Sweden. Authorities in Sweden "consider The Brotherhood to be a criminal organization in regards to the EU criteria for organized crime." Formed by Danny "The Hood" Fitzpatrick, the Brotherhood joined with the ASA MC outside of prison, with members of the Brotherhood still inside becoming the Wolfpack. All were involved in one way or another with the Great Nordic Biker Wars.

✛

BROKE JOKERS - A three-piece-patch club out of Delaware.

BROTHERHOOD - Brotherhood may win for the "name most shared." And that's about right, because it's one of those key words that are so important and descriptively integral to this entire lifestyle—so, here we go:

Brotherhood MCs made the law enforcement map in New York, Ohio, Indiana, Michigan, Wisconsin, Illinois, Nevada, Florida, and North Carolina.

In New York, the club was established in 1972. It was founded on some solid principles of brotherhood: "A family of Brother bikers that no matter what it was they would be there for each other... If one was troubled they all were there to help find the answer and to solve it...No need to look over your shoulder to see if your Brothers are there; they will be there. This vision still stands today with the members of the Brotherhood Motorcycle Club and always will. Black & Red Till Dead."

There are Brotherhoods in Antwerp, Belgium; Karlstad, Sweden (established in 1977); Montreal, Canada (established in 2007); and in Austria.

Established in 1954 is the Brotherhood that was started by "Seven men on a mission," as an old member recalls, "On a base of Camaraderie, Brotherhood, and Support for its members...they flourished on the South Side of Chicago until the mid '80s, when Outlaws MC came to the South Side, liquidating many local independent clubs. As chapters were eliminated, the Outlaws decided to absorb the Brotherhood; instead of burning all the patches as they did with many other clubs (American Breed, Devils Disciples, and many others fell by the wayside), The Brotherhood survived. Most members were moved to Southern Illinois to form the Joppa Chapter."

There's a Brotherhood in Lake Tahoe, California/Nevada.

And an HAMC support Brotherhood in Russia, established in "mid-1990s but came of age in 2003."

And an Outlaws support Brotherhood in the U.K., established in 1998.

Whew!

+

BROTHERS - Established in 1969 in Illinois. They didn't make the law enforcement map in Illinois, but there is a great mug-shot (kind of) of one of their member's tattoos on the Genoa, Illinois, PD's "Gang Information" site!

+

BROTHERS IN LAW - Established in 1999 in Lithuania. One of the Euro *"Hangaround clubs to Red and White world."*

Brother Speed

- ♦ ESTABLISHED: 1969
- ♦ PLACE OF ORIGIN: Boise, Idaho
- ♦ FOUNDER(S): A group of high school friends (including three elementary school buddies!)
- ♦ CHAPTER LOCATIONS: Oregon, Washington, Utah, Idaho, and Montana
- ♦ CLUB COLORS: Black and Gold
- ♦ CLUB PATCH: Winged skull with the helmet, goggles, and scarf
- ♦ CLAIM TO FAME: Often ranked within "Top Ten" motorcycle club lists

BROTHER SPEED - Established in 1969 in Boise, Idaho, but settled into Portland, Oregon, with their mother chapter. They made the law enforcement map in Oregon and Idaho as well as Washington and Utah. Oregon's Department of Justice also has "a list" and rates Brother Speed as one of six "outlaw motorcycle gangs" in the state. Brother Speed is also listed as an "outlaw motorcycle club" by the Idaho Department of Corrections gang information website. Brother Speed was started by a group of high school friends and the motorcycle club has grown into a major-leaguer.

No discussion of the club can be made without a mention of the tragedy that landed on them in September 2009. The worst fear of any club that travels in a pack exploded on them when a mass crash occurred on I-5 near Wilsonville, Oregon. The smash-up left one member dead, one critically injured, and ten in the hospital.

+

BROTHERS WORD - A three-piece-patch club out of Kansas City, Missouri. They made it onto the law enforcement map in the Show Me State!

+

BRUDENSCHAFT - This motorcycle club made the law enforcement map in Nebraska!

+

Buffalo Soldiers

- ◆ ESTABLISHED: 1994
- ◆ PLACE OF ORIGIN: Chicago, Illinois
- ◆ FOUNDER(S): Ken "Dream Maker" Thomas
- ◆ CHAPTER LOCATIONS: Over 90 chapters in 33 U.S. states
- ◆ CLUB COLORS: Black and Gold
- ◆ CLUB PATCH: A Buffalo Soldier
- ◆ CLAIM TO FAME: High-profile African-American club, named after Black Civil War–era military regiments

BUFFALO SOLDIERS - This is the first African-American club alphabetically on our list—and they are big and high profile. Established in October 1994 in Chicago by Ken "Dream Maker" Thomas, who believed "It was time to establish a modern progressive motorcycle club whose focus was to promote a positive image among African Americans that would be respected in the community and throughout the country."

The name comes from the Black Civil War–era military regiments—the 9th Cavalry Regiment, the 10th Cavalry Regiment, the 24th Infantry Regiment, and the 25th Infantry Regiment.

BSMC popularity grew as members attended the National Roundup and rallies held in various cities throughout the country. By August 1999, there were eleven chapters. These chapters formed the National Association of Buffalo Soldiers/Troopers Motorcycle Clubs (NABSTMC). Today the NABSTMC has over ninety chapters in thirty-three states, including Hawaii.

✠

BULLDOGS - There are at least three Bulldogs running loose in Europe:

One, established in 1996, is a three-piece-patch club in Greenland.

Germany has a Bulldogs Bandidos Support club.

There's another, established in 1999, in Finland.

✠

BULL FIGHT - Established in 1981 in Belgium with seven guys on mopeds! You gotta give these guys a mention for their longevity, and for one of the more interesting names.

✠

BUNKER - Established in 2003, a 1% diamond-patch club out of Germany

✠

DEM DEUTSCHEN VOLKE

Born to Be Wild MC, Germany. *Courtesy of Lommel and Born to Be Wild MC*

CHAPTER 2

Caballeros-Dukes

CABALLEROS - One of a myriad Bandidos support motorcycle clubs in Germany.

☩

CAES DA PALAH - A three-piece-patch-wearing, diamond-patch club out of Portugal.

☩

CALAVERA - Another of the German Bandidos support clubs.

Cannonball

- ♦ **ESTABLISHED:** Unknown
- ♦ **PLACE OF ORIGIN:** Finland
- ♦ **FOUNDER(S):** Unknown
- ♦ **CHAPTER LOCATIONS:** Six chapters in Finland
- ♦ **CENTER PATCH:** Flaming cannonball
- ♦ **CLAIM TO FAME:** Biggest one percent club in Finland, and integral in the "Great Nordic Biker Wars" of the 1990s
- ♦ **CLUB ASSOCIATIONS:** Has support clubs in five Finland locations

CANNONBALL - Referred to as "the biggest 1% club in Finland," this motorcycle club was one of the major cast members in the media/law enforcement drama that was the Great Nordic Biker Wars.

CARNICEROS - Established in 2005, a three-piece patch Bandidos support motorcycle club out of Spain. Motto: *"Caniceros MC ride only American and European old bikes."*

☩

CELTICS - A motorcycle club out of Switzerland celebrating their eleventh anniversary. There is also a Celtic club, AMA-chartered, in New York.

☩

CELTIC WARLOCKS - A "brotherhood and sisterhood" from Down Under that deserves a mention. Although they are a "Non-Back Patched, Non-Political, Non-Territorial Brotherhood & Sisterhood" they do seem to be very in the center of their support for the biker rights movement in Australia and their support for the major motorcycle clubs down there. And they do adhere to the hangaround-prospect-member order of things.

(On a related note, there was a Celtic Warriors Brotherhood in the U.K. that disbanded in 2006.)

☩

CELTS - A one percent club out of Austria.

☩

CENTAUROS - A motorcycle club out of Mexico. From their club history, "The word Centauros is from Greek mythological Centaur, meaning 'half-horse half-man.' This was also the nickname given to Pancho Villa when leading the Mexican Revolution."

✠   ✠

CHARTER OAKS - A club that made that crowded little blue part of the law enforcement map and list in Connecticut.

✠

CHICANOS EASTSIDE - Another of the German Bandidos support clubs.

✠

CHIEFTAINS - Established in 1976 in Lawrence, Massachusetts. They made the law enforcement map there and in New Hampshire. They also have a chapter in Norway!

Ching-a-lings

♦ ESTABLISHED: Early 1960s

♦ PLACE OF ORIGIN: New York

♦ FOUNDER(S): Unknown

♦ CHAPTER LOCATIONS: East Coast, U.S.

♦ CLAIM TO FAME: Author and media personality Chuck Zito established the New Rochelle chapter by merging his New Rochelle Motorcycle Club with the Ching-a-Ling Nomads.

CHING-A-LINGS - One of the "classic" clubs out of New York. They began as a "street gang" in the early 1960s and—reportedly influenced by the Hells Angels—eventually evolved into a motorcycle club. In the early 1970s the Ching-a-Lings settled in the Bronx.

Author and media personality Chuck Zito established the New Rochelle Motorcycle Club, which later merged with the multi-ethnic Ching-a-Ling Nomads. Zito would eventually leave to become one of the more well-known Hells Angels.

The Ching-a-Lings made it onto the law enforcement map in Virginia.

✠

CHOPPER CLUB - A United Kingdom motorcycle club just celebrating their thirtieth anniversary. It's refreshing to see the main focus of a motorcycle club be on building their bikes: *"The men and the machines."*

✠

CHOPPER FREAKS - Established in 1986, a three-piece-patch club in Norway.

✠

Chosen Few

- ♦ **ESTABLISHED:** 1959
- ♦ **PLACE OF ORIGIN:** Los Angeles, California
- ♦ **FOUNDER(S):** Lionel "Li'l Frank" Roger, "Hawk," "Slim," Shirly Bates, and "Champ"
- ♦ **CHAPTER LOCATIONS:** Los Angeles area
- ♦ **CLUB COLORS:** Blood-Red and White
- ♦ **CLUB PATCH:** An oval sea of red blood with white human crossed bones
- ♦ **MOTTO:** *It's not about the size of the few in the fight, it's about the size of the fight in the few.*

CHOSEN FEW - Here's another name that not only has "classic" ties but it has also been chosen by a few motorcycle clubs.

In Belgium and beyond, there is a full-on diamond patch Chosen Few that evolved through the 1990s. They use a portion of the Confederate flag in their patch. They "ride all kinds of bikes, but prefer customized bikes with a personal touch."

There is a Chosen Few in Iowa, established in 1969.

The real "classic" Chosen Few, however, comes out of Los Angeles, established in 1959. Their "blood red" patch with a white cross of human bones has become a familiar sight flying in the L.A. area, for generations. They pride themselves on being "the first fully integrated outlaw MC."

Another Chosen Few MC, established in Buffalo, New York, in 1966, wears a center patch that features a classic beatnik, indicative of the era and area in which they were formed. This club has had more than its share of interesting interactions with other clubs in the Northeast, but through it all has maintained an adage promoting unity: "If we all rode together, imagine how strong we could be!"

✠

Jennifer Thomas

Jennifer Thomas

✠

CIRCLE OF PRIDE - Established in 1990, this Iowa motorcycle club was founded in a "titty bar" by a group that included a guy named "Possum." Perfect! At their property near Conesville, Iowa, they put on big events that have "no rules...and where nudity and vulgar language run rampant!" Again, perfect! Two of the bashes are called the "Hog Wild Rodeo" and "Thunder In The Sand" with all the proceeds going to local and national charities. And, as expected, they did make the law enforcement map in the Hawkeye State.

✠

✠

COCHISE RIDERS - A three-piece-patch motorcycle club, HAMC (Hells Angels Motorcycle Club) supporters that made the law enforcement map in Arizona.

✠

COBRA, COBRAS - There are a few Cobra clubs snaking around:

One is the Cobra MC, established in 2007, beginning life as Triple Cobra MC. They are a Bandidos support club out of Denmark.

There's a three-piece-patch club that made the law enforcement map in Florida (certainly not to be confused with another Sunshine State club, C.O.B.R.A. MC, a law enforcement club!). This club has some poignant philosophy when it comes to this entire "public-and-the-patch" thing: "A serious MC club commands respect for one reason. Those who are correctly informed recognize the deep level of personal commitment and self-discipline that a man has to demonstrate and sustain in order to wear a patch...The goal is to be admired and respected by the general public rather than feared."

There is a Cobra MC in the UK and a Cobra's MC, established in 1977, in Belgium.

✠

Coffin Cheaters

- ♦ **ESTABLISHED:** Early 1960s
- ♦ **PLACE OF ORIGIN:** Long Beach, California
- ♦ **FOUNDER(S):** Unknown, but with roots back to "Preacher" in 1963
- ♦ **CHAPTER LOCATIONS:** Ohio, Pennsylvania, Florida, Louisiana, Alaska, Colorado
- ♦ **CENTER PATCH:** A coffin draped with a swastika-emblazoned red flag
- ♦ **MOTTO:** *Often imitated never duplicated*
- ♦ **CLAIM TO FAME:** Original members appeared alongside HAMC members in the 1966 Roger Corman film. . . *The Wild Angels*

COFFIN CHEATERS - Big, "classic," international, with a name shared by two motorcycle behemoths:

The "classic" club ("*Often imitated never duplicated*") was established in or around the early 1960s in Long Beach, California. Legend has it that a serviceman named "Preacher" spent some time in 1963 with the Long Beach boys, wound up getting a club charter for his own chapter in his hometown of Cleveland, and kept the name after the Southern California bunch patched over to another club.

So began one of the tightest lineages in the motorcycle club world: "You cannot join the Coffin Cheaters, you must be born into it or be a blood relative, hence our patch ('Blood In Blood Out'). Exception, if you hang out for five years and have 100% membership approval, then you can be patched in as a full patch holder. NO PROSPECTS.

We once had a probate that hung out and prospected for thirty years before becoming a full patch holder."

Members of the original CCMC, along with members of the HAMC, appeared in the 1966 Roger Corman film, *The Wild Angels*.

- ♦ **ESTABLISHED:** Early 1970s (or earlier)
- ♦ **PLACE OF ORIGIN:** Australia
- ♦ **FOUNDER(S):** Unknown
- ♦ **CHAPTER LOCATIONS:** Australia, Norway
- ♦ **CENTER PATCH:** Aboriginal-style devil's head with wings
- ♦ **CLAIM TO FAME:** On the Aussie "most dangerous" lists

Somewhere around 7,500 miles from Long Beach is Australia and the other Coffin Cheaters MC, established "at least back to the early '70s." With three chapters in Perth, two in Victoria, two in New South Wales, two in Queensland, and three Norwegian chapters, the CCMC Down Under make all the Aussie "most dangerous" lists. They are true international heavyweights.

The Norway chapters were established in 2004 as an evolution of Wild Wheels, Forbidden Few, and MC Lillestrom.

Comanchero MC

- **ESTABLISHED:** Late 1960s/early 1970s
- **PLACE OF ORIGIN:** Sydney, Australia
- **FOUNDER(S):** William George "Jock" Ross
- **CHAPTER LOCATIONS:** Australia
- **CLAIM TO FAME:** One of the major motorcycle clubs in Australia

COMANCHERO MC - Established in the "late '60s–early '70s" in Sydney, Australia, by William George "Jock" Ross, a Scottish immigrant. Legend has it that the name was chosen after Jock saw the classic John Wayne flick *The Comancheros*. More handed-down history has a second Comanchero chapter formed in 1982 by Anthony Mark "Snoddy" Spencer after he challenged Ross' authority. Spencer was said to have traveled to Texas where he formed an alliance with the Bandidos—the result would be that Spencer's Comanchero MC would patch over and become Australia's first Bandidos chapter.

There is a Comancheros (yes, Comancheros, not Comanchero) three-piece-patch motorcycle club in Catalunya, Spain.

✠

COMBATANTS - A three-piece-patch club out of New Hampshire that made the law enforcement map there in the Granite State.

✠

COMBAT VETERANS - Established in 2000, a one percenter veterans club out of Belgium.

✠

COMPADRES - Another of the Bandidos Euro support clubs, this motorcycle club is out of Norway.

✠

COMPANEROS - A stateside Bandidos support club that made the law enforcement map in Texas.

✠

CONDEMNED FEW - Diamond-patch motorcycle club that made the big time on the law enforcement map in New York.

✠

CONDORS - There are a couple of Condors MCs flying around:

A three-piece-patch motorcycle club out of Hungary, established in 1996.

Another European Condors club: the Norweigian *klubben*, established in 2002. They are a "friendship club" (support-like) with No Name MC.

✠

CONFEDERATES - A big three-piece-patch club with chapters throughout the Netherlands. Another of the Euro clubs with the Confederate flag in their patch.

⊹

CONFEDERATE GYPSIES - An Outlaws support motorcycle club out of North Carolina.

⊹

CONTRAS - Another of the bounty of German Bandidos support clubs.

⊹

CORREZE - And that bounty extends into France with this Bandidos support motorcycle club.

⊹

COSSACKS - Established in 1969, a "classic" club that made the law enforcement map in Texas:

Cossacks

- ◆ **ESTABLISHED:** 1969
- ◆ **PLACE OF ORIGIN:** Texas
- ◆ **FOUNDER(S):** Unknown
- ◆ **CHAPTER LOCATIONS:** Texas
- ◆ **CLUB COLORS:** Gold on Black
- ◆ **CLUB PATCH:** A cossack: a nomadic horseman and warrior
- ◆ **MOTTO:** *We take care of our own.*
- ◆ **CLAIM TO FAME:** One of the major motorcycle clubs in Australia

"In the Days of old, COSSACKS were nomadic horsemen and warriors defending their faith and territory from the forces of Europe. It was written some four hundred years ago that 'The COSSACKS are always on horseback, always ready to fight, and always alert.' Today, in modern times we traded our horses for motorcycles…Though we doubt seriously that any of us actually descended from the 'Russian warriors of old,' we have consequently adopted their name and sense of brotherhood. Our motto is: 'WE TAKE CARE OF OUR OWN' And our colors are Gold on Black. Always ready—Always in the wind."

⊹

COYOTES - A three-piece-patch motorcycle club howling in Hungary.

CRAWLING DEATH - Out of Germany, this club has reportedly become part of the Golden Drakes MC, Germany (that may just mean that the name is available!).

✣

CRAZY DEVILS - Established in 1982, a three-piece-patch motorcycle club in Bavaria. They even have their own song!

✣

Crazy in the Dark

- ◆ **ESTABLISHED:** Roots back to 1990
- ◆ **PLACE OF ORIGIN:** Lithuania
- ◆ **FOUNDER(S):** Young rockers
- ◆ **CHAPTER LOCATIONS:** Lithuania
- ◆ **CLUB COLORS:** Black and White
- ◆ **CLAIM TO FAME:** Rode only at night, making noise and looking crazy, to avoid and deter the "militia"

CRAZY IN THE DARK - Established with roots back to 1990 in Lithuania. Like most motorcycle clubs in that politically rocky part of the globe, they had to deal with especially harsh law enforcement/government suppression. To avoid the police, they would often have to ride only at night and they looked like they were mad! Hence the name, Crazy in the Dark!

✣

CREW - Another of the chromed crowd of Euro Bandidos support clubs—this one is out of Norway.

✣

CRIMINALS - A short 5,000-mile putt from the Crew, another Bandidos support club: the Criminals out of Chiangmai, Thailand.

✣

CROSSROADS - Established in 1986, a motorcycle club out of Baltimore, Maryland. There is also a Christian club in New York with the same name.

✣

CROSSED RIFLES - A three-piece-patch club for veterans out of North Carolina.

✣

CRUCIFIERS - This motorcycle club made the law enforcement map in California. It has made other news as well. In one of those weird, Unibomber-like tales of isolation, a Crucifiers member—and his apparent crime—was featured in a 1992 piece in the *Los Angeles Times*:

FUGITIVE IN 1981 MURDER CASE CAPTURED

Led by a tip to a Santa Cruz Mountains canyon so remote that locals call it "the belly of the beast," authorities have arrested a man for his involvement in the 1981 killing of a fellow motorcycle gang member in Van Nuys, Los Angeles, police said Friday.

Arthur La Vern Schlosser, 42, eluded detectives for more than a decade by using two aliases, hiding in a cabin two miles from the nearest town, and living off the land, said police and Santa Cruz County Sheriff's Department officials.

This week, as he met his son at a rural school bus stop, Schlosser was arrested by deputies who had been watching him for several weeks—ever since two Van Nuys detectives learned of his hide-out through an informant, said Van Nuys chief homicide Detective Stephen Fisk.

Sporting a large tattoo of Adolf Hitler on his back, Schlosser was taken into custody without incident, said Santa Cruz Sheriff's Deputy Kim A. Allyn.

He has been returned to Los Angeles County and charged with the June 2, 1981, murder of Michael Henry, 26, who was shot during a dispute, Fisk said.

Henry was actually shot by Van Nuys resident Timothy Elby, then 24, as he defended himself against Henry and Schlosser, Fisk said. Henry and Schlosser, who belonged to a bikers gang called the Crucifiers, had gone to Elby's home on Decelis Place to beat him because Elby had given Henry's ex-girlfriend a ride on his motorcycle, police said.

Fisk said Elby was never charged in the case because the shooting was considered self-defense. But Schlosser, formerly of Sunland, disappeared. Detectives believe that he settled in the Santa Cruz Mountains, near the town of Felton, shortly after the killing.

Although Schlosser did not directly cause his companion's death, he can be held responsible under California law because it occurred while they committed a crime in which the victim feared for his life, said Deputy Dist. Atty. Leonard J. Shaffer. The men also provoked Elby into defending himself, he said.

Shaffer, who handled the case in 1981, said Schlosser's disappearance did not exactly haunt him all these years. "I've had too many matters between then and now," he said.

The Crucifiers were also mentioned in an *L.A. Times* article about Hells Angels' George Christie's famous Olympic run in 1984:

As a Ventura County participant in the 15,000-mile torch relay—[Christie] ran a kilometer to the cheers of fellow bikers from the Hells Angels, Crucifiers and Heathens motorcycle chapters—Christie was asked to name a youth organization to receive the money he had paid.

And in yet another of those eBay treasure hunts, in 2010 a priceless part of Crucifiers' history came out of a dusty attic:

RARE 1950's ERA CRUCIFIERS LAMC OUTLAW BIKER GANG BANNER for CLUBHOUSE

You are admiring an ultra-rare find indeed. We are proud to offer an original 1950s era Crucifiers outlaw biker gang banner. Recent pawn with two (2) other outlaw vests from a collection. We have never seen one of these before. Measures 53´ Inches Long by 33´ Inches Wide. Very large size. Perfect for display in both your classic car or motorcycle outbuilding. Features leather reinforced working snaps. Embroidered with felt patches. Some stains thru out banner which in our opinion add character...

And, finally, maybe a few of us remember that the fictional motorcycle club in the 1981 cinematic masterpiece *The Cannonball Run* was, yes, the Crucifiers.

✠

CRUSADERS - Established in 1969 in Lewiston, Idaho. This motorcycle club specifically notes that they "are NOT a Christian MC."

Then there's a diamond-patch motorcycle club out of South Africa with the Crusaders name: "Brotherhood is the common bond of our lifestyle and our way of life…We believe strongly in tradition and adhere to the old ways of the 1%er way of life. We respect and honour the 1%er way of life, and choose to live life with the same values as they do."

✠

CURRAHEE - A three-piece-patch club out of Tennessee.

✠

CUSTOM RIDERS - Established in 1970 in the southern part of the U.S., a three-piece patch motorcycle club but also an AMA charter.

✠

CYCLE TRAMPS - Existed in the mid-1980s in Birmingham, England, and reportedly became part of the Outlaws MC.

✠

DARING EAGLES - Established in 1982, a three-piece-patch out of Germany

✠

DARK DIVISION - Our first descent into the deep "darkness" of names…out of Germany, the Dark Division is a support club for Germany's Rolling Wheels.

✠

DARK FACES - Established in 1977 in Germany with their "46" in a diamond patch. (We will be seeing a fair number of clubs that correlate numbers with the initials of their name [D=4, for the fourth letter of the alphabet, F=6]; many then put the numbers in a diamond or other-shaped patch).

✠

DARK FAMILY - A support club for the Black Iron MC out of Brazil.

✠

DARK FIGHTERS - A three-piece-patch club out of Bischofszell, Switzerland, that just celebrated their Silver Anniversary.

✠

DARK FORCES - A three-piece-patch motorcycle club out of Germany.

✠

DARK HEROES - A three-piece patch out of Germany with their "48" in a diamond.

DARKRAGE - Another of the teeming team of Bandidos support clubs in Deutschland.

✠

DARK RIDERS - Two clubs carry this slightly ominous and brooding name:

One in Montreal, established in 2004, with a chapter in Denmark.

And one in South Carolina, U.S. of A.

✠

DARKHORSE - Established in 2002, a three-piece-patch motorcycle club out of Florida.

✠

DARKSIDE - A three-piece-patch club out of New York.

✠

DC Eagles

- ◆ **ESTABLISHED:** 1963
- ◆ **PLACE OF ORIGIN:** Chicago, Illinois
- ◆ **FOUNDER(S):** "DC Danny" LeDesma
- ◆ **CHAPTER LOCATIONS:** Illinois
- ◆ **CLUB PATCH:** An eagle head
- ◆ **CLAIM TO FAME:** Gave up the one percenter patch but replaced it with a "99% NFG" patch

DC EAGLES - Established in 1963: "A club that gave up the 1% patch." But they still made the law enforcement map in the Land of Lincoln.

The late "DC Danny" LeDesma founded the DC Eagles MC in Chicago, Illinois. During the "turbulent" early days of the club and the crazed Chi-town club scene, the club had to make some concessions that came out of the beginning of a federation of motorcycle clubs. One of the concessions was to stop wearing the one percenter patch—but that changed into the wearing of a diamond patch that says "99% NFG," which all DC Eagles wear above their heart. The club says that, "This patch is as or even more important to a DC Eagle than his back patch…We say that all of these brothers got their training in previous clubs; now they are getting their PHD in BROTHERHOOD."

✠

DEATH MARAUDERS - This motorcycle club made it onto the law enforcement map and list in Illinois.

DEATHMEN - This motorcycle club began in Manchester, England, by their founder, "Charley." Ten years later they expanded into San Diego, California, "after a long road of negotiation with some of the most notorious Clubs in the world...and 3 piece MC struggles within the toughest Motorcycle Club State in the U.S.—California...This Club is the definition of determination."

✠

DEATHTRAPS - Out of California, this interesting club is based on some real old-school stuff. Their "mindset" is that "The DeathTraps are trying to revive a lost lifestyle that has been buried under lame fat tire bikes and between the pages of ridiculous 'builder' magazines. Thirteen guys who are only doing what has been done forever, but until recently has been replaced by theme bikes and fucking circus shows."

✠

Defiant Souls

- ◆ **ESTABLISHED:** 2006
- ◆ **PLACE OF ORIGIN:** Muscatine, Iowa
- ◆ **FOUNDER(S):** Unknown
- ◆ **CHAPTER LOCATIONS:** Iowa
- ◆ **CLUB COLORS:** Red and White
- ◆ **CLUB PATCH:** A skeleton riding a bike with big apes
- ◆ **MOTTO:** *A wise man knows when to speak, and when to shut up and listen.*
- ◆ **CLUB ASSOCIATIONS:** Support club for the Sons of Silence

DEFIANT SOULS - Established in 2006 in Muscatine, Iowa, the Defiant Souls is a support club for the Sons of Silence. They have a near-biblical motto: *"A wise man knows when to speak, and when to shut up and listen."*

✠

DEGUELLO - A Houston one percent Bandidos support club.

✠

DEMON KNIGHTS - A three-piece, diamond-patch motorcycle club out of New York that made the law enforcement map there.

✠

DERANGED FEW - Also making the law enforcement map were the Deranged Few—they made it down in Virginia.

✠

DESPERADO - A three-piece-patch, "Official hangaround MC to the Red & White" in Tata, Hungary.

Desperado's

- ♦ **ESTABLISHED:** 1975
- ♦ **PLACE OF ORIGIN:** Johnston County, North Carolina
- ♦ **FOUNDER(S):** Unknown
- ♦ **CHAPTER LOCATIONS:** North Carolina, Virginia
- ♦ **CLUB COLORS:** Black and Blue
- ♦ **CLUB PATCH:** The bandana-covered face of a desperado
- ♦ **CLAIM TO FAME:** Another of the clubs with modified punctuation. "We aren't stupid," they assert. "It was a misprint on the original patches in 1975...We choose to keep it...as a reminder of our roots."
- ♦ **CLUB ASSOCIATIONS:** Friends to the HAMC

DESPERADO'S, DESPERADOS - Okay, another of the shared names to explore:

One, the Desperado's, was established in 1975 in Johnston County, North Carolina. And, yep, they made the law enforcement map there. They're pretty straightforward in their self-analysis: "We are not a motorcycle club for everyone. We are an 'old school' club with very high standards that will not be compromised for anyone... We are not a support club, but we're damn sure not a 'fence walking' club either. We are proud to call the Red and White our friends and do support them worldwide."

And, like the Red and White, they answer the burning question about the misplaced apostrophe in their name: "Yes we know it doesn't belong there. We aren't stupid. It was misprinted on the original patches in 1975. We have had many chances to change it as our patches have been made and refined several times. We choose to keep it in its original form as a reminder of our roots. Besides, it sets us apart from others that have chosen to use the DESPERADO name and really have no idea what it's all about."

The Desperado's also made the law enforcement map in Virginia and they were mentioned in the huge Alexandria, Virginia, Grand Jury June 2010 indictment of at least 27 members of the Outlaws MC on a variety of charges:

8. Maintaining the Outlaws' Control Over Specific Areas—*At all times relevant to this indictment, the Outlaws organization was focused on achieving and maintaining control of the specific Region and Chapter areas occupied by the Enterprise. This control was achieved by asserting control over a particular area by directing the members, probationary members, and official hangarounds to engage in acts of violence against other competing motorcycle gangs, including the Hells Angels Motorcycle Club (HAMC), Desperados Motorcycle Club (Desperados MC), Renegades MC, and the Diablos MC.*

And there are more Desperados around the world. There is a Desperado MC, an HAMC support club in Hungary. There is a Desperados Bandidos support club in Texas. And in Calgary, Canada, there is another HAMC support club: "We ride for freedom, as a brotherhood. Proud supporters of Hells Angels."

✠

DESTRALOS - In Washington State, this Bandidos support club made it onto the law enforcement map.

✠

DEVASTATORS - A three-piece-patch club out of Denmark.

✠

Devil Dolls

- ◆ **ESTABLISHED:** 1999
- ◆ **PLACE OF ORIGIN:** San Francisco, California
- ◆ **FOUNDER(S):** A group of women riders, including the famous/infamous "Goth Girl" (who is no longer with the club)
- ◆ **CHAPTER LOCATIONS:** California
- ◆ **CLUB COLORS:** Red and Black
- ◆ **CLUB PATCH:** A Bettie Page–esque she-devil surrounded by flames
- ◆ **CLAIM TO FAME:** An all-female club—and a club that definitely rides.

DEVIL DOLLS - Established in 1999 in San Francisco. This begins our relationship with the Devil in his various shapes, matters, and forms. And it's a good way to start the selling of our souls, with one of just a couple of female clubs on this list—and the mention is well worth it. The Devil Dolls really don't keep a low profile! Their patch is a coy Bettie Page–like she-devil surrounded by flames. And they *do* ride. They are definitely not just another pretty face.

✠

DEVIL DRIVER - A three-piece-patch, one percent club out of Germany.

✠

Devils

- ◆ **ESTABLISHED:** 1985
- ◆ **PLACE OF ORIGIN:** Hungary
- ◆ **FOUNDER(S):** High school friends ("motor-freaks")
- ◆ **CHAPTER LOCATIONS:** Budapest, Debrecen, and Kecskemét, Hungary
- ◆ **CLUB COLORS:** Red and White
- ◆ **CLUB PATCH:** A hairy, bearded devil
- ◆ **CLAIM TO FAME:** Once told by Hungarian authorities, "If you do not stop gathering immediately, we will do in everyone!"

DEVILS - Established in 1985 in Hungary, the Devils are another of those motorcycle clubs in a part of the world where the cops and government are hardened and serious: "In 1985 one could in no way call our country democratic. It was rather a police state controlled by politics…this was the time when the community life of our club started! Our fellowship began at the time we went to high school. The few motor-freaks were characterized by their common interest—nothing but the motor mattered. We met every day, we worked on our motors and knocked around. We spent our money on our motors rather than on food.

Our club faced several times bothering from local authorities: 'If you do not stop gathering immediately, we will do in everyone!'"

The club survived and now has chapters in Budapest, Debrecen, and Kecskemét.

DEVIL'S ADVOCATES - A three-piece-patch motorcycle club based in Luxembourg.

✠

DEVILS BREED - One of just eleven motorcycle clubs to make the law enforcement map in the Hawaiian Islands. Mahalo!

✠

DEVILS BRIGADE - A three-piece-patch club with chapters in Detroit and Holland.

✠

DEVILS CHOICE - Another of the "official support clubs of the 81 world" out of Denmark.

✠

Devils Diciples

- ◆ **ESTABLISHED:** 1967
- ◆ **PLACE OF ORIGIN:** Fontana, California
- ◆ **FOUNDER(S):** 12 original members
- ◆ **CHAPTER LOCATIONS:** U.S., Ireland, and England (though the European chapters are essentially separate entities, with different colors, patches, and spellings)
- ◆ **CLUB PATCH:** A wheel and trident.
- ◆ **CLAIM TO FAME:** A true "classic" club, grown from Vietnam War years

DEVILS DICIPLES - Established in 1967 in Fontana, California, this is a true "classic" club, growing from vets of the Vietnam War years—and growing from the social earthquakes of the time. Beginning with twelve original members, the DDMC has become worldwide. We've seen, and *will* see, a lot of creative variations on wording, punctuation, and spelling as we comb through MC names—here, "Diciples" was intentionally tweaked so that the club wouldn't be confused as having any "religious affiliation."

A little personal anecdote—I don't think I've ever felt more of a connection and a bridge between the biker world's corner of the 1960s and current times as when I spent an evening at the DD clubhouse in Los Angeles. It's a de facto museum—a shrine not only to their club, but to all the eclectic energy that may have had that big boost in the 1960s but has remained truly timeless throughout this entire lifestyle.

Below is a female perspective of the commitment of a patch holder to his club—a DDMC ol' lady gives her views:

A MAN OF VALUE

Holly, ol' lady of Skinz, Devils Diciples MC

Relaxing in a Las Vegas casino bar, Skinz says to me, "Tell my brother Casino, here, what you just told me about how you view patch holders and marriage."

So I explained that I saw no higher or stronger bond between people than a marriage. There is no other ceremony or ritual or acknowledgment that means as much as a marriage means—at least in the "real" (i.e., fake) world.

I do feel that some patch holders hold their club right up there on a level even with marriage.

And I see that as a good thing!

I know this is the opposite of how it is perceived by most people, especially women who are ignorant of the motorcycle club scene. Many times a jealous ol' lady will allow herself to blame her man's commitment to his club for the problems between them in the home, and will view his club involvement only as a bad thing.

But that's from the eyes of a jealous ol' lady.

I see that kind of commitment as proof that a relationship filled with meaning, respect, loyalty, honor, love, support, protection, pride, and selflessness is cherished and desired. And these men are exhibiting the same traits and values within their club that are both paramount and fundamental to a strong marital bond. Furthermore, these men hold the bonds of brotherhood on a level equal to marriage. So, my take on being with a patch holder is that if you happen to be with one who wants *both* a club and marriage in his life, then you have found a pretty special man—a righteous man.

And to me, there's no better man!

Lil' Jon is the "P" of the Mountain Chapter of the Devils Disciples MC in California. He discusses a dilemma faced by many in the MC community— on one hand they are shunned and feared but on the other hand there is a strong vicarious interest in the lifestyle:

In all my years as a member of the Devils Disciples Motorcycle Club, our policy has always been that our business is our business and nobody else's. But now somebody wants me to tell my club's history so that any Tom, Dick and Harry can read about it. I don't know why any club member would talk to someone about their club knowing that it will be read by some of the very people whom we take great measures to keep out of our lives.

There's nothing that I enjoy more than sitting at the clubhouse, having a beer with my brothers and swapping stories of good times and bad. But that is only for us. That is why we have club-houses; so we can control who comes into our life. That's why we prospect people so we can control who comes into our life.

Most people outside of my club wouldn't give us the time of day. Bars won't let us in because we are in a club, cops harass us because we are in a club, the general public may give us a nod as we ride by but wouldn't stop to help us as we sat on the side of the road. These are not the kind of people that I want to share my life with.

I have had a great life and have met many amazing people riding with the Devils Disciples Motorcycle Club but unless you are one of us or run in our circle, that's all you will ever know from me.

Courtesy of "Skinz" and Devils Diciples MC

✠

DEVILS GRIP - This motorcycle club made it onto the law enforcement map in Virginia. In 2009, members were mentioned in newspaper reports as having attended the funeral for Pagan MC member "Jimbo" Hicks, after Hicks was killed by police during a raid on his home.

And the club is mentioned in that same, huge Alexandria, Virginia, Grand Jury June 2010 indictment of the Outlaws MC, cited as having "formed an alliance" with the OMC to "fight a common enemy."

✠

Devils Henchmen

- ♦ **ESTABLISHED:** 1973
- ♦ **PLACE OF ORIGIN:** Christchurch, New Zealand
- ♦ **FOUNDER(S):** Unknown
- ♦ **CHAPTER LOCATIONS:** Christchurch and Timaru, New Zealand
- ♦ **CLAIM TO FAME:** "The original South Island outlaw motorcycle club"

DEVILS HENCHMEN - Established in 1973, New Zealand's Devil's Henchmen MC is out of Christchurch and Timaru. It is recognized as "the original South Island outlaw motorcycle club."

✠

✠

DEVILS OWN - A three-piece-patch club out of another hotbed of motorcycle club activity: Arizona.

✠

DIABLOS - Well, we leave the Devils and now shake hands with the various incarnations of Diablos:

The Diablos out of Virginia are among the many clubs that made the pages of the epic Alexandria, Virginia, Grand Jury June 2010 indictment (see *Desperados*).

In California, Diablos made it onto the law enforcement map. They also go way back in legends and history. Reportedly back in 1958 or 1959 the *Los Diablos* patched over to another California motorcycle club but returned to "their roots" as Diablos in 1961, retaining the sacred and holy "'Berdoo" bottom rocker.

Connecticut Diablos also made their state's section of the law enforcement map. But back in 1998, members of the Meriden chapter were jailed on various charges, ranging from murder-for-hire to heroin conspiracy.

In August 2007, the Comancheros MC Germany was reportedly renamed Diablos and is a Bandidos support club.

Finland also has a Diablos Bandidos support club as does Belgium, established in 2004.

Diablos, Spain, established in 1993, is a three-piece-patch motorcycle club out of Ciudad Condal.

✠

DIABLOS LOBOS - This long-running motorcycle club out of Arkansas made the law enforcement map in the Natural State. The cops may not like them, but the kids love 'em—they have put on a major toy run for the last twenty-five years or so!

DIABSIN FRATER - This motorcycle club out of South Africa might not exactly be a group of one percenters, but they have a hot center patch that looks like Hellboy before he lost his horns.

✝

DIE GOTZEN - A three-piece-patch motorcycle club out of Russia, they express some compelling intro-spection: "We rarely communicate quite isolated from the outside, sometimes even aggressive. Too cruel was the world around us, so we built our own and try to live it, faithful to his ideals, the Holy Spirit of fraternity, avoiding of villainy and betrayal, unfortunately so common nowadays."

✝

DIRE WOLVES - There are a couple of dens of these wolves:

One, established in 2010 in Union County, North Carolina.

Two in Georgia: one established in 2008, the other in 2010. They do have different patches but they are linked. The boys out of Union County have a very cool and matter-of-fact philosophy: "Ride with me, drink with me, party with me, make memories with me, defend our lifestyle with me, but whatever else you do, don't fuck with me."

Good advice all the way around!

✝

DIRT & GRIME - This motorcycle club made its smudge on the law enforcement map in Washington State.

Dirty Dozen

- ◆ **ESTABLISHED:** 1960s
- ◆ **PLACE OF ORIGIN:** Arizona
- ◆ **FOUNDER(S):** Billy Burr, Nic-a-tic, and close to 30 others
- ◆ **CENTER PATCH:** Pair of winged dice
- ◆ **CLAIM TO FAME:** Their landmark merger with the Hells Angels in Arizona

✝

DIRTY DOZEN - This is our first look at a phrase and a name that has been part of the biker vocabulary and leathered lexicon forever. Many clubs have used this specialized designation to mean many things within their motorcycle clubs; but as a full club name, we need to look to Arizona—with yet another of those landmark-legends from the 1960s. The Dirty Dozen MC was "classic" in every way. The looks, the bikes, the actions—they were the perfect "what you see is what you get" characters, just like those they portrayed in *Angel Unchained*, another of the American International stable (or maybe *un*-stable) of "B" biker flicks in the 1960s. Their legend is especially deep because of their ties to the Hells Angels. In his book, *Hell's Angel*, Sonny talks about the Dirty Dozen's merger into the HAMC—going into the Red and White in the early/mid-1990s after having been an AZ-only motorcycle club and "friend and allies" of the Angels for twenty-five years.

✝

✠

✠

DOMINEERS - This East Coast bunch made it onto the law enforcement map and list in Massachusetts.

✠

DRAGON OF THE ROAD - A Bandidos support club based in Belgium.

✠

DRAMMENS - The club's history started back in 1990 in Norway, when five friends started a motorcycle club called Bullock MC. They started things out with a bit of (future) Euro-irony, as their first clubhouse was where the current police station lies.

In January 2003, they were accepted as a hang-around club to the Chieftains.

DRUIDS - Established in 1978, the Druids *North* is a motorcycle club out of Sheffield, England. There is also a Druids MCC, established in 1990, based in Ireland.

✠

DUKES - Established in 1996, a motorcycle club in West Rand, South Africa.

✠

Courtesy of Jennifer Thomas

CHAPTER 3

Eagle Riders-Gypsy Jokers

EAGLE RIDERS - Established in 1994, a three-piece-patch motorcycle club soaring through Estonia.

✠

East Bay Dragons

- ◆ **ESTABLISHED:** 1950s
- ◆ **PLACE OF ORIGIN:** Oakland, California
- ◆ **FOUNDER(S):** Tobie Gene Levingston
- ◆ **CHAPTER LOCATIONS:** Northern California
- ◆ **CENTER COLORS:** Red, Gold, and Green
- ◆ **CENTER PATCH:** A green dragon
- ◆ **CLAIM TO FAME:** One of the earliest Black motorcycle clubs, featured in Levington's *Soul on Bikes: The East Bay Dragons MC and the Black Biker Set*

EAST BAY DRAGONS - Established in the 1950s in Oakland, California, by Tobie Gene Levingston. The Dragons began as a car club, evolving into "the nation's most elite exclusively black motorcycle club."

In 2003, Tobie Gene wrote *Soul on Bikes: The East Bay Dragons MC and the Black Biker Set*. The book is more than just data on the Dragons, it's a social commentary that comes from a perspective that other biker culture chroniclers of the time just don't have:

We were already up and running strong by the time the Black Panthers came around during the 1960s to lobby for our support. They had moved into offices just a couple of blocks from our clubhouse. Black Panthers co-founders Huey Newton and Bobby Seale and chief of staff David Hilliard came in and ate in Joe's restaurant...To a lot of Dragons, the Black Panthers, their legacy, and their programs represented a bold, strong presence in the Black community. Many of the Black Panther party leaders came around the clubhouse to rally support for their causes, and we were invited to come down and represent ourselves at their functions.

✠

EAST COAST RIDERS - A club reportedly absorbed into Nova Scotia's Bacchus MC.

✠

El Forastero

- ◆ ESTABLISHED: 1962
- ◆ PLACE OF ORIGIN: Sioux City, Iowa
- ◆ FOUNDER(S): Two guys who were turned down from starting a Satans Slaves chapter in Iowa
- ◆ CHAPTER LOCATIONS: Midwest, U.S.
- ◆ CENTER COLORS: Purple and Gold
- ◆ CENTER PATCH: Big ape hangers with the 1%er diamond in the middle
- ◆ CLAIM TO FAME: Among their ranks was *Easyrider* magazine's Dave Mann, the most renowned biker artist of all time
- ◆ CLUB ASSOCIATIONS: Affiliated with Galloping Goose MC

EL FORASTERO - Established in 1962 in Sioux City, Iowa, by "Tiny and Fugle"—two guys who had apparently asked the Satans Slaves for permission to start an SS chapter in Iowa. That idea wasn't exactly warmed up to by the Slaves, so El Forastero MC (the outsiders/the strangers) was born. They are a one percent motorcycle club and made the law enforcement map listing in Iowa, Missouri, Wisconsin, Minnesota, and South Dakota.

Besides their early 1960s founding, the other factor that makes the EFMC one of our "classic" clubs is that they had among their brotherhood the Normal Rockwell of the biker world, Dave Mann. Mann became a founding member of the El Forastero Kansas City chapter

and the legend has it that it was Tiny and Fugle who prompted Dave to focus his art more on bikes and less on pin-up chicks and hot rods. It proved to be damn good advice!

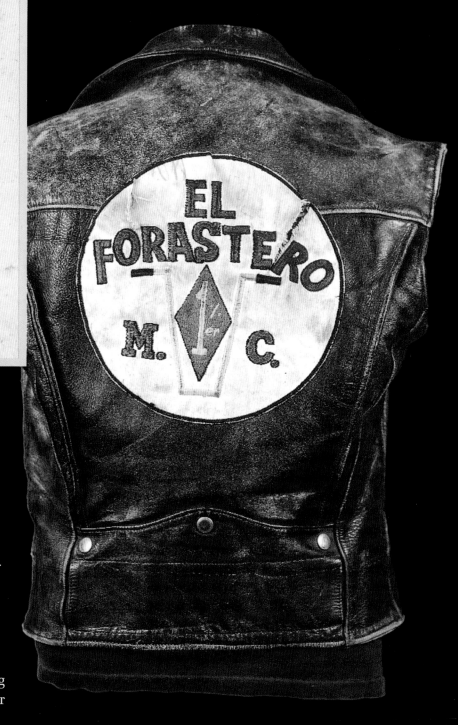

EMPTIES - They fully made it onto the law enforcement map in Idaho. They also had a commemorative fortieth anniversary "rock" carved for the club, courtesy of Pocatello Cycle. The precision graphics on the rock feature a noose around an empty bottle of Coors. Now, I don't know if that's because they don't like Coors or if it's because they do and just don't like seeing an empty bottle.

⊹

Enola Gay

- ♦ **ESTABLISHED:** 1993
- ♦ **PLACE OF ORIGIN:** Czecho-Moravian Highlands, Czech Republic
- ♦ **FOUNDER(S):** Unknown
- ♦ **CHAPTER LOCATIONS:** Czech Republic
- ♦ **CENTER PATCH:** Eagle with a bomb in his talons
- ♦ **CLAIM TO FAME:** A crew member from the Enola Gay, the infamous B-29 bomber that dropped "Little Boy" on Hiroshima, was from the founding area
- ♦ **CLUB ASSOCIATIONS:** They support Hells Angels, Bohemia

ENOLA GAY - Established in 1993, a three-piece-patch club in Czech Republic with a very unique historical tie-in. The club was named, of course, after the famous WWII B-29 bomber that dropped its package on Hiroshima. One of the crew members,

Joseph Stiborik, was from the Czech Republic, from the town of Nove Mesto na Morave, where the motorcycle club is based. The club is also an HAMC (Hells Angel Motorcycle Club) supporter.

⊹

EOD - Okay, you can have a blast with this club. The EODMC is a club out of Florida for veterans of explosive ordinance disposal! They are a "traditional motorcycle club" with the hangaround-prospect-member sequence. They do not accept law enforcement, they do wear a three-piece patch, and they do differentiate between themselves and a riding club with a similar name also for EOD vets.

⊹

71

Epitaph Riders

- ◆ **ESTABLISHED:** Unknown
- ◆ **PLACE OF ORIGIN:** New Zealand
- ◆ **FOUNDER(S):** Unknown
- ◆ **CHAPTER LOCATIONS:** Christchurch and Greymouth, New Zealand
- ◆ **CLAIM TO FAME:** Monetarily liquidated by the IRD in 2005
- ◆ **CLUB ASSOCIATIONS:** Part of a New Zealand federation of clubs known as "the A-Team," along with the Outcasts MC, the Forty-Fives MC, the Southern Vikings MC, Satan's Slaves MC, Sinn Fein MC, and the Lost Breed MC

EPITAPH RIDERS - Another of the clubs on all of the "lists" in New Zealand. The Epitaph Riders are based in Christchurch and Greymouth. They are one of the few clubs to suffer severe financial hardships as a result of some lengthy legal entanglements. Trouble with the IRD (the Kiwi equivalent of America's evil IRS) culminated in the gang being sold to an ex-member for $1 in 1999, and finally liquidated in 2005.

A stark reminder of, as a local calls it, "a testament to the darker side of Christchurch history," is the abandoned ERMC clubhouse in the middle of Addington. It's a bit creepy and I'm sure filled with ghosts in leather.

The Epitaph Riders are also a part of a federation of clubs known as "the A-Team," along with the Outcasts MC, the Forty-Fives MC, the Southern Vikings MC, Satan's Slaves MC, Sinn Fein MC, and the Lost Breed MC.

ESCORPIONES - "The Scorpions," a three-piece patch motorcycle club stinging in Pais Vasco (Basque Country), Spain.

✠

ESCUDEROS - Another of the loud-piped packs of German Bandidos support clubs.

✠

EVEL ROWDIES - Established in 1980. A three-piece-patch club in Switzerland and, yes, they do spell their name like the King of the Snake River, rather than bad guys.

✠

Evil Crew

- ◆ **ESTABLISHED:** A few years back
- ◆ **PLACE OF ORIGIN:** Sweden ("down in the suburbs where we all used to raise some hell")
- ◆ **FOUNDER(S):** Unknown
- ◆ **CHAPTER LOCATIONS:** Sweden
- ◆ **CENTER COLORS:** Red and Blue
- ◆ **CENTER PATCH:** A tribal horned "death head"
- ◆ **MOTTO:** Ten tigers are always stronger than a hundred lambs
- ◆ **CLUB ASSOCIATIONS:** "Evil Crew MC is not bound to any motorcycle brand and does not support anyone but ourselves."

EVIL CREW - A one percent motorcycle club in Sweden with some sharp philosophies and statements: "Ten tigers are always stronger than a hundred lambs...Evil Crew MC is not bound to any motorcycle brand and does not support anyone but ourselves...Because this is what it means to be a 1%er, which we pride ourselves in being. . . . A 1%er is always free, never supporting anyone, never being told what to do by others, and always loyal to his colors. No one chooses Evil Crew; they choose you."

✢

EVIL LOYALTY - A Bandidos support club in Denmark.

✢

EVOLUTION - A club evolving in upstate New York, founded by "six men that have lived and enjoyed the life of brotherhood."

✢

EXILES AND EXILE RIDERS - Another mix of clubs with the same/similar names:

Exiles MC made the map in Maine.

Then there is a three-piece patch club in Abu Dhabi in the United Arab Emirates.

But then we have the Exile Riders in California with a three-piece-patch cut that looks as "outlaw" and as one percent as anything I've ever seen. They actually do discuss the reason for the three-piece patch—that it represents something that is earned, not merely given. But...all that said...they are a law enforcement motorcycle club!

✢

EXTERMINATORS - Established in 1984, this three-piece-patch motorcycle club is out of Denmark. They do have a very cool buzzard for a center patch.

✢

EYE OF RA - WOW! While certainly not an outlaw club, this organization has "connections" to the one percent world by actually being featured on the weird Last Combat website—a site that apparently features video games (or something like that) of motorcycle club vs. motorcycle club (kind of like sports video games pitting one team against another). Eye of Ra is matched up in battles with the Boozefighters, the Outlaws, the Warlocks, the Pagans, the Jewish Motorcyclist Alliance, the Moped Army, and more! The club itself is located in South Wales.

✠

FARAONS - Established in 2003 in Slovakia, these *Pharaohs* are HAMC supporters.

✠

FAT MEXICAN SUPPORT CLUB - Based in Australia, it's kind of obvious that this a Bandidos support club, taking its name from its affectionate and accepted referral to the Bandidos center patch (it's also the title of Alex Caine's *The Fat Mexican: The Bloody Rise of the Bandidos Motorcycle Club*, an enigmatic book that was really more about one specific incident—Canada's so-called "Shedden Massacre"—than an overall examination of the Bandidos' growth into motorcycle club prominence).

✠

FEW GOOD MEN - An HAMC support club out of New York.

✠

Filthy Few

- ◆ **ESTABLISHED:** Unknown
- ◆ **PLACE OF ORIGIN:** New Zealand
- ◆ **FOUNDER(S):** Unknown
- ◆ **CHAPTER LOCATIONS:** Tauranga, Rotorua, Waihi, and Matamata, New Zealand
- ◆ **CLAIM TO FAME:** Takes its name from a common idiom seen on patches throughout the motorcycle culture— often ascribed to mean that the wearer has killed for his club

FILTHY FEW - Taking its name from a phrase that has been around the motorcycle club world for a long time (Filthy Few is a patch "idiom" often thought to mean that the wearer has committed murder for a specific cause of his club), this New Zealand motorcycle club is located in Tauranga, Rotorua, Waihi, and Matamata. In April 2010, New Zealand's *Bay of Plenty Times* reported that the club had been "shut down" during a police raid of the club's bar, which was deemed illegal by authorities.

Alcohol harm prevention officer for the Western Bay of Plenty, Sergeant Nigel McGlone said the laying of such charges was unusual, but that illegal bars would not be ignored either: "It doesn't matter whether you are a club, a gang, a school PTA running fundraising quiz nights, or whatever—the rules are the same for everyone."

Hmmm…if you say so…

✠

FINAL DAWN - A full-on one percent motorcycle club out of Austria.

Finks

♦ **ESTABLISHED:** 1969

♦ **PLACE OF ORIGIN:** Adelaide, South Australia

♦ **FOUNDER(S):** Unknown

♦ **CHAPTER LOCATIONS:** Australia

♦ **CLUB COLORS:** Black and White

♦ **CENTER PATCH:** Court jester Bung from the *Wizard of Id* comic strip, to which the club name refers

♦ **CLAIM TO FAME:** An oft-listed top club in the crowded Australian "bikie" scene

FINKS - Established in 1969 in Adelaide, South Australia. It's another of the many Australian motorcycle clubs to make this list. The Finks got their name from the *Wizard of Id* comic strip and the peasants' loud and frequent proclamations that "The King is a fink!" Their *colours* are that of Bung, the jester in the strip.

In February 2011, *The West Australian* reported on a less-than-*Law & Order* kind of court scene involving members of the Finks:

As West Australian Chief Justice Wayne Martin sentenced four Finks bikie members to jail for maintaining their code of silence out of fear of

retribution, he was told he had "no idea about the streets".

The motorcycle gang members had refused to answer questions or to be sworn in at a secret Corruption and Crime Commission (CCC) hearing into organised crime last year.

The Finks members Tristan Allbeury, Stephen Silvestro, Troy Crispin Smith and Clovis Chikonga had been called in relation to a brawl between them and rival gang the Coffin Cheaters.

The brawl had broken out at the Perth Motorplex on October 3 and left Silvestro and Smith with injuries.

All four men had kept quiet during the CCC hearing and were charged with contempt of court for refusing to be sworn in to give evidence.

*Allbeury was subsequently charged with insulting Commissioner Len Roberts-Smith by refusing to answer 18 separate questions before telling him to "f*** off" and "get f****d".*

✠

FIRESTARTERS - A three-piece patch club out of Slovenia. Their center patch is the Rune Gebo (the Big X), which symbolizes the greatest gift to a devoted warrior: devotion and passion.

✠

Flaming Knights

- ◆ **ESTABLISHED:** 1968
- ◆ **PLACE OF ORIGIN:** New Haven, Connecticut (in the garage of Leroy "King Dragon" Bolden)
- ◆ **FOUNDER(S):** Leroy "King Dragon" Bolden and others
- ◆ **CHAPTER LOCATIONS:** International
- ◆ **CLUB COLORS:** Red and Gold
- ◆ **CENTER PATCH:** A flaming knight!
- ◆ **MOTTO:** *Born to wander*
- ◆ **CLAIM TO FAME:** Fully racially integrated club

FLAMING KNIGHTS - Established in 1968 in New Haven, Connecticut, the Flaming Knights Motorcycle Club started in the garage of Leroy Bolden, a.k.a. "King Dragon." The motorcycle club is an integrated three-piece-patch international club.

⊹

FLYING HORSES - Established in 1973, this one percent diamond-patch club out of Germany is in "K-town" (Kaiserslautern, but called K-Town by the 50,000 NATO and American military personnel stationed there): "The Flying Horses 1% Motorcycle Club K-Town is no supporter club for anybody!"

⊹

FLYIN' IRON - Made the law enforcement map in New Hampshire. In 2009, one of their members appeared on New Hampshire's Most Wanted list for a failure to appear. He was considered "Armed and Dangerous." Special sections of his mug shots feature some pretty nice tattoos!

⊹

FLYING WHEELS, FLY-IN WHEELS - Established in 1977, the Flying Wheels MC Association was founded in Georgsmarienhütte OT Holzhausen and is the biggest club in the Osnabrück region of Germany. A three-piece-patch club, but they don't consider themselves one percenters.

The Fly-In Wheels MC was established in Flint, Michigan, "over five decades ago" and this national club made the law enforcement map in Florida. In 2006, a member was under indictment in Michigan for narcotics and firearms violations—the indictment refers, of course, to the club as a gang but the club does officially say that they are not a one percent club.

Fly-in Wheels

- ♦ **ESTABLISHED:** Pre-1960s
- ♦ **PLACE OF ORIGIN:** Flint, Michigan
- ♦ **FOUNDER(S):** Unknown
- ♦ **CHAPTER LOCATIONS:** Michigan, Colorado, Florida, and Pennsylvania
- ♦ **CLUB COLORS:** Blue and White
- ♦ **CENTER PATCH:** A winged motorcycle wheel
- ♦ **CLAIM TO FAME:** Club claims to not be "1%" but made the law enforcement list of "OMGs" in Florida

FLYING WHEELS - There is a Flying Wheels riding club established in 1965 by moped riders out of Arizona. They *didn't* make the law enforcement map anywhere.

✠

FORAJIDOS - A major diamond-patch one percent club throughout Spain.

✠

FORBIDDEN - This motorcycle club made the law enforcement map in the crowded house that is Connecticut. They also made some dismal news reports in 2008 when their "P" was shot and killed.

The Associated Press would report:

Kevin Campbell of Watertown is charged with murder in the shooting death of 51-year-old Roland LaGasse of Torrington, who was president of the Forbidden Motor Cycle Club. Campbell, who was also in the club, has said he acted in self-defense and the gun accidentally fired.

Litchfield Superior Court Judge James Ginocchio heard testimony on Tuesday indicating that the shooting occurred during a dispute over whether to give a new member of the club his first-year patch.

One witness testified that Campbell deliberately shot LaGasse after LaGasse slapped Campbell's brother across the face.

✠

FORBIDDEN ONES - Established in 1992, this motorcycle club is out of New York.

✠

FORBIDDEN WHEELS - A long-running motorcycle club out of Michigan that slid into a sad side note in the early 1980s with a trial that saw their "P," Paul Allen Dye, convicted of a double murder. The *Detroit Free Press* would report:

A Detroit district judge Thursday called for a grand jury probe of a motorcycle club whose president has been charged in the slaying of two women inside the club's headquarters.

Tried by a jury for the third time, petitioner Paul Allen Dye was convicted in the Recorders Court in Detroit, Michigan, on two counts of murder and one count of possession of a firearm during commission of a felony. His defense in each of his three trials was that the crimes were committed by one of the prosecution's key witnesses, who was present at the scene of the crime.

As of 2009, Dye was still fighting to have his sentence commuted.

✠

FORTRESS - This HAMC support club is based in Poland. There's also a Fortress MC in Russia.

✠

FORTY FIVE - One of the clubs on the many "lists" in New Zealand. This Auckland-based motorcycle club is also a part of the "A-Team" federation, along with The Epitaph Riders, the Outcasts MC, the Southern Vikings MC, Satan's Slaves MC, Sinn Fein MC, and the Lost Breed MC.

✠

FOUR HORSEMEN - In Norway, this is a support club for the HAMC.

There is also a long-lived club, the 4 Horse Men—a primarily Black motorcycle club—with chapters in Pasadena and San Diego, California.

✠

FOURTH REICH - There are at least *three* Fourth Reichs:

There was one Fourth Reich in Salt Lake in the late 1960s. Some old members have been trying to dig up a reunion lately.

And then there's Michigan, where the Fourth Reich became another of those not-so-good newsmakers when, in 2006, Sherry L. Priemer was convicted of manslaughter (though not first-degree murder as originally charged) for killing Gregory (Sigmund) Getty, "a veteran of two tours in Vietnam and a member of the Madison Heights–based Fourth Reich Motorcycle Club," by shooting him in the back of the head.

New South Wales, Australia, is the "bikie" home of our third Fourth Reich, another commanding Australian motorcycle club, with chapters in Albion Park and Wollengong.

✠

FREEDOM SEEKERS - Established in 1969, this motorcycle club is from the Tennessee Hills.

✠

FREE EAGLES - Established in 1975, this three-piece-patch motorcycle club from Germany didn't just come together based on their love of bikes and the lifestyle—the founding members were also part of a Doors fan club.

✠

FREE MEN, FREEMEN - There are a few unrestrained Free Men roaming the globe:

One is a three-piece-patch Free Men, established in 1979, in Germany.

There is a Freemen three-piece-patch club out of Russia—a "hangaround club to the 81 world."

And a Freemen MC in Minnesota.

✠

Free Souls

- ♦ **ESTABLISHED:** 1968
- ♦ **PLACE OF ORIGIN:** Eugene, Oregon
- ♦ **FOUNDER(S):** Unknown
- ♦ **CHAPTER LOCATIONS:** Throughout Oregon and one in Washington
- ♦ **CLUB COLORS:** Blue and White
- ♦ **CENTER PATCH:** An ankh—the ancient Egyptian symbol of eternal life
- ♦ **CLAIM TO FAME:** Considered one of Oregon's "big five," alongside the Vagos, Brother Speed, Gypsy Jokers, and the Outsiders, and listed in one source's "Top Ten of America's most notorious biker gangs"

FREE SOULS - Established in 1968, in Eugene, Oregon, this motorcycle club made the law enforcement map in the Beaver State as well as Washington. They are considered one of Oregon's "big five," alongside the Vagos, Brother Speed, Gypsy Jokers, and the Outsiders.

✠

FREE SPIRITS - Another of those clubs that gave up the one percenter patch. This New Jersey club dates back to the 1960s but was forced to "disband due to many members' arrests and to general disorder. That club and all ties to the 1% world ended totally & completely."

Today, they are an AMA-sanctioned club.

There are other riding clubs around with the Free Spirits name and an all-female club in Michigan.

✠

Vince Clements/shutterstock.com

79

Freeway Riders

- ◆ ESTABLISHED: 1970s
- ◆ PLACE OF ORIGIN: Hagen, Germany
- ◆ FOUNDER(S): "A few young guys who rode their motorbikes and celebrated"
- ◆ CHAPTER LOCATIONS: 20-plus chapters throughout Germany
- ◆ CLUB COLORS: Red and Black
- ◆ CENTER PATCH: Winged skull with riding cap accompanied by crossbones
- ◆ MOTTO: *E.F.I.F.: Einmal Freeway Immer Freeway* (Once Freeway Always Freeway)

Freewheelers

- ◆ ESTABLISHED: 1968
- ◆ PLACE OF ORIGIN: Chicago, Illinois
- ◆ FOUNDER(S): A group of riders "who had been running together for some time"
- ◆ CHAPTER LOCATIONS: Illinois
- ◆ CENTER PATCH: A freewheelin' Grim Reaper
- ◆ CLAIM TO FAME: Their interwoven history to the Devil's Ushers, Hell's Henchmen, and Hells Angels
- ◆ CLUB ASSOCIATIONS: Ties to the Hells Angels

FREEWAY RIDERS - Established "thirty-five years ago" in Hagen, Germany, by "a few young guys who rode their motorbikes and celebrated." A thundering, straight-ahead, diamond-patch one percent club with chapters throughout Germany and roots that go back "to the time of jean jackets, long hair, and sideburns."

✠

FREEWHEELERS - Two heavy-duty—and freewheeling—motorcycle clubs share this name:

One was established in 1968 in the western suburbs of Chicago. In a scene reminiscent of the HAMC discovering early on that two groups had taken the name, two presidents of two Freewheelers in Illinois discovered each other at a bike show

and—again, like the HAMC—formed a bond and merged the clubs. Members of one of those factions later became Hell's Henchmen. Other members eventually became Devil's Ushers. Hell's Henchmen eventually all patched over to the HAMC. The ties remained strong among all the clubs and members and the Freewheelers kept ties to the HAMC.

Established in 1979 in Waterford City, Ireland, the Freewheelers there would become huge in the European biker world. Beginning with twelve members, the Freewheelers MC "were the first of the 1% clubs to build and ride customised Harley-Davidson motorcycles now considered the norm for 1% clubs worldwide."

The club is responsible for The South East Custom and Classic Bike Show—an event that began in 1987 and still runs to this day in Tramore Racecourse, County Waterford.

Freewheelers

- ♦ **ESTABLISHED:** 1979
- ♦ **PLACE OF ORIGIN:** Waterford City, Ireland
- ♦ **FOUNDER(S):** Twelve original members
- ♦ **CHAPTER LOCATIONS:** Ireland
- ♦ **CENTER PATCH:** A winged freewheeling skull
- ♦ **CLAIM TO FAME:** First one percent club to build and ride customized Harleys

Lenny is the "P" of the Freewheelers, Ireland:

All in all, we walk a fine line but have had no interference up until now.

Freewheelers MC was founded in Waterford City, Ireland in 1979. It was one of the first homegrown Irish one percenter clubs to exist in Ireland in the 1970s. From the outset we were destined for the long haul. We still have five original members from the twelve who started in '79, including our two founding members, John Blue O' Shea, and Claudio Clau Giani.

The Brotherhood that is Freewheelers MC is as strong now as it was at the beginning and it is a true bond. It is what we have lived for. It is what we would die for. It is what has made us what we are, true one percenter's, true brothers, which is something that can be lost if numbers become the game, which is all too often the case.

Our policy from day one was to keep Ireland free of international politics, which for the most part, thirty-two years later, we have achieved. Our alliance with the other three true Irish one percent clubs has been and is a major part of this policy, and it is an alliance that we intend to nurture into the future.

After thirty years I still get the Buzz. I still get the rush of being out there with my bros. It's what it is all about: Harleys, freedom, brothers, and the wild times that this mix creates.

My advice to all is to be true to the one percent lifestyle! Live it, love it, protect it!

—Lenny 1%er, President,
Freewheelers MC Ireland. F.F.F.F.

✠

FUCKING FREAKS - Established in 1987 in North Tavastia, Finland. (And no, I don't know if they have an FFFFFF patch!)

✠

FUGARWE TRIBE - This club made the law enforcement map in Illinois. It's a notable motorcycle club for their name (from the old Indian—I'm sorry, Native American—joke, "Where the Fugarwe?") and their longevity. Established in 1948 as the Road Kings, in 1955 they became the Fugarwe Tribe.

✠

FULL OF ENERGY - A three-piece-patch club out of the Czech Republic that really demonstrates the universal struggles it takes for a motorcycle club to become established—politically and protocolwise. This club began with roots in 1991; they nearly ran out of energy and took a three-year pause from 2000 to 2003, and then refilled themselves with energy, and eventually became a full club in 2005.

Galloping Goose

- ◆ **ESTABLISHED:** 1949–1950
- ◆ **PLACE OF ORIGIN:** Los Angeles, California
- ◆ **FOUNDER(S):** Dick Hershberg, one of thirteen original members
- ◆ **CHAPTER LOCATIONS:** Nationwide, U.S.
- ◆ **CLUB COLORS:** Purple and Gold
- ◆ **CENTER PATCH:** The famous "running finger" designed into a patch by renowned So-Cal artist John Altoon
- ◆ **CLAIM TO FAME:** They're a "classic club" with long roots, featured in a *Gangland* episode "Beware the Goose!"

GALLOPING GOOSE - With roots that go back to the early 1940s, the GG are "pioneers *and* classic" in the club world. And they're another of the clubs whose name gets bastardized a lot—it is singular: Galloping Goose. That's mainly because the name came from a motorcycle called the "Galloping Goose" owned by a guy named Dick Hershberg. The famous "running finger" in their patch was painted on the bike's tank. They're another of those post-WWII good ol' boy groups that got together by hanging out in the still-relaxing classy ambience of a Los Angeles bar—theirs was the Pullman, near downtown's Union Station. The group came together as a formal club in "1949 or 1950" with thirteen original members.

Their patch, which began as a combination of the tank painting and drawings on a cocktail napkin, has an even more L.A./Hollywood connection, in that its final design was the creation of the famous So-Cal artist John Altoon—an eccentric painter described by art historians as having an "outsized personality and reckless intensity."

The Galloping Goose MC made the law enforcement map in Cali, of course, and they were the subject of the *Gangland* episode "Beware the Goose!"

✠

GERONIMO - Long-lived three-piece patch club in Hungary that evolved from that country's Angels MC—they are closely allied with HAMC.

There is also a Geronimo MC in Germany with a completely different patch.

✠

GHOST ANGELS - Established in 1976, a three-piece-patch club out of Maxhutte, Germany.

✠

Ghost Mountain Riders

- **ESTABLISHED:** 1982
- **PLACE OF ORIGIN:** Santa Cruz Mountains, California
- **FOUNDER(S):** "Lompico Lyle"
- **CHAPTER LOCATIONS:** Northern California
- **CLUB COLORS:** White on Black
- **CENTER PATCH:** Rider storming from the mouth of a skull-shaped mountain
- **MOTTO:** *Mi Vida Loca* and *Qué Viva Los Tamales!*
- **CLAIM TO FAME:** Known for their "truck surfing" and "tamale passing"; featured in the 2000 documentary *American Biker*
- **CLUB ASSOCIATIONS:** Monterey Bay Confederation of Clubs

GHOST MOUNTAIN RIDERS - Established in 1985, "on a ridge high in the Santa Cruz Mountains" of Northern California, the Ghost Mountain Riders made the western edge of the law enforcement map and were featured in several segments in the seminal film documentary *American Biker* in the mid-2000s.

They also have some pretty solid lore about their club; a few million tales from the road; and some definite ideas about the meaning of one percenter. Felicia Morgan—a badass and brazen biker-photojournalist whose hard-butt riding habits are right up there with Gypsy Raoul and *Easyrider*'s late

Roving Editor George "Rip" Rose—had a long sit-down with the founder of the Ghost Mountain Riders, "Lompico Lyle," GMRMC Nomad President Tony "Loco," and other brothers of the GMRMC:

Lyle: *The name Ghost Mountain Riders was actually created in 1979, but the GMRMC as a club officially began in 1985. It started with three guys sitting up on a ridge in the Santa Cruz Mountains, near Loch Lomond.*

We heard a long time ago that there's an old Indian burial ground up there, and that's what our club is based on. We figure we're up there riding with ghosts, the people who were here before us.

The way it happened was that we were sitting around one evening up under the redwood trees. The Indians used to live up there along with the grizzly bears and all that stuff, in kind of an idyllic existence, 'til Whitey came up and raped the land and took out a lot of the trees. Now a lot of redwoods are protected through selective logging and other things, so we're enjoying second- and third-growth redwoods, which have captured a lot of the atmosphere of the way things were.

Anyway, we're enjoying a quiet winter's evening, sitting up there around a campfire behind my house. Me and my buddy—we're smoking some, drinking some—and we get to tripping out: "Wow, we're up here with the ghosts of the Indians past…they used to be here!"

"Yeah, we're hanging around with ghosts!"

"We're on a ghostly mountain. We ride our motorcycles on this mountain. Yeah, we're ghost mountain riders!"

Yeah, it started with something stupid like that. Ghost Mountain was never the real name of the place—it's our name for it. But after a while a T-shirt was made, and the T-shirt thing kind of caught on with several of the guys who lived up there.

Now most of the people who live there have started calling it Ghost Mountain.

✠

GHOST RIDERS, GHOSTRIDERS - There are a lot of Ghost Riders in the skies of the biker world:

One Ghost Riders was established in 1971 in Tennessee—and made the law enforcement map there!

Then there's the Ghostriders, an AMA club in Northern California.

Established in 1961 is a Ghostriders in Texas, and they are very vehement that they were the first with the Ghostrider spirit—and name: "Nobody tells us nothin'!" They made the map listing down there!

We have a Ghost Riders three-piece-patch sport bike club in Phuket, Thailand, and yet another sport bike herd, the Ghost Ryderz Extreme Motorcycle Club from New York and into the south.

Ghost Riders MC haunts Malaysia and there are Ghost Riders out of Singapore

Man, it's spooky to think about there being so many Ghost Riders!

✠

GHOST'S - Established in 1989, these Euro-specters are a three-piece-patch club in Hungary.

✠

Gladiators

- ♦ **ESTABLISHED:** 1963
- ♦ **PLACE OF ORIGIN:** Australia
- ♦ **FOUNDER(S):** Unknown
- ♦ **CHAPTER LOCATIONS:** Australia
- ♦ **CLAIM TO FAME:** Author Arthur Veno credits them with kicking off the one percenter motorcycle club movement in Australia

GLADIATORS - Legend has it that the Gladiators MC, established in 1963, was Australia's original one percenter motorcycle club. In June 2005, one of the Gladiators got into a bit of a bind for possessing weapons...of the type never seen in the Coliseum. *The Daily Examiner* explained:

A Gladiators Motorcycle Club member was yesterday found guilty of possessing unregistered and prohibited firearms.

A jury found Steven Gardiner, 48, of Kungala, guilty on the charge of possessing one semi-automatic, sawn-off shotgun and four Chinese-made rifles.

The firearms were found in a police search of a storage unit at Hi-Tech Self Storage in Toormina on November 20, 2002. Gardiner, who was the president of the Grafton chapter of the Gladiators at the time, had taken out the lease on the storage unit in his name in October 1999, but in court claimed it had been used by many members of the motorcycle club.

He told the court he had no knowledge of the firearms and suspected he had been set up by a disgruntled member of the bike club or by the police.

The Crown asserted the unit was intended for Gardiner's personal use and under the Firearms Act he was required to prove he did not know, or could not reasonably be expected to know, the firearms were there.

The jury found Gardiner not guilty of six charges of possessing prohibited weapons.

Gardiner is being held in custody and will be sentenced in the Coffs Harbour District Court today.

There is also a three-piece-patch Gladiators motorcycle club out of Karbach, Bavaria.

✠

GOLDEN DRAKES - Established in "early 1975," this three-piece-patch motorcycle club was formed in Italy and later expanded into Germany. They have support clubs and reportedly absorbed the Crawling Death MC.

✠

GRAVE DIGGER, GRAVE DIGGERS - Time to exhume some of the clubs that have undertaken to use the Gravedigger name:

I'm sorry, I know I said that there would be no mentions of fictitious clubs, but since we already mentioned the Crucifiers from *The Cannonball Run*, we need to mention the Grave Diggers MC featured in the 1974 nearly Emmy-winning feature, *Stone*.

The trailer itself was downright terrifying: "Members of the Grave Diggers Motorcycle Club are being knocked off one by one, and someone needs to find out why!"

Stone was touted as director Sandy Harbutt's "timeless Australian cult film about a bunch of renegades riding Kawasaki 900s."

Okay, now back to the real world. There is a living Grave Diggers MC, established in 1980 in Bayreuth, Bavaria, Germany, and a Grave Digger MC nearby in the Netherlands.

✠

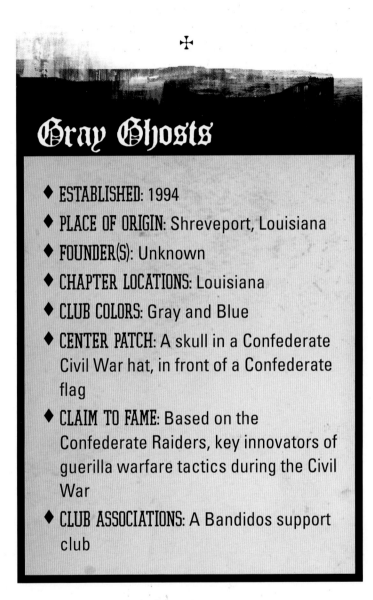

Gray Ghosts

- ◆ **ESTABLISHED:** 1994
- ◆ **PLACE OF ORIGIN:** Shreveport, Louisiana
- ◆ **FOUNDER(S):** Unknown
- ◆ **CHAPTER LOCATIONS:** Louisiana
- ◆ **CLUB COLORS:** Gray and Blue
- ◆ **CENTER PATCH:** A skull in a Confederate Civil War hat, in front of a Confederate flag
- ◆ **CLAIM TO FAME:** Based on the Confederate Raiders, key innovators of guerilla warfare tactics during the Civil War
- ◆ **CLUB ASSOCIATIONS:** A Bandidos support club

GRAY GHOSTS - Established in 1994 in Shreveport, Louisiana, this motorcycle club is based on "the Confederate Raiders under the command of Colonel John Singleton Moseby. Moseby's Raiders, as they were often called, were key innovators in the tactics of guerilla warfare during the Civil War."

The Gray Ghosts are a Bandidos support club and they made the law enforcement map in Louisiana.

✛

GREASY DOGS - Yet another motorcycle club that has made all the lists in New Zealand. In March 2011 the *Bay of Plenty Times* reported on a big rumble Down Under:

Nine members of the Greasy Dogs motorcycle gang have been fined $500 each following a standoff with rival gang the Filthy Few last month. . . . Police were alerted to tensions between the two gangs about 11.30 am on February 5 after Filthy Few members wearing gang patches rode motorcycles into Matapihi—an area known to be occupied by Greasy Dogs. . . . About 3 pm, about 20 Greasy Dogs members travelled to the Filthy Few gang pad at Birch Ave. An altercation followed between the two groups, during which police say some of the Filthy Few armed themselves with weapons including hammers, a spade and a baseball bat. When police arrived, the Greasy Dogs members began dispersing but 13 were arrested and charged with unlawful assembly.

✛

GREAT SPIRITS - A three-piece-patch club from Japan. They have a really non-PC center patch with a Chief Wahoo–type character with a bloody hatchet!

✛

GREEN MACHINE - A major club in its own right in Southern California and recognized as the main support club for the Vagos.

✛

Jennifer Thomas

Jennifer Thomas

Gremium

- ♦ **ESTABLISHED:** 1972
- ♦ **PLACE OF ORIGIN:** Mannheim, Germany
- ♦ **FOUNDER(S):** Unknown
- ♦ **CHAPTER LOCATIONS:** 110 full and prospect chapters, in Austria, Spain, Venezuela, Germany, Italy, Poland, Slovenia, Bosnia Herzegovina, Thailand, Serbia, Turkey, Chile, and in the Canary Islands
- ♦ **CLUB COLORS:** Black and White
- ♦ **CENTER PATCH:** Rising sun and a clenched fist stretching up through the clouds
- ♦ **CLAIM TO FAME:** Largest motorcycle club in Germany and leading worldwide motorcycle club
- ♦ **CLUB ASSOCIATIONS:** "We support nobody—but lots support us!"

GREMIUM - Established in 1972 in Mannheim, Germany, this is one of the big dogs in the European motorcycle club landscape. Gremium's Markus7 gives us their history from the "inside":

GREMIUM MC

by Marcus7
Press Agent, GMC NRW

In 1972, the Gremium MC was founded in Mannheim, Germany. Today, our club is the biggest MC in Germany and one of the leading MCs in the worldwide biker scene.

Our back patch shows a rising sun and a clenched fist that stretches itself into the sky through the clouds. We changed our colors slightly in 2004, because the patch also had a Celtic Cross that could have been mistaken for the Christian Cross in the Muslim states of the former Yugoslavia. Since then, all members ride under the lettering of their own country and under the Iron Cross between the letters. The only exception to this rule is given to our Polish brothers, because the Iron Cross is not welcome in Poland.

After its foundation, the Gremium MC grew fast and strong like no other MC with German roots. With almost two thousand members and double that number of supporters and friends in Europe, America, Asia, and all over the world, we represent a certain power. The members are organized in more than 110 full and prospect chapters, nationally and internationally. Our brothers are present in Austria, Spain, Venezuela, Germany, Italy, Poland, Slovenia, Bosnia Herzegovina, Thailand, Serbia, Turkey, Chile, and the Canary Islands. In spite of the immense distances, our club brothers maintain strong relationships to each other and very special friendships.

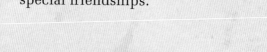

In 1978, we organized the so-called "Presidents Rally" with the Bones MC, to be a meeting of the German motorcycle clubs, held on the Friesenheimer Insel in Mannheim. In the years 1983, 1986, and 1995, we organized this event on our own.

We organize several annual runs. The biggest runs are the Euro Run (all European and non-European countries are invited) and the NRW Run, which is carried out by the chapters that belong to the German county of Nordrhein-Westfalen. These two events are visited on average by one to four thousand brothers, family members, and friends of the Gremium MC.

Unfortunately, these events are always accompanied by a large police detachment.

✠

EURORUN 04.-06.Juli 2008

Both photos courtesy of Gremium MC

Grim Reapers

- ◆ **ESTABLISHED:** 1958
- ◆ **PLACE OF ORIGIN:** Alberta, Canada
- ◆ **FOUNDER(S):** Unknown
- ◆ **CHAPTER LOCATIONS:** None
- ◆ **CLAIM TO FAME:** Were one of the "big four" in Alberta
- ◆ **CLUB ASSOCIATIONS:** Patched over to Hells Angels in 1997

GRIM REAPERS - I know you're dying to know how many Grim Reapers MCs there are. A few have crooked their fingers at us from the shadows:

Established in 1965, the Grim Reapers Motorcycle Club was established in Louisville, Kentucky, and has expanded into other states. They made the law enforcement map in the Bluegrass State, Illinois, and Tennessee.

In Calgary, Alberta, Canada, the GRMC was established in 1958, growing to be a "dominant club" in the 1970s and 1980s. Reportedly, "along with the Rebels, the Warlords, and King's Crew, they were once a "big four" in Alberta prior to 1997. In 1997, they became part of the Hells Angels in a patch-over ceremony held in Red Deer, Alberta."

There is also a Grim Reapers MCC in the UK.

✠

GRINGO'S, GRINGOS - Established in 1988, the Gringo's MC began in the town of Terhagen, Belgium. There are two other chapters, a nomad chapter and a chapter five thousand miles away in Denver, Colorado.

There is a Gringos MC, Germany—another of the Deutsch Bandidos support clubs.

And there are Gringos in the Netherlands.

☩

GUERRILLEROS - And another of the Harley-hordes of Bandidos support clubs in Germany.

☩

Gypsy

- ◆ **ESTABLISHED:** 1932
- ◆ **PLACE OF ORIGIN:** Marysville, Tennessee
- ◆ **FOUNDER(S):** Lee Simerly
- ◆ **CHAPTER LOCATIONS:** U.S., Germany, and Mexico
- ◆ **CLUB COLORS:** They wear signature gold-colored cuts
- ◆ **CENTER PATCH:** A pickle riding a motorcycle (after being called "the sour pickles of society")
- ◆ **CLAIM TO FAME:** One of the oldest "pioneer clubs" in the world

GYPSY - Established in 1932 in Marysville, Tennessee, by Lee Simerly—making this "pioneer" club one of the more unique in the MC world. With their gold cuts and their "pickle" patch, they really are unlike anyone else out there! The pickle patch itself is one of the first "let's turn this around on 'em" kinds of statements we see in the biker culture. Much like the one percenter label came to be embraced, the Gypsy center patch of a crazed pickle on a bike was in response to the club being called "the sour pickles of society" by members of that other 99%, long before that little socio-mathematical equation came our way. Their powerhouse really is in Texas but they are in many states and into Germany and Mexico.

GYPSY MOTORCYCLE CLUB—OUTLAW OR FAMILY CLUB?

By Gypsy Raoul

Gypsy history summaries from as early as 1979 suggest that we were once an "outlaw" club, but we reorganized to become an American Motorcycle Association (AMA) or "family" club.

I don't believe that the Gypsy MC was ever an "outlaw" club in the sense that many clubs are portrayed today—those referred to by law enforcement as OMGs. There was a time, however, when Gypsy member's behavior and attitudes leaned far more toward "outlaw" than we do now. The club's transition from a rough-and-tumble, hard-ridin', hard partyin' club to our current family orientation didn't happen overnight; it took a number of years to complete.

When the club was started in 1932, the word "outlaw" was not widely recognized in motorcyclist's vernacular. It was when those non–AMA-sanctioned events—the "Outlaw Gypsy Tours"—were organized during the post-WWII era that the term was solidified as virtually synonymous with "1%er."

The Gypsy MC (no relationship to AMA Gypsy Tours, Jackpine Gypsies, or Gypsy Jokers MC) was chartered as a motorcycle club by the AMA as early as 1968, only a couple of years after "Papa Jack"—the son of founder Lee Simerly—established the club in Texas; in fact, Papa Jack, "Blue," and several other early members competed in AMA flat track races in the late '60s and early '70s. The club has maintained an AMA charter ever since, and has never been banned from membership.

As the club grew through the '60s and '70s, some clubs, who became known as 1%ers, distanced themselves (through their behavior) from traditional motorcycle clubs. They created the "bikes, booze, and broads" biker lifestyle and adopted outrageous acts like wearing German helmets, swastikas, and various colored "wings." As time went by, these clubs evolved from this generally harmless antisocial behavior to at least a perceived criminal behavior.

While starting out with the same "bikes, booze, and broads" approach as the early 1%ers, the Gypsy MC maintained the philosophy of having fun instead of creating a business from club activities. Beginning in the early 1970s, the Gypsys included women as patch members, although many were more "associates" than full members. Associate membership for women became a formal membership status in the late 1970s and continued until 2001. Throughout the '70s, members' motorcycles ran the gamut from Harleys to British and German bikes, and also included the very popular four-cylinder Hondas.

In the early days in Corpus Christi, the Gyspys rode and hung out with the dominant 1% Texas motorcycle club. The clubs coexisted and many of the members became close friends. However, periodic skirmishes between members of the two clubs were not uncommon. Leadership of both clubs inevitably worked hard to contain these incidents and prevent them from spreading. In those days, the Gypsy MC was just a "good-ole-boys" motorcycle club; members rode their motorcycles, camped at roadside parks, and hosted parties for members, families, and friends. But the majority of our members prepared for the worst; they began riding in groups and many carried weapons wherever they went. This is when Papa Jack recognized that being labeled "outlaw" or 1% would put us in a continual conflict with other 1% clubs.

Jack struggled to lead the club, mostly by example, to maintain diplomatic relations with all clubs and law enforcement throughout the

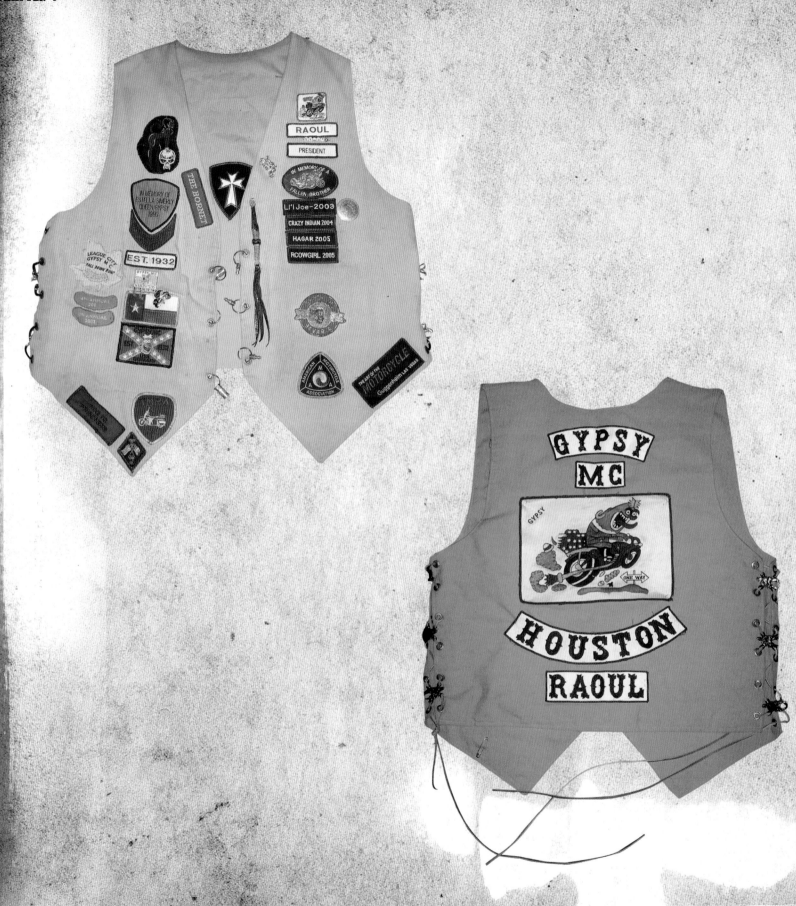

1970s. But it wasn't until 1979, following Jack's marriage to Jaynie Phillips, that a leadership decision was made to make a concerted effort to change our image—to become a "family" club. Many members feel that it was Jaynie's influence that led Jack to force this change.

In June 1979, Papa Jack called a meeting of his chapter (the Black Rockers) and the other Gypsy chapter presidents to decide the future of the Gypsy MC. Minutes of this meeting indicate that the direction of the club—either outlaw or AMA—was decided by a vote. The forty-to-four outcome was in favor of AMA or family. Jack made a strong statement to the members, especially the leaders, that changes were expected. The meeting minutes stated that colors must be clean, and that International Officers would attend runs in "full uniform" and conduct themselves in a manner becoming a leader. Patches and pins worn on the outside of club colors were limited, and restrictions were placed on wearing outlaw or obscene patches.

Ever since that meeting, the Gypsy MC has held steadfast to establishing the club's "family lifestyle." Immediate change is seldom possible; after all, the club had over fifteen years of culture to overcome and many members would have preferred to keep the status quo. But over the years, the Gypsy MC has continued to move closer and closer to a true family club—although we still wear a three-piece-patch, which is the traditional trademark of an "outlaw" motorcycle club.

Papa Jack's philosophy for influencing the culture of the Gypsy Motorcycle Club was based on priorities: Family first, then Job, and then the Club. It's this philosophy that has gone a long way towards making the Gypsy Motorcycle Club what it is today.

✜

GYPSY ACES - A Galloping Goose MC support club out of Leavenworth, Kansas.

✜

Gypsy Jokers

- ◆ **ESTABLISHED:** April 1, 1956 (April Fool's Day)
- ◆ **PLACE OF ORIGIN:** San Francisco, California
- ◆ **FOUNDER(S):** Unknown
- ◆ **CHAPTER LOCATIONS:** U.S. Pacific Northwest, Australia, Germany, Norway, and South Africa
- ◆ **CLUB COLORS:** Black and White
- ◆ **CENTER PATCH:** A smiling skull
- ◆ **CLAIM TO FAME:** Always on the "lists" of top motorcycle clubs

GYPSY JOKERS - Established on April Fool's Day, 1956. A true "classic" club that began in San Francisco, was allegedly run out of 'Frisco by the Angels, and settled in the Pacific Northwest in 1967. Expansion took them into Australia, Germany, Norway, and South Africa. They make the "lists" in Australia and they made the law enforcement map in Oregon and Washington.

CHAPTER 4

Hangmen-Kvillebacken

Hangmen

- ♦ **ESTABLISHED:** 1960
- ♦ **PLACE OF ORIGIN:** Richmond, California
- ♦ **FOUNDER(S):** Ray Aho and eleven other charter members
- ♦ **CHAPTER LOCATIONS:** Western U.S. and Germany
- ♦ **CENTER COLORS:** Black and Gold
- ♦ **CENTER PATCH:** A noose
- ♦ **CLAIM TO FAME:** Included in three Dave Mann/Ed Roth collaborative paintings

HANGMEN - Established in 1960 in Richmond, California, by Ray Aho and eleven other charter members. They are a "classic" club.

One of the club's former members, Tom McMullen, started a short-lived magazine called *Outlaw Chopper*—a low-budget but very real publication like the iconic and equally short-lived *Colors* magazine on the other coast.

Another relic in the "classic" stable of the Hangmen is the art of Dave Mann and Ed "Big Daddy" Roth that included their club. The early work that Mann and Roth did was pure biker gold when it comes to history. Like the untitled piece they did with the Vagos' god, Loki, looking over a Bakersfield run, the pair did three pieces that featured Hangmen.

In another untitled work, the Hangmen colors are seen in front of the Devil. A second work, titled "Tijuana Jail Break," shows Hangmen "Moose" on his motorcycle with his shirt open looking back at the jail, holding a rope with a noose. A third,

"El Forastero New Year's Party," shows Hangmen "Skip" in a black Russian hat, holding a rope with a noose.

✠

HARAMI - Another German Bandidos support club that also has a chapter in Turkey: "Sevgi, Sadakat, & Saygi" (Love, Loyalty, and Respect).

✠

HARD NOSES - Full one percent motorcycle club out of Asere, France.

✠

HARLEKINS - Three-piece-patch club in Germany with their "8" in a diamond.

✠

HAWGS - There's a Hawgs in Toten, Norway, and a Hawgs in Massachusetts. The boys in Mass had a little trouble with cops at their clubhouse in 2005. The *Patriot Ledger* reported about the chaos:

HANSON—Police have shut down what they say is an illegal barroom run by a motorcycle club, but members are complaining that officers unnecessarily wrecked their clubhouse.

"The whole place is completely smashed up," Thomas Nava, 41, a member of the Hawgs motorcycle club, said of the New Year's Eve raid. "Pool cues were broke in half, the pool table was bashed in and turned over. They seized the

jukebox, TV, VCR; they even ripped pictures off the wall. I just don't get it."

Police Chief Edward F. Savage III said his officers appropriately dismantled and seized all items that could be used to run an unlicensed bar at the rented music rehearsal studio.

✛

HAWGZ - Established in 1982 in a basement at Kungsgatan, in the center of Malmo. One of the oldest clubs in Malmo, Sweden.

✛

HEAD HUNTERS, HEAD-HUNTER'S - Watch your neck, there are a few heavyweights with the Head Hunters name:

There is a multi-chapter Head Hunters MC in Poland, one of the "official support clubs of the big red machine world."

There are Head Hunters in Malaysia.

Head-Hunter's MC was established in Germany in 1979.

And there are the Head Hunters Down Under who are another of the clubs making all those "lists" in Australia/New Zealand. It is considered by authorities to be "one of the fastest growing motorcycle clubs in the country." It has chapters in Auckland, Wellsford, Northland, Tauranga, and Wellington, New Zealand. Reportedly, in late 2010, members of the Sinn Fein MC patched over to the Head Hunters.

✛

HEADSMEN - This club was the reported core of the July 2002 establishment of the Middlesex, Massachusetts, charter of the Red Devils MC.

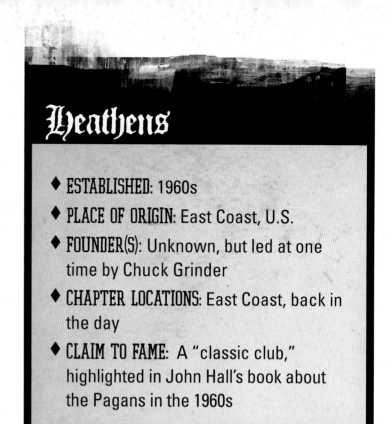

Heathens

- ♦ **ESTABLISHED:** 1960s
- ♦ **PLACE OF ORIGIN:** East Coast, U.S.
- ♦ **FOUNDER(S):** Unknown, but led at one time by Chuck Grinder
- ♦ **CHAPTER LOCATIONS:** East Coast, back in the day
- ♦ **CLAIM TO FAME:** A "classic club," highlighted in John Hall's book about the Pagans in the 1960s

HEATHENS - There is a current motorcycle club known as the Heathens in Wisconsin; they made it onto the law enforcement map there. In 2009, one of their members was indicted in the Brown County Circuit Court for allegedly killing his girlfriend's dog—and putting it in the oven.

But there was also a Heathens MC on the East Coast back in the day. John Hall describes them and some of the universal flavor of the 1960s in his book about the formative years of the Pagans MC, *Riding on the Edge: A Motorcycle Outlaw's Tale:*

And while the Heathens may not have been the biggest club on the East Coast, they were one of the most respected, thanks to the leadership of a former paratrooper named Chuck Grinder.

The Heathens were a large club, and Chuck ran Reading like a feudal warlord. He had the cops scared, he had the mob scared, and he had the citizenry scared. Independent motorcyclists avoided riding in packs through his town, and they never wore denim jackets with cut-off sleeves, much less one percenter patches, because they knew this was an invitation to getting hit in the head with a chain while sitting at a stoplight.

Hellbent

- **ESTABLISHED:** 1959
- **PLACE OF ORIGIN:** Sacramento, California
- **FOUNDER(S):** James "Mother" Miles and his brother, Patrick "Mighty Mouse" Miles
- **CHAPTER LOCATIONS:** Three chapters in Northern California: Sacramento, Nomads, and Tri-county 823 crew
- **CLUB COLORS:** Fiery Orange and Black
- **CENTER PATCH:** Flaming skull wearing WWII helmet and goggles
- **CLAIM TO FAME:** James "Mother" Miles went on to become one of the most legendary of the Hells Angels.
- **CLUB ASSOCIATIONS:** The original Hellbent became the North Sacramento chapter of the HAMC (Hells Angels Motorcycle Club). Hellbent has been twice restarted, once by Pat and now by Pat's son James, with continued ties to the Red and White.

HELLBENT - Established in 1959 in Sacramento, California—originally as Hellbent for Glory—by James "Mother" Miles and his brother, Patrick "Mighty Mouse" Miles. The club began around the same time the Bay Area Hells Angels were forming, a club that would come to define legendary status in the motorcycle club universe. As they grew, Hellbent for Glory and the Angels became close, and eventually Hellbent became the North Sacramento chapter of the HAMC. Later, because of growing police harassment, Miles and most of his chapter, excluding his brother, Pat, who decided to go to San Bernardino and became a Berdoo member, would move to the Bay and become the Red and White Nomads chapter out of Richmond.

James Miles was killed in 1966 in a head-on motorcycle collision. Between his multi-mentions in Hunter Thompson's beatified book and the one simple-yet-screaming-a-thousand-words power photo of his massive funeral in *LIFE* magazine, Mother Miles shed a light on what leadership and brotherhood truly meant—and means—in a motorcycle club.

James was buried in his hometown of Sacramento. His brother, Pat, buried his own colors with James, never to wear a death's head again. In the year 2000, Pat's son, James Meredith Miles, "unfolded" Hellbent and the history began again.

Sitting down with our indefatigable road-correspondent Felicia Morgan, Mother Miles' widow, Ruby, and his nephew, James Meredith Miles, give us a look into the deep red and bright white history of Mother's legendary Hellbent for Glory Motorcycle Club:

Ruby: Jim was in a car club, the Throttle Jockeys, before he met me.

James Meredith Miles: I guess he just had a thing for speed, because he was into the cars first, and then that got him into motorcycles. Because the next thing you know, he's quit that and started Hellbent for Glory.

Ruby: I met him in 1958, and he had a bike then. He started Hellbent in '59, and he flew the Hellbent colors here in Sacramento. The club was definitely here for a while before they decided to go with the Red and White.

JMM: In early '64, they folded Hellbent and started the original North Sac Hells Angels.

Back then, all charters had to be sanctioned out of the Mother Charter, which was Berdoo. So Hellbent went down to Berdoo, turned in their stuff, grabbed new patches, and came back as HAs. Their new chapter was in North Sacramento, so they wore "No. Sacto." rockers.

Ruby: Even though he was only in the Hells Angels for a year and a half, Jim became famous because he was in the newspapers for all the shit the cops tried to pin on him that he didn't do. He was arrested for rape, but never actually charged. Typical cop bullshit: Line up some bikers and say, "Okay, girls. Pick four of 'em out." So that didn't go anywhere.

There were other incidents too—and they're reported inaccurately all over the place.

Jim was very popular. Wherever Jim and I lived, it was like the clubhouse; that's where everybody was all the time.

JMM: That's how he got his nickname, "Mother"; he treated everyone like they were his kid!

JMM: My dad said that when they started their HA chapter—my dad was in it too—they didn't last here but seven to eight months; they couldn't get but two or three blocks without getting pulled over and being harassed by the cops.

The cops actually told Hellbent before they even went down to Berdoo: "If you come back as Hells Angels, we're gonna just shut you down." And they pretty much did. Back then, if they wanted to shut you down, they shut you down.

So that's when Miles moved to the Bay and No. Sacto. became the Red and White Nomads chapter out of Richmond.

Ruby: Jim died in January of '66. He actually died of pneumonia in the hospital after his wreck. He was coming back from hanging out with Sonny and the boys and got hit by an old guy in a white pickup. He died seven days later and never did regain consciousness. He was only twenty-nine.

It was ironic—Jim had a thing about being thirty, a "God, I don't want to turn thirty!" type of thing—and he died a just few hours before that milestone.

JMM: My dad and Jim had made a pact with their mother that since they were the only men left in the family and both in the club, if either of them died, the other one would lay down his patch. So when Jim died, my dad did leave the club. And he wouldn't get into any other club or do anything with my grandmother around. But when my grandmother died, he said screw it, and he restarted Hellbent.

This was the second version of the original club.

From '76 to '79 my dad had Hellbent back again in Sacramento—but he didn't get permission to start the club. And after a while Hellbent started getting big, and he was told, "No, no, you didn't do it right."

So version number two of the club ended. From 1979 to 2000 there was no Hellbent in Sac.

In October of '99, when I was thirty-three, I went to the Sac HAs and told them I wanted to start Hellbent back up. Since the club had folded and become HA, out of respect, it was the correct thing to do. They laughed at me and told me the club was part of history and should stay there!

So I just kept hanging around. I befriended an officer in the club. He asked if I was serious about this and I said yes.

He said, "Well, I don't know…"

I called Ruby and told her they probably wouldn't support me in starting it back up. She said, "Let me see what I can do."

She talked to some people and I got called back in. I was told, "Get your guys together and hang out for a year or so. If you can keep these guys together for a year, then we'll talk."

It ended up being just over a year, and after that, I was like, "What's up?"

"Well, you kept 'em together so..."

There were still a couple original Hellbent members alive at the time who were still HAs. So we sought their approval too. They were called and informed of all the steps I had already gone through to get the club back up and running.

The first thing they asked was "Well, who's trying to do it?"

They were told it was Mother Miles' nephew.

"Okay," they said. "That's cool."

Thank god I was who I was and Ruby was around, 'cause they wouldn't have let me restart the club otherwise. No one else could have done it. No way. It was just because of my family history—I had links to the original club. And they like Ruby!

At one point, we made Ruby an honorary member.

Ruby: In the original Hellbent, I had my own patch and was secretary of the club.

JMM: We got our new patches in September of 2000. When I restarted the club, I wanted a "No. Sacto" rocker to go back to the original history. We're still trademarked as "Hellbent for Glory" so that's our real name.

My dad died in 1994 of cancer.

After I was born, my dad had been sent to prison and my mom took off with another HA, so my brother and I grew up in foster homes and were later adopted by my aunt and uncle. So I didn't see my dad for twenty-something years of life.

My uncle and my dad—Jim and Pat.

My brother and me—Pat and Jim.

My brother, Pat, died about a week before his thirtieth birthday, just like my Uncle Jim did.

When I was about to turn thirty, I called in sick and stayed home for two weeks! I was completely paranoid.

Me, Uncle Pete, and Turk are the only charter members still in the club. The reason is that a lot of people just can't find a medium between their personal life and the club.

And that's nothing new.

Courtesy of Felicia Morgan

Both photos courtesy of Felicia Morgan

CHAPTER 4

All photos courtesy of Felicia Morgan

HELL RAZORS - There are two Hell Razors MCs. While neither may actually be a one percent club in the strictest sense, the name alone is worth a mention. One club was established in 1993 in South Africa. The other is in the United Arab Emirates.

✠

Hells Angels

- ♦ **ESTABLISHED:** 1948
- ♦ **PLACE OF ORIGIN:** Fontana/San Bernadino area of inland Southern California
- ♦ **FOUNDER(S):** Otto Friedl, Arvid Olsen, and others from the P.O.B.O.B. MC
- ♦ **CHAPTER LOCATIONS:** Worldwide
- ♦ **CLUB COLORS:** Red and White
- ♦ **CENTER PATCH:** The patented death's head
- ♦ **MOTTO:** (One of many) *When we do right, nobody remembers. When we do wrong, nobody forgets.*
- ♦ **CLAIM TO FAME:** Where do we begin? From Sonny Barger to the Lynch Report to the 1960s biker flicks—by far the most media-exposed club ever
- ♦ **CLUB ASSOCIATIONS:** Has support clubs worldwide

HELLS ANGELS - First, the basic nuts and bolts of the most publicized motorcycle club in the galaxy—and well beyond. As always, the best history lessons are taught by those who lived that history, who got their hands dirty as they built it, got bloodied in the bad times, and got rewarded in the good. A couple of those teachers within the ranks of the HAMC would be Sonny, of course, and his book, *Hell's Angel: The Life and Times of Sonny Barger and the Hells Angels Motorcycle Club.* It's *the* text and required reading. And then there's a history that was written by a member of the Charleston, South Carolina, chapter, which has made the rounds in various forms and reads like an A-plus university thesis. The combination of these two works provides an objective and very subjective history of the club.

The generally accepted nuts and bolts of the story is that the club began in 1948 in the Fontana–San Bernardino inland area of Southern California with Otto Friedl, Arvid Olsen, and some others from the P.O.B.O.B.s. Sonny's account of how, unbeknownst to the SoCal boys, *another* Hells Angels began to grow, up North in the Bay area is more than interesting. His account of their chance meeting in 1957 is more than stunning.

Obviously, they have expanded universally since then and have made every map and list and every form of notoriety, fame, infamy, and publicity that there is. We all know that. But among the many impacts that the HAMC has had on every corner of biker culture, the sheer wallop of what leadership can do in this lifestyle has been shown again and again in the HAMC. The public has always tended to see the leaders in motorcycle clubs as simply being the biggest and baddest, with rises in the structural hierarchy—again, always—being achieved only by a constant battle royal. Survival of the physically fittest.

While I've certainly seen plenty of guys—from many different clubs—with an officer's tab on their cut who could decimate a WWE Smackdown or kill a bus with their bare hands, there are far more who

have achieved on another level. Sonny has proved that for decades. As has George Christie, Donny Petersen, Jim Elrite, and so many more. This is not a lifestyle solely based on jungle law. There's a lot of brain that comes along with that biker brawn.

Donny Petersen is the author of the entertaining yet technically brilliant epic, *Donny's Unauthorized Technical Guide to Harley Davidson 1936–2008, Volume 1: The Twin Cam*. He is known as "The World's Most Read Harley Technical Journalist" and has had a monthly column called Techline in *American Iron* magazine since 1992. He hosts Tech-Talk on Biker TV and has operated Heavy Duty Cycles in Toronto, Canada, since 1974. His from-the-heart, from-real-experience comments on this entire lifestyle should also be on that required reading list—for history but also for just exactly what this lifestyle means. Here is just one example:

GREED IS THE ENEMY

By Donny Petersen, HAMC

Sooner or later, outside forces will knock a motorcycle club down to the mat. How a club deals with adversity determines the quality of that club. A strong, well-organized one will rise from the mat. Many times, the club will become more powerful than before. Why? Their internal structure, with membership values of brotherhood placing the club's interests above their own will bring the spirit to lift themselves up to rebuild. Internal value systems determine the strength or weakness of a club much the same as with the individual.

If there is weakness on the inside, a different scenario will certainly ensue unless the cancer is cut out. Weakness may derive from letting wrong people join. A member or members may come to feel they are more deserving than their fellow members. Jealousy may sow its divisive seeds.

Greed is what drives many of these faults. Greed causes one to bend or break long-established rules. It causes one to put himself above the rest. It destroys the concept of brotherhood. Further, it gives those on the outside the lever they need to hurt the room. Like a rear drive chain, a club is only as strong as its weakest link.

Bikerdom has changed much over the years. The short answer for this is money. Money and greed fucks everything up and erodes the old values. The old days were the best days. We flew under the radar. Yeah, we got nickel-and-dime hassled, sometimes brutally, but not on the level of today where massive organized resources launch repeatedly against us. No longer do the huge ex-footballer cops attempt to regulate us with the blunt instruments of intimidation, fists, and phony charges. The new controllers have college degrees and use their brains to apply complex laws to insidiously manage the biker threat (whatever that is).

The new truth is that a bike club, or a biker for that matter, cannot survive today without money. When I started riding in the late sixties, most of us had no money nor did we care about it. As long as we had rent for our flophouse rooms, a case of beer, our bikes, and three-dollar club dues, we were happy as can be.

COMMUNICATION

Communication has altered the world of the biker. No matter the time of the day, a click of the mouse lets me know what is going on in the one percent world anywhere and everywhere on the planet. The Internet has turned the slow, orderly, and careful growth of bike clubs into rapid expansionary efforts. The teachings and sometimes the bastardization of biker core values can occur at light speed. Motorcycle clubs of every flavor proliferate. Expansion can take

Sonny Barger. *Courtesy of Ken Karagozian*

on a life of its own, becoming the sole reason for existence.

There isn't the necessary time to absorb and internalize the values required for enduring success. Some clubs, parts of clubs, or groups of members fall victim to the devastating sin of bikerdom, which is misused power driven by greed. These aberrations reflect little on the basic original values.

THE PRETENDERS

There are thousands of motorcycle clubs and groups emulating homogenized versions of the outlaw lifestyle. H.O.G. became an instant success and becomes the largest bike club in the world. However, one percent (1%) outlaw bikers reacted in disgust at the theft of their lifestyle by Harley-Davidson. I am not criticizing H.O.G. members or any other biker since I welcome all those on two wheels into the fold.

However, as far as the original clubbers are concerned, Harley-Davidson has turned their back on the core group that supported the Motor Company through thick and thin. They feel that H-D steals their colors, insignia, and way of life. Worse, the clubbers think Harley-Davidson pasteurizes their lifestyle to allow a safe walk on the wild side for the mainstream Harley enthusiasts.

Nevertheless, Harley-Davidson must move forward with the majority conformist population to survive. Small core groups of loyalists cannot adequately support H-D survival; for Harley-Davidson also craves and seeks expansion. Furthermore, the image problem of outlaw clubs is troubling for mass marketing mainstream appeal. Yet, the outlaw clubs of the day personified freedom, old-West ruggedness, and individualism.

H.O.G. seeks this image to market and quite effectively so. Despite the differing points of view, H.O.G. is the most brilliant marketing tactic by Harley-Davidson in a sea of dazzling strategies that obscures the one chink in Harley-Davidson's armour.

There are a myriad of other types of bike clubs that would twist Freud's analytic brain. I welcome them all to the mix. I respect their right to be free and nonconformist to explore their individuality and freedom. With this said, I ask the rhetorical questions of why law enforcement groups form their own outlaw-type clubs basing on the gangs they love to hate? Do the Jesus clubs relate to the outlaw lifestyle because their salvation is also based in rebellion against the establishment Roman Empire? Females entering the fold on Sportsters was one thing, but what would Freud think about them graduating to the Big Twins, growing balls, and forming their own clubs with no men allowed, in this previous male-only haven? Perhaps he would not view this in a testicular way, but as simple vibratory gratification. I prefer a simpler answer that the reason-to-be is there is no other feeling quite like riding in the wind.

BIKE MAINTENANCE

Today, Harley-Davidsons are reliable. Many forget or ignore checking their oil, which was a religious rite in days past. In the Knuckle, Pan, and Shovelhead days, even a guy like me with no technical background whatsoever was forced joyfully into mechanics. Why? If you were broken down and didn't know how to string broken chain onto the sprockets with a clothes hanger lying on the side of the road or set a points ignition with a cigarette paper (or rifle a good used set from a rusting derelict car, or a magneto from a tractor sitting idle in a nearby field), you weren't going anywhere until you fixed the problem.

You always had help, because bikers would stop to lend assistance and wouldn't leave until you were okay. There was nobody riding by pretending they didn't see you. In fact, riding by without offering help was the ultimate sin for which one would be cast from the fold.

Present day, the cell phone calls a tow truck and a pizza-to-go while waiting for someone else to fix your problem as you relax by the pool in a local motel with your credit card at the ready.

THE PARTY IS ON THE ROAD

There were no credit cards because we had no credit. It didn't matter—motels wouldn't rent a room to us anyway. We slept outside wherever we felt. The party was wherever we were. The destination wasn't where we were headed; it was just the reason to be on the road. The road was the destination. It was the party, the brotherhood, and the reason to be.

THE WAY IT WAS

I remember one time my engine blew. I was riding about thirteen hundred miles to Canada's east coast with a riding partner appropriately nicknamed "Harley from Toronto" on our chopped Shovelheads.

Two hundred miles into the trip, the return-oil-pump key sheared in my oil pump. I diagnosed this at 60 miles per hour fairly quickly because the engine was filling with too much oil, causing oil blow-by past the rings into the combustion chamber. Resultant billowing blue smoke out my drag pipes and oil forcing out of the bottom engine casing vent splattering all over the rear of my chopper were the symptoms of too much oil in the bottom end of my engine. Sluggish performance is also a result of too much oil-drag on the churning flywheels.

As I gingerly slowed to a stop on my oil-soaked rear tire, the engine quit because of oil-fouled spark plugs. Harley and I pushed my Shovel into a deserted shed behind a weed-strewn gas station. We spent the next three days rebuilding the engine with tools we always carried and some more tools that Harley rode many miles to borrow. We did not really need to rebuild the engine as rebuilding the oil pump would have sufficed, but that was the mantra in those days.

Harley rode off with my heads fifty miles in one direction to recut the valve seats at some old automotive machine shop in some no-name town. Then he rode seventy-five miles in another direction to the closest Harley-Davidson dealer to buy piston rings, gaskets, and the all-important oil pump keyway.

Each night, we rode two-up to the nearest and only bar in Nowhereville to shoot some pool and drink beer. We were dirty and skuzzy with greasy long hair and beards wearing the dirt and oil from rebuilding and sleeping on the asphalt.

There were no showers so there was no need for soap.

The locals did not like us.

As we left the bar the second night, Harley's Shovel would not fire. Someone had stolen his spark plug wires. I knew what was about to happen. I had to back his play in the middle of nowhere, in the middle of the night, without my own means of getaway. Oh, did I forget to mention the local yokels outnumbered us big time?

It was on; the ferocity of Harley's temper kept them at bay, with me as his backup shadow, as he crudely but effectively determined who had his plug wires. Plug wires in hand, we beat a hasty retreat before the crowd could regroup.

We blasted into the darkness, the straight pipes shattering the nighttime air.

We slept on the asphalt another night until the hot sun woke us with our usual and quite normal hangovers.

I dumped a half-quart of oil into the bottom end over the bearings before installing the top-end. We greased or oiled all internal parts during assembly. Finally, my '66 Shovel was purring like a kitten. Unbeknownst to us, the oil-pump-feed key broke on initial startup.

I did not ride the bike hard because of the necessary break-in procedure.

So how far will a Harley engine run in very hot summer temperatures in this condition? At about 200 miles, the bike began to feel sluggish. I saw heat wafting off the engine...but the day was hot. At around 225 miles, my bike began to labor. At about 240 miles, my bike began to slow as I gave her more gas. The poor old girl slowed to a seized stop.

Harley hung tough. I made a pay phone collect call back to Toronto and some brothers hopped into an old pickup and made the long trip to bring the parts I needed and to lend assistance. Helping me out was more important than anything else, including work.

Ahh, the life of a biker was not always easy. Looking for adventure and whatever came our way was not always fun. Yet, I remember this experience with fondness thirty years later.

Well, let us get back to the subject at hand.

BIKE MAINTENANCE WAS HALF THE FUN

Half the trip was working on your bike. There was nothing better than sitting down with a case of beer on a Saturday afternoon and twisting wrenches with your bros...and we learned our lessons hard. Take the beginnings of my first bike shop in the wrong side of Toronto, a place where only bikers were happy.

In the hardcore machismo days of the early seventies, when bikers were men, and women were double-breasted, there was no room for sensitivity. Me and my bro Tramp were working on a 1947 Knucklehead chopper. The bike was a beauty with a raked frame and a real long front end, with a skinny spool wheel without brakes or a front fender. This was in a dirt floor garage in the city's seedy tenderloin, where if

you weren't strong you were a victim. Our dogs were as big and mean as we could be. Me and Tramp lazily drank our beer on a hot weekend while taking turns kick-starting the radical beast that refused to start.

Tramp took the breather off the brass plumbing, also known as a Linkert carburetor, and

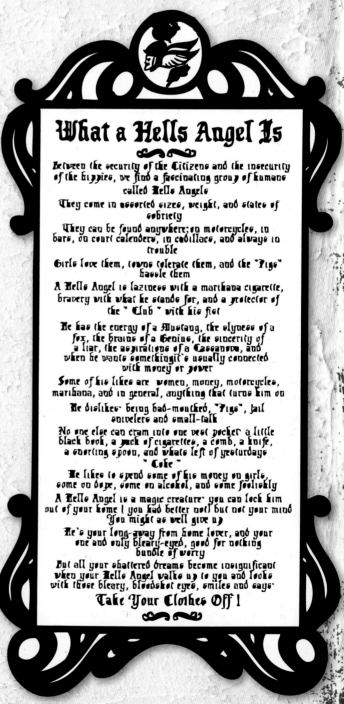

What a Hells Angel Is

Between the security of the Citizens and the insecurity of the hippies, we find a fascinating group of humans called Hells Angels

They come in assorted sizes, weight, and states of sobriety

They can be found anywhere; on motorcycles, in bars, on court calendars, in cadillacs, and always in trouble

Girls love them, towns tolerate them, and the "Pigs" hassle them

A Hells Angel is laziness with a marihana cigarette, bravery with what he stands for, and a protector of the "Club" with his fist

He has the energy of a Mustang, the slyness of a fox, the brains of a Genius, the sincerity of a liar, the aspirations of a Cassanova, and when he wants something it's usually connected with money or power

Some of his likes are women, money, motorcycles, marihana, and in general, anything that turns him on

He dislikes being bad-mouthed, "Pigs", jail snivelers and small-talk

No one else can cram into one vest pocket a little black book, a pack of cigarettes, a comb, a knife, a snorting spoon, and what's left of yesterdays "Coke"

He likes to spend some of his money on girls, some on dope, some on alcohol, and some foolishly

A Hells Angel is a magic creature; you can lock him out of your home (you had better not) but not your mind You might as well give up

He's your long-away from home lover, and your one and only bleary-eyed, good for nothing bundle of worry

But all your shattered dreams become insignificant when your Hells Angel walks up to you and looks with those bleary, bloodshot eyes, smiles and says:

Take Your Clothes Off !

Vintage poem, author unknown.

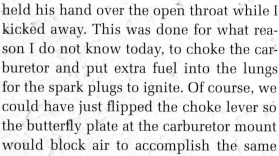

Both photos courtesy of Felicia Morgan

held his hand over the open throat while I kicked away. This was done for what reason I do not know today, to choke the carburetor and put extra fuel into the lungs for the spark plugs to ignite. Of course, we could have just flipped the choke lever so the butterfly plate at the carburetor mount would block air to accomplish the same thing. This is just the way things were done back then. I guess if I bared my soul, I would have to say that we really didn't have a clue—but a real man could not admit that. Instead, we authoritatively fiddled with stuff like taking the breather off so we could convince ourselves and anyone else, particularly a woman looking on, that we were on top of our game.

Back in those days, we didn't like the black gas line hose that also happened to be fire resistant because we could not see if there was gas in the line going into the carburetor. Yes, we had to be able to observe if the dreaded and omnipresent vapor lock was preventing gas flow. The automotive shops sold this line we all used that

was clear hose that yellowed with use. It never occurred to us that the yellowing meant that it was not for use with gasoline. Details. We had no time for insignificant details. We were into big picture stuff; the stuff that really mattered. We were men of action who took bold steps, especially into the unknown. You know, I can make a lot of fun of myself and the other hard-core riders of the day, but to put this all into perspective, it would have been very poor judgment to question us or dare laugh at us back then...after all, we were men of action. We knew only one direction and that was forward.

Anyway, Tramp removes his hand and we see lots of gas in the carburetor throat. As I continued to kick, we see air forcing back out of the carburetor throat, mixing with the liquid gas. Today, I would kick once, see this and proceed to check ignition timing. Bikes used distributors with points and condensers back then. It was very easy to install the distributor so that the timing was 180 degrees out. When this happens, the bike can sometimes start and run with great difficulty but there is lots of backfiring especially back out the carburetor because the piston movement and valves are sort-of going in the wrong direction when the spark plug fires. If the plug is not firing at the appropriate time, only a vapor backfires out through the throat.

However, if the spark plug is firing with vapor present, sometimes the backfire would contain a temporary ball of fire that most times goes out because the evaporate gas in the air depletes.

I finished a kick, with my leg still on the kicker pedal as I looked down at the carburetor. A ball of fire accompanied a backfire. This time it didn't go out as it found a fresh source of fuel. I couldn't believe my eyes. The momentary ball of fire burned through the clear hose substituting as a proper gas line in a fraction of a second. Gas poured out all over the side of the poor old Knucklehead feeding the rapidly spreading fire.

Where was the fire extinguisher? What fire extinguisher? We never took precautions. I grabbed a shop smock and tried to beat out the flames. I was pretty good at spreading a fire and not so good at putting one out. Tramp threw a bucket of water on the flames. The fire was now raging. I ran out of the shop and down the street to a local car garage, raced in, demanded where their fire extinguisher was, and proceeded to rip it off the wall. I ran out without explanation, none was needed since it was sensible to sidestep a near-hysterical 275-pound biker with greasy hair halfway down his back and a full beard obviously on a mission. By the time I raced back into the garage, the fire was still raging as black smoke from the burning tires

choked me back. I fired off the extinguisher and got the flames out. The bike was burned to the ground. Nowadays, it would be a write-off, but everything was rebuildable back then.

Tramp and I popped open a couple of more beers and surveyed the damages. Ahh well, luck was partially with us, as my garage had cement block walls and a very high roof—not the old dried-out and termite-infested rotting wood found in most garages in the area. Stoically, Tramp took a swig of beer and remarked that the Knuckle needed a new paint job anyway. The good news was that we now had a major project to complete. We were progressively becoming more excited as we realized that we would be taking apart and rebuilding our first Knuckle engine. Our old ladies (wives) had now shown up. Tramp and I did not notice the successive eye rolls they were subjecting us to. We didn't care anyway. This was in an era where your bike and brotherhood was way more important than a girlfriend or wife. Half the trip back then was working on your scoot. It was as much fun as riding.

TIMES CHANGE

The old days are just that: the old days. They will not repeat. Young bikers have trouble with the old guys that have the power. They feel repressed, for they have so much to offer. The old guys strain to accept and bring the youngsters along. The young bikers are busy reinventing the wheel. I wish I knew as much as these new young guys. The old guys marvel at their stupidity and cockiness. Most times they fail to remember they were exactly the same.

Original bike clubs had a young membership demographic, but that has changed big time. I once felt the greatest challenge to bike clubs was the generation gap, and for some it was. Bike clubs may never change, but they sure can adapt to and deal with what threatens them. This generational membership problem resolved itself as successful bike clubs recognized three generations of members that coexist and learn from each other. These are the keys to regeneration.

Patience on all sides is key and is arguably the most difficult part of the process. The old ones are like grandparents (mostly advisers and sometimes officers); the middle-aged are like the parents (active officers); and the young (members) are the salvation for the future. However, I watch some clubs or club charters where the youngest member is secretary. In this case, the young are likely more qualified than their elders. Why? They are usually the most tech savvy with computers.

For a bunch of supposedly ignorant Neanderthal clubbers, their core values and ability to survive can surpass the legendary brilliance of others. Look at the modern manufacturing and marketing marvel, Harley-Davidson. Harley-Davidson now suffers much economic malaise because it catered to only one age grouping, the post–WWII baby-boom. Harley never welcomed nor garnered the next generation of youth into the fold. It failed to ensure its own salvation. Harley could have learned much from the outlaws they eschewed. H.O.G will face the same multigenerational situation. We shall see if the good guys and gals can fare as well as the bad guys.

The old biker club lifestyle is the template for the new one. However, the past is the past and those who will not or cannot adapt fall by the wayside. The new bikers are well aware that greed is the real enemy that will eat them from the inside out. The cancer of greed is always lurking in the background waiting to ensnare the weak.

Successful bikers may be dinosaurs, but they are one particular breed dinosaur: The Adaptosaurous.

Hells Lovers

- ◆ **ESTABLISHED:** 1967
- ◆ **PLACE OF ORIGIN:** Chicago, Illinois
- ◆ **FOUNDER(S):** Frank "Claim-Jumper" Rios
- ◆ **CHAPTER LOCATIONS:** Nationwide, U.S.
- ◆ **CENTER PATCH:** Iron cross with a skull
- ◆ **MOTTO:** Death is my sidekick and the highway is my home.
- ◆ **CLAIM TO FAME:** One of the first integrated clubs in Chicago

✠

HELLS LOVERS - Established in 1967 in Chicago, this multi-ethnic group made the law enforcement map in Illinois and Missouri. It was one of the first integrated biker clubs in Chicago and was founded by Frank "Claim-Jumper" Rios after he was denied membership in another motorcycle club. The club's motto is "Death is my sidekick and the highway is my home."

In 2010, that "sidekick" came to "claim" Claim-Jumper. *The Chicago Tribune* talked about his life:

A Harley-Davidson buff who was turned down when he tried to join a motorcycle club in the late 1960s, Frank "Claim-Jumper" Rios started the Hell's Lovers, one of the first integrated biker organizations in Chicago.

"He got to know people across the United States, and he knew the different clubs," said his son, Demetrius Guyton. "He enjoyed the wide-open road. The fun part of the road trips was hanging with his bros, even with the breakdowns."

Mr. Rios, 62, died of cardiac arrest attributed to complications from diabetes Monday, Dec. 28, at Aurora St. Luke's Medical Center in Milwaukee, his son said. Mr. Rios had moved from Chicago's West Side to Milwaukee in 1997.

A Mexican-American from the West Side, Mr. Rios was an outsider among existing motorcycle clubs when he started the Hell's Lovers in 1967.

"He put the name on his back, and it took off," his son said. "He hooked up with a childhood friend, and they formed a nation."

Overseeing his own club allowed him to meet others who danced to their own rhythm, his longtime friend, Andrew "Poolie" Poole said.

"When people liked the way we lived, they jumped onboard with us," said Poole, also a founding member of the Hell's Lovers. "We believed in each other."

The Hell's Lovers have about 50 members in Chicago and claim more than 1,500 members across the country in states like Tennessee, Colorado, Texas, Georgia and Maryland, Guyton said.

"When you'd see us coming, you'd wonder, 'How'd they all get together?'" said Ralph Collier, who joined in 1972. "We'd freak people out because we had all kinds of people: black, white, Mexican."

Many motorcycle clubs have an outlaw reputation, and members of the Hell's Lovers had occasional scrapes with the law over the years. But Mr. Rios managed to stay out of serious trouble.

"It got to be wild and crazy at times," Collier said. "Half our stories can't be put in print. There were times when tears had to be shed. But you lived to see what would happen the next five minutes…"

✠

HELL'S OUTCASTS - The "oldest documented OMG in Minnesota" according to the St. Paul Police Department. Naturally, they made the law enforcement map listing there. The vintage jacket below indicates that there might be some inconsistancy with the spelling of the club's name.

113

HENCHMEN - There are a few Henchmen waiting to grab you:

First is the "Black & Blue Crew," a long-running Henchmen MC out of Northern California who made the map on the left coast.

There is also a Henchmen from North Wales that was patched over to the Outlaws MC many years ago and a Henchmen MC that made the law enforcement map in Tennessee.

HERMANOS - A Bandidos support club in Wyoming.

HERMANOS UNIDOS - A Bandidos support club in Texas—interesting in that they are also an AMA-chartered club.

✠

✠

Hessians

- **ESTABLISHED:** 1968
- **PLACE OF ORIGIN:** Costa Mesa, California
- **FOUNDER(S):** Tommy Maniscalco
- **CHAPTER LOCATIONS:** U.S. West Coast, out as far as Colorado and Oklahoma
- **CLUB COLORS:** Black and White
- **CENTER PATCH:** An iron cross and a saber-pierced skull
- **CLAIM TO FAME:** In addition to being a truly "classic" club with a lot of longevity, the Hessians Motorcycle Club was the subject of one of the most acclaimed film documentaries on the biker culture, *Hessians MC*.

HESSIANS - There is only one good way to present the history of this "classic" club, and that's through the words of "Spike," the president of the Hessians Mother Chapter Orange County, California:

The Hessians Motorcycle Club started back on March 7, 1968, by Tommy Maniscalco and the initial founding group in Costa Mesa, Orange County, California.

The name of the Club was inspired by the mercenary soldiers of Hesse, Germany. The Hessians were a fierce, well-oiled fighting machine, hired by the English to fight the American patriots. The Hessians were revered by many.

When Hessians MC set up in 1968, it faced many challenges—challenges from major clubs, law enforcement, and just the task of starting and growing something new.

The club prevailed and developed into a formidable, respected MC in the biker community. The Hessians grew from strength to strength, creating a platform and national reputation that still stands today, nearly fifty years later.

A groundbreaking documentary with the straight-ahead title Hessians MC was created about the club by film producer Randall Wilson of Guerrilla Docs. The violent legacy of this hard-riding, hard-fighting, and hard-partying outlaw club is well documented by personal stories and anecdotes of its members surviving the biker wars, the lifestyle, law enforcement, and the day-to-day dangers of life on the road.

The Hessians are one of those authentic age-proven clubs that have always produced awe and respect. They're one of those rare clubs that—both then and now—carry clout along with the mystique. In the world of motorcycle clubs, they are the real deal.

✠

Jennifer Thomas

HIGHLANDERS - Established in 1996, there are Highlanders in the Smoky Mountains of Tennessee. And according to the book *Hells Witness* by Daniel Sanger, former Halifax Hells Angel Mike McCrea formed a Highlanders at one point up in Nova Scotia.

HIGH PLAINS DRIFTERS - They made the law enforcement map in New Mexico and Colorado and also received some discouraging words in The National Drug Intelligence Center's Colorado Drug Threat Assessment Report in May 2003.

Highway 61

- ◆ **ESTABLISHED:** Unknown
- ◆ **PLACE OF ORIGIN:** New Zealand
- ◆ **FOUNDER(S):** Unknown
- ◆ **CHAPTER LOCATIONS:** New Zealand and Australia
- ◆ **CLAIM TO FAME:** Largest outlaw motorcycle club in New Zealand
- ◆ **CLUB ASSOCIATIONS:** Bandidos MC

HIGHWAY 61 - The Highway 61 MC is considered the largest outlaw motorcycle club in New Zealand—and that's saying a lot considering the sheer weight of biker stuff down there. They have chapters in Auckland, Hastings, Wellington, and Christchurch, New Zealand, and in Brisbane and the Gold Coast in eastern Australia.

Highwaymen

- ◆ **ESTABLISHED:** 1954
- ◆ **PLACE OF ORIGIN:** Detroit, Michigan
- ◆ **FOUNDER(S):** Unknown
- ◆ **CHAPTER LOCATIONS:** Michigan, Florida, and other states
- ◆ **CLUB COLORS:** Black and Silver
- ◆ **CENTER PATCH:** A winged skull with a vintage motorcycle "cap"
- ◆ **CLAIM TO FAME:** Very high-profile "classic" club, on many "top clubs" lists

HIGHWAYMEN - Another biggie, another "classic." The Highwaymen Motorcycle Club was established in 1954 in Detroit, Michigan. The years 1954, 1973, 1987, and 2007 saw FBI and other law enforcement investigations of the club—the largest in the Detroit area. They have chapters in several states and made the law enforcement map in Michigan and Florida.

In 1955, the Highwaymen actually had an AMA sanction.

That went down and some issues with the law came up. In 2007 the FBI arrested forty members and associates on a "variety of charges." In 2010 their clubhouse became subject to forfeiture as a "drug den."

And an especially rough issue happened a couple of years before, in 2008, as reported by the *Detroit Free Press*:

Four metro Detroit police officers and a member of the Highwaymen Motorcycle Club were indicted Wednesday by a federal grand jury in Detroit on charges stemming from a four-year FBI investigation into drug trafficking and other crimes, according to the U.S. Attorney's Office in Detroit.

As the cut below shows, there have been other clubs using the name "Highwaymen."

✠

HOG RIDERS - A three-piece-patch club out of Iceland. *Brrrrrr!*

✠

HOLE IN THE WALL - This motorcycle club joined the crowd on the law enforcement map listing in Connecticut.

✠

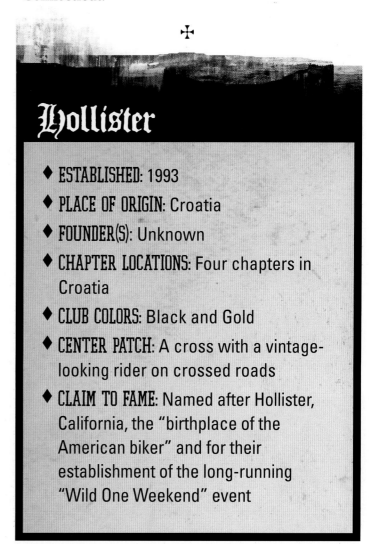

Hollister

♦ **ESTABLISHED:** 1993

♦ **PLACE OF ORIGIN:** Croatia

♦ **FOUNDER(S):** Unknown

♦ **CHAPTER LOCATIONS:** Four chapters in Croatia

♦ **CLUB COLORS:** Black and Gold

♦ **CENTER PATCH:** A cross with a vintage-looking rider on crossed roads

♦ **CLAIM TO FAME:** Named after Hollister, California, the "birthplace of the American biker" and for their establishment of the long-running "Wild One Weekend" event

HOLLISTER - Established in 1993 in Croatia as a very nifty tribute to "the Birthplace of the American Biker"—6,100 miles away! The club began under the name "N.U.B.G.Z," which in the local dialect stands for, "Independent Good-for-Nothing Association of City of Zagreb." The club "decided on that name because it was the beginning of the 1% scene." In 1996 they organized the first party at their clubhouse and called it, what else, "The Wild One Weekend."

✛

HOMBRES - Established in 1994, a Bandidos support club in Washington.

✛

HORSEMEN - Out of Ridgetown, Ontario, Canada, this motorcycle club has been making the news for the extra attention that law enforcement has been paying them. The *Ontario News* gets into some of the daily interaction between the club and the cops:

> A Chatham-Kent–based motorcycle club has set up shop in Lambton County and members say they're being regularly harassed by Sarnia police.
> The Horsemen Motorcycle Club, which originated in Ridgetown, moved into a club house in Mooretown 18 months ago. They insist they're not a gang and not involved in organized crime, but are subjected to frequent police stops and have their events closely monitored.
> Members, friends, and family are regularly photographed and videotaped by police, they say.

✛

HUHU - Set up in Tokoroa, New Zealand, the Huhu MC is yet another club on all of the "lists of gangs" down there. And these guys go way back, beginning as a "bush crew" in the 1950s and morphing into a motorcycle club in the 1970s.

✛

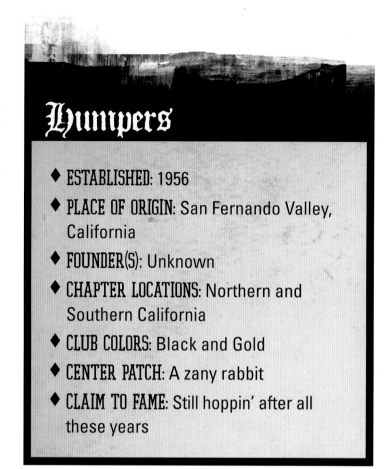

Humpers

- ◆ **ESTABLISHED:** 1956
- ◆ **PLACE OF ORIGIN:** San Fernando Valley, California
- ◆ **FOUNDER(S):** Unknown
- ◆ **CHAPTER LOCATIONS:** Northern and Southern California
- ◆ **CLUB COLORS:** Black and Gold
- ◆ **CENTER PATCH:** A zany rabbit
- ◆ **CLAIM TO FAME:** Still hoppin' after all these years

HUMPERS - Another club that should be noted for their longevity and because they made the law enforcement map in California. Humpers MC was established in 1956 in the San Fernando Valley and now have chapters in Northern Cali and down south in Costa Mesa: "We are a serious MC club that has been around for 54 years. We attend rallies and charity fund raising events to support other clubs and show respect. We ride to promote brotherhood and freedom."

✛

HUNOS - The Hunos (Spanish for *Huns*) are located in, yes, Spain. This is a serious, 1%, diamond-patch club. In 2005, they opened their clubhouse in the town of Berriozar, near Pamplona, and named it "The Scourge of God."

HUNS - There are two Huns MCs that we'll meet

Huns (California)

- **ESTABLISHED:** Late 1950s
- **PLACE OF ORIGIN:** California
- **FOUNDER(S):** Jessie "Scooter J" Sinka
- **CHAPTER LOCATIONS:** Arizona and New Mexico
- **CENTER PATCH:** A Hun skull
- **CLAIM TO FAME:** The first sanctioned motorcycle club in the state of Arizona

Huns (Connecticut)

- **ESTABLISHED:** Around 1957
- **PLACE OF ORIGIN:** Connecticut
- **FOUNDER(S):** The founders included Roger Skeffington, Leroy Dunn, Eddie Ioulo, and Jim Barquin (Tommy Bartone and John "Rogue" Herlihy weren't far behind)
- **CLAIM TO FAME:** A true "classic" club and an MC that was on the pioneering end of the fights for bikers' rights

and share hugs with here. And they both have histories that nearly go back to Attila himself. Both can also be considered "classic" clubs—one is alive and well in Arizona, the other was an East Coast club that produced a ton of history and influenced the entire direction of this lifestyle.

First, the bunch out in the desert: Established "in the late 1950s and brought to Arizona by its founder, Jessie 'Scooter J' Sinka in 1968," the club became the "first sanctioned motorcycle club in the state of Arizona." They have chapters in the Grand Canyon State as well as in Alamagordo in their neighboring state of New Mexico—the Huns made it onto the law enforcement map in both!

Now we go back east. The Huns out of Bridgeport, Connecticut, were one of those clubs that truly helped to define the image. They rode; they produced members like John "Rogue" Herlihy, who became one of the most well-known biker-photojournalists ever; and they became deeply involved in the early fight for bikers' rights. They were legislative pioneers, with prophetic looks into a future that would see a hell of helmet laws and other restrictions designed to neuter a lifestyle that is the

antithesis of impotence. They were there to begin the fight.

And somewhere along the line, "Rogue" found the time to get involved with one of the first biker magazines to hit the stands. *Colors* didn't last too long, but it was the incubation pod for all the slick super mags like *Easyriders* to do what they have done to make this way of life a commercial giant. This was just more pioneering.

"Padre" was there in the late 1960s. He tells us what it was like becoming a Hun:

THE HUNS: PARTIES, PUTTS, & POLITICAL PIONEERING

By Padre

It was the winter of 1969—right after the summer of Woodstock. I was riding with a casual group called the Iron Cross Riders out of Pittsburgh, Pennsylvania. Four of us caged it up to Bridgeport, Connecticut, to meet with a club called the Huns.

We arrived that night at their clubhouse at #1 Islandbrook Avenue, where we met "Rabbit," the president of the Mother Chapter. After a number of brews, I also started a close friendship with "J.B.," "Tree," "Druggest," and "Buzzard." We spent the night at the clubhouse, and the next day, I met "Nigger" and "Rogue." Life has not been the same since.

When we awoke, we went outside to check out our surroundings in the daylight. We were in a large industrial complex with a junkyard on one side and tall buildings on the other. You couldn't see the road from the front of the clubhouse, nor could nosey folks see us from the road. We later learned the adjacent junkyard was owned by Huns members as well. So the privacy factor was ideal.

We Pittsburgh folks spoke to Rogue about the possibility of becoming a part of their organization. Rabbit showed up and we were told they needed to know us better before talking any business. So we relaxed and had a good time for the rest of the weekend. We were treated like brothers by bikers who had just met us.

And so began a fine relationship between Pittsburgh and Connecticut.

I started traveling to Bridgeport at least once a month—often more—and continued throughout the winter. Eventually my riding group became a prospective chapter.

We were told that prospective members had to get their bikes up to Bridgeport on Memorial Day. All members and prospects would meet at the Mother Chapter and ride en masse to a host chapter for a party. So my buddy Riz and I hit the road. We carried the bikes in a van because Riz just finally got his rebuilt heads back right before we had to leave. It was a seven-plus-hour ride in a cage (six on a scoot). I drove while Riz wrenched!

When we got there, we learned that the party was being held in New London, Connecticut. We parked the cage and our ride to New London became the break-in ride for Riz's new engine.

Twenty-five or more Huns and their friends rode from Bridgeport to New London my first year. At least forty more Huns were at the New London clubhouse when we arrived, and even more flowed in as the day went on. A great first Mandatory for me.

Great, because I got to see how big the club was, but mostly because I met Pappy.

When we got there, I met Bryan, their chapter's president, and Donald "Pappy" Pittsley—the oldest biker I had met up to that point of my life. Pappy and I hit it off from the start. Pappy rode a Sportster that had more chrome than I had ever seen on a scoot. That chrome was always sparkling—and so was he. He was a military man, self-disciplined, with a free spirit, and he didn't like the government telling him that he needed to wear protective headgear. So he was developing ways to fight back.

The Huns had already stepped up to argue with local government concerning motorcycles not being allowed in a city park on the waterfront. They had gone to court and won! They had shown that bikers would stand together and could use their numbers to help themselves. Pappy wanted state and federal officials to see that we had the votes to make changes.

The Huns had three other mandatory runs that year, as in previous years. I discovered there were chapters throughout Connecticut, as well as one in Massachusetts. By the time I retired, we had Hun chapters in Pennsylvania, New York, New Jersey, Connecticut, Massachusetts, and Quebec. Our club grew rapidly in the early seventies because of the new helmet law and riders' desire to stop it.

The Huns was a laid-back club that loved to ride and party. The only time we pushed our weight around was in the courts or with lawmakers. We learned how our government works, and how to make the government work for us.

With the help of his Hun brothers, Pappy started the Connecticut Motorcycle Association (CMA) and used it to recruit more bikers into banding together. He told me that I should start a motorcyclists' rights organization in Pennsylvania.

The Huns organized many protest rallies. We tried to make each one bigger and better. We started locally, holding protests near our chapters. Our protests received newspaper coverage all over Connecticut; many of those articles are still available and are quite interesting. It wasn't long before we had the numbers to head to the Capitol and make an impression.

I took Pappy's advice and started WPMA (Western Pennsylvania Motorcyclists Association). My chapter began doing the same things in Pennsylvania that the club was doing in Connecticut. Hun chapters all over the East Coast followed suit. We each pushed in our own states for helmet-law repeal, and won as often as not.

The Huns Motorcycle Club was a group of men who loved to ride and have a good time, and who were passionate about promoting motorcyclists' rights. As a member, I was loved and respected. We helped one another in any way we could. We shared what we had. We were family!

✠

HURRICANES - Established in 1979 in Italy, this three-piece-patch club also has chapters in Switzerland and Austria.

✠

ILLUSIONS - A motorcycle club celebrating their twenty-second anniversary. They made the law enforcement map in Virginia, but say that they're not a one percent club.

✠

IMMORTALS - This is a name that will likely last for a long, long time...and there are several clubs that will back that up.

One is a diamond-patch motorcycle club, established in 1969 in New York.

There is an Immortals MC in Sweden, established in 1988, looking toward a never-ending future.

The Immortals Motorcycle Club in Australia was established in 1971 in a local suburb of Melbourne. They are "Loud & Proud."

An Immortals MC in Pawtucket, Rhode Island, was established in 2002.

Ten years before that, a Bangkok MC became *Immortal.*

✠

In Country

- ◆ **ESTABLISHED:** 1994
- ◆ **PLACE OF ORIGIN:** Illinois
- ◆ **FOUNDER(S):** Small group of Vietnam vets who had served in country
- ◆ **CHAPTER LOCATIONS:** U.S. and Germany
- ◆ **CLUB COLORS:** Red, Gold, and Green
- ◆ **CENTER PATCH:** A dragon
- ◆ **MOTTO:** *Vets helping vets*

IN COUNTRY - Established in 1994, this is a big club—national and international. Founded by a "small group of Vietnam veterans in Illinois who had served in country."

✠

INDEPENDENT SOLDIERS - Another of the motorcycle clubs mentioned on one of the strangest (and never-ending) "anti-gang" websites in the universe as an associate club of the HAMC in Canada.

✠

INDIAN BIKERS - Established in 1996, a three-piece-patch club out of Matera, Italy, that evolved over many years from a loose riding club called Motorskull. The group caught the attention of the clubs in the area, for their dedication, and their apparent "embracing of the philosophy of the 1%er."

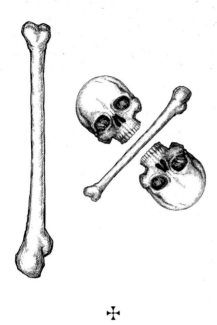

Invaders

- ♦ **ESTABLISHED:** 1965
- ♦ **PLACE OF ORIGIN:** Gary, Indiana
- ♦ **FOUNDER(S):** "Mad Doctor," Charley, Ed Smith, and others
- ♦ **CHAPTER LOCATIONS:** Indiana, Illinois, and Colorado
- ♦ **CLUB COLORS:** Black and White
- ♦ **CENTER PATCH:** A variation of the crazed pickle
- ♦ **CLAIM TO FAME:** Their longevity and their distinctive white cuts

INDIANS - Established in 1993, this is a full-on one percent motorcycle club out of Croatia: "Love, loyalty, respect. These three words became basic, essential values of the club."

☩

INFIDELS - Established in 2006, the "original" Infidels MC is a national club founded by a security contractor working in Iraq named "Slingshot." They have very strong political views. There is also an American Infidels MC with equally focused political views.

☩

INTRUDERS - A three-piece-patch club out of Slovakia; an HAMC hangaround club.

☩

INVADERS - Established in 1965 in Gary, Indiana. This is a "classic" club that made the law enforcement map in Hoosier-land. Their original white cuts proved to be very distinctive—a definite departure from the norm in the motorcycle club world of fashion. Another impressive distinction is that this motorcycle club has retained so much of their history and they like to share it—important stuff for those just climbing onto the saddle to begin their ride with all of this.

There is also a three-piece-patch Invaders out of Poland.

☩

IRON CHARIOTS - With a steely determination, we now begin our look into the Iron-oriented motorcycle clubs. The first is the Iron Chariots MC, a club

123

based in Singapore that believes in "Brotherhood and the open road…beliefs based on the three pillars of Courage, Honour, & Respect…qualities that are represented by the Lambda symbol…which we wear proudly on our hearts."

✠

Iron Coffins

- ◆ **ESTABLISHED:** 1966
- ◆ **PLACE OF ORIGIN:** Toledo, Ohio
- ◆ **FOUNDER(S):** Unknown
- ◆ **CHAPTER LOCATIONS:** Ohio
- ◆ **CLUB COLORS:** Black and White
- ◆ **CENTER PATCH:** A skeleton riding a winged chopper
- ◆ **CLAIM TO FAME:** Their center patch was designed by the famous Ed "Big Daddy" Roth.

IRON COFFINS - Established in 1966 "in the north end of Toledo, Ohio" as a club with the Chosen Few name. They've evolved into the Iron Coffins and made a serious mark in motor-culture history by having Ed "Big Daddy" Roth design their center patch—that is so, so cool! (Roth had also designed a decal entitled "Iron Coffin" that featured a Vietnam War–era tank tearing things up in what he called "fifty-two tons of rolling death"!) Not surprisingly, the Iron Coffins made the law enforcement map in Ohio!

Other clubs also used the name "Iron Coffin" (above cut), although none of them sported artwork by Big Daddy Roth on their center patch.

✠

IRON CRIMINAL - A diamond-patch 1% club out of Russia.

✠

IRON DEMONS - This diamond-patch motorcycle club made the law enforcement map in New Jersey!

✠

IRON DRAGONS - A long-running Bandidos support motorcycle club out of Germany. They have "94" in their diamond and have, yes, an iron dragon for a center patch.

✠

IRON EAGLE(S) - Established in 1982, we have an Iron Eagle MC in Germany. There is also an Iron Eagles, non-one-percent club in Pennsylvania.

✠

IRON HORSE - A three-piece motorcycle club in Northern Ontario, Canada. Their center patch reads "RHB"—respect, honor, brotherhood.

✠

IRON HORSEMEN - Established "in the mid 1960s," this is a big club and it's a "classic" club. Founded in Cincinnati, Ohio, the club has chapters in Kansas, Pennsylvania, Tennessee, Indiana, California, Kentucky, Maine, New Jersey, Massachusetts, Maryland, and New York—and it made it onto the law enforcement map in most of them. They have a very catchy motto: *"Ashes to ashes, dust to dust, if it weren't for the Iron Horsemen, the highways would rust."*

In 2007 the club was the target of an ATF/DEA investigation called "Operation Trojan Horse."

The Iron Horsemen in Australia are also a powerful and "classic" club, founded in Melbourne in 1969. They are a full-on, diamond-patch 1% motorcycle club with a very vocal support of the military. And they are active—the club participates in many runs like the Lap of the Bay, Run to the Hills, and the Graveyard Run.

✠

Iron Horsemen

- ◆ **ESTABLISHED:** Mid-1960s
- ◆ **PLACE OF ORIGIN:** Cincinnati, Ohio
- ◆ **FOUNDER(S):** Unknown
- ◆ **CHAPTER LOCATIONS:** Kansas, Pennsylvania, Tennessee, Indiana, California, Kentucky, Maine, New Jersey, Massachusetts, Maryland, and New York
- ◆ **CENTER PATCH:** Winged metallic horse's head
- ◆ **MOTTO:** *Ashes to ashes, dust to dust, if it weren't for the Iron Horsemen, the highways would rust.*
- ◆ **CLAIM TO FAME:** The target of a 2007 ATF/DEA investigation called "Operation Trojan Horse"

- ◆ **ESTABLISHED:** 1969
- ◆ **PLACE OF ORIGIN:** Melbourne, Australia
- ◆ **FOUNDER(S):** Unknown
- ◆ **CHAPTER LOCATIONS:** Australia
- ◆ **CENTER PATCH:** A bird over an iron cross
- ◆ **CLAIM TO FAME:** One of the oldest clubs in Australia

Iron Horses

- ◆ **ESTABLISHED:** 1966
- ◆ **PLACE OF ORIGIN:** Fürth, Germany
- ◆ **FOUNDER(S):** American GIs
- ◆ **CHAPTER LOCATIONS:** Italy, Wales, Hungary, and Germany
- ◆ **CLUB COLORS:** Black and Gold
- ◆ **CENTER PATCH:** An armored horse with crossed battle axes
- ◆ **CLAIM TO FAME:** Founded by American GIs who brought their patches with them overseas

IRON HORSE, IRON HORSES - The Iron Horses were established in 1966 in Fürth, Germany, by American GIs who "had already brought their colors with them from the U.S." In 1971, the first German members joined. The club has expanded to Italy, Wales, Hungary, and Northern Germany.

There is also a diamond-patch 1%er Iron Horse MC, in Jakarta, Indonesia.

✠

IRON RAGE - They made the law enforcement map listing in Nebraska!

✠

IRON SLEDS - Established in 1976, a long-lived motorcycle club out of Macoupin County, Illinois.

IRON THUNDER - Established in 1980, an East Coast motorcycle club with a history as told by their "Prez," Iron Man:

Our original name was going to be Iron Cross, but we found out there was already a club called Iron Crosses MC so we shit-canned that name. Then I see an ad for a '79 Harley-Davidson Lowrider; the ad said, "Turn On Your Thunder!" It sounded good, so we kept the original "Iron" part of our name and used the "Thunder" from the ad. We became Iron Thunder in 1980 and fired up in Westminster, Maryland—our eleven charter members all grew up in Cranberry. We now have expanded with a chapter in Pennsylvania.

✠

IRON TRIBE - One of the mere dozen motorcycle clubs to make the law enforcement map listing in North Carolina!

Jackpine Gypsies

- ♦ **ESTABLISHED:** 1936
- ♦ **PLACE OF ORIGIN:** Sturgis, South Dakota
- ♦ **FOUNDER(S):** Clarence "Pappy" Hoel
- ♦ **CHAPTER LOCATIONS:** South Dakota
- ♦ **CLAIM TO FAME:** Founded by "Pappy" Hoel! In Sturgis!! Do you need more?

JACKPINE GYPSIES - Established in 1936 in Sturgis by Clarence "Pappy" Hoel, in the ultimate "pioneer"-pairing. The club's simple purpose was essentially "racing and touring." Pappy also bought an Indian dealership in Sturgis in 1936. Two years later, on August 14, 1938, the first "Black Hills Classic" was thrown by his Jackpine Gypsies; the tale is told that there were nine participants and just one race. The club is still enjoying its purpose of that "racing and touring," and I understand that the rally itself has expanded to more than just those nine racers...

✠

JAMES GANG - Straight-up, diamond-patch 1% motorcycle club that made the law enforcement map in Connecticut.

✠

JESTERS - No kidding around here, there are a lot of Jesters!

Established in 1983, there are Jesters in the UK.

Established in 1996, there are Jesters in Thailand.

There is a Jesters MC that was just one of eleven clubs to make the law enforcement map in Hawaii.

And there is a Jesters Motorcycle Club that is *yet another* of the motorcycle clubs mentioned on one of the strangest (and never-ending) "anti gang" websites in the universe, as an associate club of the HAMC in Canada.

✠

JOKERS - While we're still in a fun mood, let's deal a few Jokers.

Established in 2002, there is a Jokers MC in Wiltshire, England, that evolved from members of clubs like the Ravens, Annwn BC, Sentinels, and Lowlanders. They throw a twist on the 1% patch by putting the "1%" in a pair of rolling dice.

There is a Jokers MC in Michigan.

And a full-on, diamond patch 1% motorcycle club in Kaluga, Russia.

Established in 1995, there's a three-piece-patch club in Spain.

✠

JOKERS WILD - Pulling another card from the motorcycle club deck, we see that there is a Jokers Wild MC "near the West Virginia/Virginia line" and a riding club in Nova Scotia.

✠

JOURNEYMEN - Established in 2005, in Prescott, Arizona. This three-piece patch is loud, proud, and vocal when it comes to their thoughts on the fact that it's not "illegal" to be a patch holder and "to value true brotherhood above all else."

Yes, some motorcycle clubs dressed like this in the '30. *Jeff Thrower/shutterstock.com*

Juneau

- ◆ **ESTABLISHED:** 1930s
- ◆ **PLACE OF ORIGIN:** Juneau, Alaska
- ◆ **FOUNDER(S):** Unknown
- ◆ **CHAPTER LOCATIONS:** Now defunct
- ◆ **CLAIM TO FAME:** The first documented motorcycle club in Juneau

JUNEAU - North to Alaska—this is a genuine "pioneer" club from way, way up there! Dating back into the 1930s, this club was "perhaps the first documented motorcycle club in Juneau." Gee, ya think?!

Jus Brothers

- ◆ **ESTABLISHED:** 1990
- ◆ **PLACE OF ORIGIN:** Tracy, California
- ◆ **FOUNDER(S):** Michael Patrick "Irish Mike" McCusker
- ◆ **CHAPTER LOCATIONS:** Stockton, California
- ◆ **CLUB COLORS:** Royal Blue and Silver
- ◆ **CENTER PATCH:** An eagle head with seven stars over it on a Route 66–shaped sign
- ◆ **CLAIM TO FAME:** The subject of the 2008 book, written by the founder: *A Road Without End: The Jus Brothers Motorcycle Club 1990–2007*

JUS BROTHERS - Established in 1990 in Tracy, California. This diamond-patch 1% club made it onto the law enforcement map listing out west, but they also made it onto the bookshelves when their founder, Michael Patrick "Irish Mike" McCusker wrote *A Road Without End: The Jus Brothers Motorcycle Club 1990–2007*. It was a book a lot like John Hall's book about the Pagans, in that it was more like a barroom conversation than a literary journal. In fact, read together, both the Hall book and Irish Mike's make for a nice continuum of the biker lifestyle from the 1960s to the present.

✠

KELTICS - An "Outlaws MC affiliated" club with chapters in Florida.

✠

KING COBRA - A three-piece-club patch in Franken, Germany.

✠

KINGPIN CREW - Another of the MCs mentioned on one of the strangest (and never-ending) "anti-gang" websites in the universe, as an associate club of the HAMC in Canada.

✠

KINGSMEN - Established in 1958, this is one of our "classic" clubs. They have chapters in New York, Pennsylvania, and Florida—and made the law enforcement map in all three!

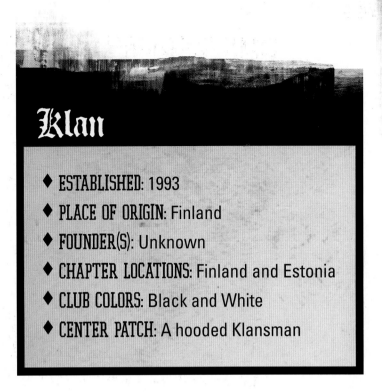

Klan

♦ **ESTABLISHED:** 1993
♦ **PLACE OF ORIGIN:** Finland
♦ **FOUNDER(S):** Unknown
♦ **CHAPTER LOCATIONS:** Finland and Estonia
♦ **CLUB COLORS:** Black and White
♦ **CENTER PATCH:** A hooded Klansman

KLAN - Established in 1993, with chapters in Finland and Estonia. This three-piece-patch club has one of the most "interesting" and ominous center patches anywhere.

✠

KNIGHT RIDERS - Established in 1969 by American GIs in Dino's Cafe in Kitzingen, "making it one of the oldest motorcycle clubs in Germany." The founding members were Champ, Jack the Snake, and Moose. As time passed, more German members came into the essentially American motorcycle club. They have their founding date of "69" in a diamond, and the red and white colors are the colors associated with the Würzburg garrison.

✠

Knights

- ♦ **ESTABLISHED:** 1975
- ♦ **PLACE OF ORIGIN:** New Jersey
- ♦ **FOUNDER(S):** Miles Hahn and others
- ♦ **CHAPTER LOCATIONS:** New Jersey, Maryland, Delaware, Pennsylvania, Florida, Virginia
- ♦ **CLUB COLORS:** Black and Gold
- ♦ **MOTTO:** *Brotherhood and Vigilance*

KNIGHTS - A three-piece-patch club in Malta. They have a motto that kind of says it all: "Forever strong, forever bikers, forever brothers. . . . Our will shall find the way!" And they are HAMC supporters.

But there is another Knights MC, an East Coast club with a history as told by one of their more loquacious members, "Weebles," KMC:

First off, we are not affiliated with any of the other Knights MCs. We started out as Jersey Knights in 1975—this was Generation I. This first phase of the club actually wanted to go AMA, but when they went to all the racing events, they took all the trophies—the AMA clubs there were pissed! So when the Jersey Knights applied for an AMA charter, the AMA turned them down. "Fuck you, AMA!" they decided.

Maryland soon joined the fold, and then Delaware. Generation I went until 1985 when Generation II came into play. With Generation II came big changes. We went with a three-piece patch, adding a sword to our center patch. And instead of being Jersey, Maryland, and Delaware Knights we joined under one banner and

became Knights MC with state rockers on the bottom. In 1987, Pennsylvania was added to the fold. Generation II went on through 2010.

Generation III went into effect in 2011. At that time, some of us dropped the state rockers and went with "EST. 1975" for our bottom rocker. Since we were scattered all over the U.S., we felt this was the right thing to do. We also decided to put our colors on leather. A lot of our older members decided they didn't want to change their old colors, so they kept them and wear a retired patch instead.

Oh, and one more thing: In all the years we have been a club, we have never been infiltrated!

Weebles also has a few very sensitive and soul-searching thoughts about those who disrespect colors, the sometimes too casual use of the term "bro," and the true meaning of that sacred biker title:

I've actually seen these jerks wearing those Sons of Anarchy colors. I've even stopped 'em and told 'em, maybe a bit too harshly, "Don't you know how disrespectful that is to the 1%er?!" And they have no clue what a 1%er is! Fuckin' clueless! I've also seen those rock colors from Zack Wilde's band. Another bad idea, and what the fuck, I seen a shirt from Sturgis made to look like a set of colors! Funny how everybody wants to be one of us; they want to play in our world, but they don't want to live in our world!

But we do—and we ride! And, man it seems like every ride we go on is an adventure. But it's always been that way, really. Some people can just get on their bikes and ride from point A to point B and back again and that's it. You ask them what they saw, what happened, what did they do along the way, and you always get the same answer: "Well, it was nice and sunny and the ride was nice and we stopped off and got gas and had a cold drink and bla bla bla and then we rode home again; we had lots of fun…" Boring!

My bike is a fourteen-year-old rat. Granted, it's a pretty good-lookin' rat and it's a rat hot-rod, but man, when you build a rat hot-rod, things fuckin' happen! Things vibrate loose; things fall off. Oops, ahh! And even if you try and keep an eye on things, sometimes things slip under the radar and then things fuck up! But, brother, it's about being a biker!

Okay, so a run that should take eight hours ends up taking close to fourteen or more—who gives a shit? It's fuckin' raining, we're fuckin' soaked to the bone, it's fuckin' freezing—who gives a shit? The sun is frying my fuckin' brains out in this fuckin' helmet! Big fuckin' deal! There's a great cold spring up here in the mountains but these fuckin' people never see any of this or experience any of this!

Man, I have tried and fuckin' tried to explain to these fuckin' barstool sidewalk commandos that the party is the ride, not the show at the end of the ride! Fuck it, man, I give up! I'm too old for this shit! This new generation of riders just ain't what we're all about!

Oh yeah, and you meet one in a bar and fuckin' instantly he's your fuckin' bro! Just add JD and beer.

I got so fuckin' mad one night in our local watering hole. This asshole called me "bro" and John, one of my brothers from outta state, was there.

I reached over and took out my pistol and handed it to the asshole and said, "Shoot me, motherfucker!" And he looked at me like I had an eye in the middle of my forehead.

My brother slipped up in front of me and said, "Motherfucker, if you're gonna shoot anyone, shoot me!" The asshole stood there lookin' at the pistol, and John just reached down and took it out of his hand. He handed it back to me and said to the guy, "Sorry—you want to play in our world, but when it comes down to it, you don't want to stay in our world. You just got a lesson in what a bro is!"

Then (John's very diplomatic, I'm not...) he goes on to say, "The word 'bro' is short for

Courtesy of Rich "Weebles" Halmuth and Knights MC

'brother'—someone who shares your beliefs, your happiness, your sorrow, and right or wrong, will stand up for you—no questions asked. If his brother gets in trouble and he sees it, he will keep his mouth shut, and if anyone asks him if he saw anything he will say he saw nothing, just like Sergeant Shultz—or as we like to say, 'Weebles'll lie and I'll swear to it!' And, like you just seen, he will walk in front of a bullet for a brother in a heartbeat!

"So look, son, we don't want to hear your BS about all your rides you go on—we've never seen you ride ever. And don't ever, never, ever again call any one of us 'bro.' Okay, now go home and think on this."

"Hey, man, my bike's outside," I say to the guy. "What say we blast up to the titty bar!"

"Oh, well," this kid says, "you know, I had to sell it. The old lady got on my ass, lost my job, dropped my cell phone in the toilet, bla, bla…"

It's the same shit, man—the same shit that I've been hearing since the '70s. Guess I'm just gettin' to be an old grumpy biker…hahahaha!

✠

KNIGHTS OF JUSTICE - I said I wasn't going to list any law enforcement clubs, but this motorcycle club out of South Africa needs a mention if for no other reason than their "rather intense" political views on the "outlaws" of the world. Their "Creed of a Knight" doesn't leave much room for giving a brother a break now and then.

✠

KNUCKLE DRAGGERS, KNUCKLE DRAGGERZ - Knuckle Draggers is a relatively new Southern Californian motorcycle club that did a textbook job of following protocol as they formed.

There is a Knuckle Draggerz three-piece-patch club for military vets of Iraq and Afghanistan that claims no states, just "the countries of war." They also have a classic set of bylaws. Number one pretty much sets the tone: "Don't be a shit bag, we got no room for dumb asses here. That will bring disgrace to the proud veterans of this club."

✠

KOA PUNA - Established in 1979, this motorcycle club was one of the "Ocean's Eleven" motorcycle clubs that made the law enforcement map in Hawaii. Founded in the Puna District of The Big Island, "Koa Puna MC has been running 'em hard since 1979!"

✠

KVILLEBACKEN - Established in 1973 in Sweden, this Bandidos support club was later joined by members of Lucifer's Bunch MC. It was in 2006 when they were admitted as an "official supporter club to Bandidos MC World."

CHAPTER 5

La Hondra-Mystic Seven

LA HONRA - As we have seen, the Bandidos Motorcycle Club has formed a giant, multi-nation support team of motorcycle clubs that are more numerous than the bullets in Pancho Villa's crossed bandoliers. La Honra in Germany is among them.

⊹

LA ONDA - This MC is also in Germany and is also a part of the Bandidos wide web of support.

⊹

LAST CHANCE - An Ontario, Canada based motorcycle club that reportedly patched over to the HAMC (Hells Angels Motorcycle Club) when the Red and White came into the province.

⊹

Last Rebels

♦ **ESTABLISHED:** 2009
♦ **PLACE OF ORIGIN:** Russia
♦ **FOUNDER(S):** Ex-members of several Russian clubs
♦ **CHAPTER LOCATIONS:** Two chapters and a hangaround club in Russia
♦ **CENTER COLORS:** Black, Red, and Silver
♦ **CENTER PATCH:** An iron cross, crossed swords, and a wheel
♦ **MOTTO:** *In union we stay! Last rebel forever, last rebels forever, forever brothers! Forever brothers!*
♦ **CLUB ASSOCIATIONS:** "81" supporters in Russia

LAST REBELS - Two Last Rebels ride across our list.

One, established in 2009, is a three-piece-patch motorcycle club in Russia that is a Red and White supporter.

The other club is the Last Rebels out of West Virginia. With chapters in Buckhannon, Huntington, Kanawha County, Wayne County, and Southeast Ohio, this Last Rebels made the law enforcement map in the Mountain State.

⊹

LATIN STEEL - This Bandidos support club in Texas won the 2010 Austin region Confederacy of Clubs (COC) award for the organization's Safety & Awareness program.

Legacy

♦ **ESTABLISHED:** 2001
♦ **PLACE OF ORIGIN:** Chicago, Illinois
♦ **FOUNDER(S):** A group of "motorcycle fanatics" who wanted to create the first Polish motorcycle club in America
♦ **CHAPTER LOCATIONS:** Chi-town
♦ **CENTER PATCH:** A shield with crossed swords
♦ **CLAIM TO FAME:** The "only Polish MC in the U.S."
♦ **CLUB ASSOCIATIONS:** They display Outlaws MC support.

LEGACY - Established in 2001 on the North Side of Chicago. The motorcycle club is recognized as the "only Polish MC in the U.S." And they do display Outlaws MC support.

Legacy Vets

♦ **ESTABLISHED:** 1998
♦ **PLACE OF ORIGIN:** California
♦ **FOUNDER(S):** Viet Nam Vets MC
♦ **CHAPTER LOCATIONS:** U.S. and Europe
♦ **CLUB COLORS:** Red and Black
♦ **CENTER PATCH:** An eagle on a world map; very similar to the Viet Nam Vets MC patch
♦ **CLUB ASSOCIATIONS:** They will be the "legacy" of the VNVMC as the 'Nam vets evolve into the inevitable.

LEGACY VETS - When the Viet Nam Vets MC was formed, it was obvious that its membership pool was finite. The Legacy Vets branch of the Red and Black opened things up to military service beyond Vietnam. These "returning warriors" are "activists and advocates for veteran's rights and related issues." And, yes, the Legacy Vets MC is an organization with chapters everywhere, but they seem to have only made the law enforcement map in Hawaii!

LES DURS - Established in 1983, a diamond-patch 1% motorcycle club out of Germany (*Les Durs* means "tough guys" in French).

LIBERTAD VAGUEROS - Another representative in the congress of clubs that is the Bandidos support body in Germany.

✠

Living Dead

- ◆ **ESTABLISHED:** 1973
- ◆ **PLACE OF ORIGIN:** Germany
- ◆ **FOUNDER(S):** "Klaus, along with fifteen boys and a girl"
- ◆ **CHAPTER LOCATIONS:** Germany
- ◆ **CENTER PATCH:** A true old-school skull and crossbones
- ◆ **CLAIM TO FAME:** The club has been the subject of a great deal of media coverage about their long history.

LIVING DEAD - This diamond-patch 1% club with chapters in Germany is stayin' alive, celebrating their thirty-fifth anniversary.

✠

LIVINGS - Established in 1991, a one percent motorcycle club out of Germany, with their "12" in the diamond.

✠

LOBO - Lobo MC Germany has itself a mighty pack, running with chapters and support clubs throughout Germany—they're a full-tilt diamond-patch 1% motorcycle club. *"Zieh mit den Woolfen!"*

✠

LOBOS - There are other packs of wolves running around as well.

Established in 1974, Lobos MC is a three-piece-patch club out of Nuremberg, Germany. There is another Lobos in Germany, too—established in 1979—with a completely different patch than the Nuremberg boys have.

There was a Lobos MC that was in the Windsor, Ontario, area of Canada that reportedly merged with the HAMC in 2001.

Roaming around in Oregon is a Lobos AMA/off-road racing group. And the Lobos Guara MC in Brazil is celebrating its twelfth anniversary.

Brazil is also the home of the Lobos Da Estrada MC in Rio.

✠

Lone Legion

- ◆ ESTABLISHED: Unknown
- ◆ PLACE OF ORIGIN: Blenheim, New Zealand
- ◆ FOUNDER(S): Unknown
- ◆ CHAPTER LOCATIONS: New Zealand
- ◆ CLAIM TO FAME: One of the New Zealand clubs that continually make the various law enforcement and other "top clubs" lists; part of the A-Team alliance of clubs in NZ

LONE LEGION - Out of Blenheim, New Zealand, Lone Legion is another of the newsmakers down there. They are another club reported to be a part of the "A-Team," an alliance that includes the Outcasts MC, the Epitaph Riders MC, the Forty-Fives MC, the Southern Vikings MC, Satan's Slaves MC, Sinn Fein MC, and the Lost Breed MC.

Loners

- ◆ ESTABLISHED: 1973
- ◆ PLACE OF ORIGIN: La Mirada, California
- ◆ FOUNDER(S): Six friends
- ◆ CHAPTER LOCATIONS: Arizona, Arkansas, California, Kentucky, and Oklahoma
- ◆ CLUB COLORS: Blue and Gold
- ◆ CENTER PATCH: A large golden "L"
- ◆ CLAIM TO FAME: A "classic" club out of SoCal that was known for their annual event in Hanford, California

LONERS - The Loners aren't really alone; there are two biggies with many charters:

Established in 1979 in Ontario, Canada, the club made news in 2001 when it got into a big legal battle to keep their club mascot on their property. Eventually their "neutered, declawed lion named Woody" was moved to an animal sanctuary. The diamond-patch 1% motorcycle club also has a nomad chapter and a chapter in Spain.

California's Loners were established in 1973 in the SoCal city of La Mirada. Founded by six friends, the club grew to a common sight among the Southern California motorcycle clubs. They made the 2010 law enforcement map in Cali and Arizona and were the driving force behind a huge biker event held for years in Hanford, California. Other clubs used the name "Loners," one of which wore the cut on the facing page.

Long March

- ◆ **ESTABLISHED:** October 2009
- ◆ **PLACE OF ORIGIN:** The People's Republic of China
- ◆ **FOUNDER(S):** Kirk Boutette, Wei Ren, H. Clay Jones
- ◆ **CHAPTER LOCATIONS:** China
- ◆ **CLUB COLORS:** Red and Black
- ◆ **CENTER PATCH:** A dragon
- ◆ **CLAIM TO FAME:** One of the few three-piece-patch clubs in the PRC

LONG MARCH - Long March is a three-piece motorcycle club that rides "outlaw" in the People's Republic of China. One member describes the experience:

The Long March MC started with the Chang Jiang 750 side-valve sidecar motorcycles. Sometime in the late '90s, a loose (non-formal) group of Chang riders decided to form a club. At this time the group was headed by an expat named "Orvo Vilila," but the club also included Chinese sidecar riders. A few years later many of the foreign members had returned to their home countries and the club name was left to me. I formed a discussion group, called Long March, which discussed vintage PLA parts for the Chang Jiang six-volt flathead. After some time, a couple of the guys who participated on the board bought Harley-Davidsons and the focus of the club begin to change. After my move to Beijing, I began to ride with some of the riding clubs like V2 and it was cool to meet new Harley riders and to go on the weekend rides and to

LONES - One more in the lengthy line of German Bandidos support clubs.

✠

LONE STAR - Established in 1993, not in Texas, but in Germany: "We say it loud—we are Lone Star and proud."

✠

lunch, but I found the rides too short with not enough riding. The idea of club life was missing from the riding clubs. A few of the guys I met at the V2 rides wanted a club that would involve living a motorcycle life instead of just riding on the weekends.

This wasn't a spur-of-the-moment decision, and the decree of becoming a proper MC was in part due to the dissatisfaction (experienced by the three original members) with the lack of motorcycle-related activities among Harley riders and the idea of elite showcasing of opulence over biker lifestyle and motorcycle culture.

We actually started this MC to be a Chinese club, although foreigners who are lifers in China are encouraged to check us out, and, in fact, two of the original founders are indeed an American and a Canadian.

Requirements for a rider's acceptance to the MC are fairly strict as the MC itself is not properly licensed in China, as you can imagine, and so we exist basically in the underground. The club has just revised the colors in a visual statement to reaffirm its dedication to the life, and members have worked hard and dedicated time and money to the building of a proper clubhouse and establishing an annex in a local non-authorized Harley shop, which is closer to town than the clubhouse and will serve as a repair station and maintenance depot.

There can be no democracy without V-twins.

—H. Clay Jones, Long March MC

✠

LOS ALIADOS - This club joins the list of German Bandidos supporters.

✠

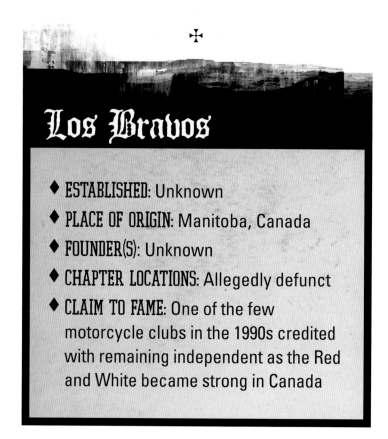

Los Bravos

- ◆ **ESTABLISHED:** Unknown
- ◆ **PLACE OF ORIGIN:** Manitoba, Canada
- ◆ **FOUNDER(S):** Unknown
- ◆ **CHAPTER LOCATIONS:** Allegedly defunct
- ◆ **CLAIM TO FAME:** One of the few motorcycle clubs in the 1990s credited with remaining independent as the Red and White became strong in Canada

LOS BRAVOS - A club that has a place in Canadian motorcycle club lore as being one of the independent motorcycle clubs out of Manitoba that "kept the Hells Angels from assuming dominance in the prairie provinces until the late nineties."

Back in the late 1990s, Los Bravos were mentioned in the law enforcement white paper, *Criminal Intelligence Service Canada 1998 Annual Report:*

In Manitoba, the Winnipeg-based LOS BRAVOS celebrated their 30th anniversary in October 1997. They have about 24 active members and nine strikers (prospects), and have allegedly joined the HELLS ANGELS as a hangaround club.

LOS ESTRAGOS, LOS LOCOS, LOS MALOS, LOS MUERTOS - All *quarto* of these *clubes de motociclismo* are part of the SYLB alliance in Germany, supporting the Red and Gold of the Bandidos Motorcycle Club.

Lost Breed

- ♦ **ESTABLISHED:** 1976
- ♦ **PLACE OF ORIGIN:** Nelson, New Zealand
- ♦ **FOUNDER(S):** Unknown
- ♦ **CHAPTER LOCATIONS:** Nelson, New Zealand
- ♦ **CLAIM TO FAME:** Part of New Zealand's A-Team alliance

LOST BREED - Established in 1976 in Nelson, New Zealand. Law enforcement calls them the "only gang in town" when they comment on their influence in Nelson. Lately, the motorcycle club has announced that they are "strongly opposed to the drug 'P' and domestic violence." The cops countered with some comments of their own, asking if they are also "against the use of cannabis and the unrestricted sale of alcohol." The Lost Breed is also a member of that "A-team" federation of motorcycle clubs that includes the Outcasts MC, the Epitaph Riders MC, the Forty-Fives MC, the Southern Vikings MC, Satan's Slaves MC, Sinn Fein MC, and the Lone Legion MC.

LOS VALIENTES - Richard "Deadeye" Hayes (no relation) grew up in St. Paul, Minnesota. He joined the Los Valientes back in the day and wrote the book, *Outlaw Biker: My Life at Full Throttle*. He describes a taste of some Los Valientes—and universal motorcycle club—flavor:

> *My club, the Los Valientes, is considered an outlaw club because we run a three-piece patch and claim an area. We ride with the best and are ready for any test—it's like the jungle because any sign of weakness will be smelled right out. Even your own brothers will push you to see that they can count on you in a tough spot. There's nothing better than a good old ass kicking to get the testosterone flowing, a good old bare knuckle, knock-down, drag-out fight. No guns or knives—most of the time.*

And, no surprise here, Los Valientes made the law enforcement map in Minnesota.

LOST DUTCHMAN - Established in 1994 in Arizona, The Lost Dutchman MC is "proactive in issues that affect the motorcycle community." And they made it onto the law enforcement map in Arizona.

Lost Tribe

- ◆ ESTABLISHED: 2007
- ◆ PLACE OF ORIGIN: Oulu, Finland
- ◆ FOUNDER(S): Unknown
- ◆ CHAPTER LOCATIONS: Finland
- ◆ CLUB COLORS: Black and White
- ◆ CENTER PATCH: An iron cross and a skull
- ◆ CLAIM TO FAME: Not engaged in Satanism!

Lucifer's Messenger

- ◆ ESTABLISHED: 1979
- ◆ PLACE OF ORIGIN: Germany
- ◆ FOUNDER(S): Ex-members of Snoopy MC and Wild Tiger MC including the last remaining original, Puchtler
- ◆ CHAPTER LOCATIONS: Germany
- ◆ CLUB COLORS: Their patches and colors seem to evolve and change frequently.
- ◆ CLAIM TO FAME: Interesting use of Shakespearean quotes surrounding the club

LOST TRIBE - We have actually found two Lost Tribes:

The first, established in 2007 with a "skull place" in Oulu, Finland. The three-piece-patch club engages in "Cruisailu, Customointi, and Heavy drinking." They also offer an important reassurance: "Heimo ei harrasta satanismia, eikä muutakaan rikollista toimintaa"—"Tribe is not engaged in Satanism, or any other criminal activity."

Our second find is The Lost Tribe that is a member of the Jewish Motorcyclists Alliance in Virginia Beach. "The members of the Lost Tribe motorcycle club don't have any rules, leaders, membership fees, dues, or commitments, but they do request one thing: Jewish pride."

✝

LOWLANDERS - Established in the mid-1990s, this three-piece-patch club has chapters in Italy and Bulgaria.

LUCIFER'S MESSENGER - A three-piece-patch out of Germany: "Independent since 1979." One of the few motorcycle clubs that uses a spin on a quote by William Shakespeare anywhere among its official stuff: "Hell is empty, and the Lucifers are here."

✝

LYON - Part of the Euro Bandidos support system. "SYLB" France.

✝

MACHO KINGS BROTHERHOOD - A three-piece-patch motorcycle club in Turkey.

Mad Dog

- **ESTABLISHED:** 1994
- **PLACE OF ORIGIN:** Philippines
- **FOUNDER(S):** Tom Leber
- **CHAPTER LOCATIONS:** Philippines, Thailand, Singapore, Japan, Hong Kong
- **CLUB COLORS:** Red, White, and Black
- **CENTER PATCH:** What else? A mad bulldog!
- **CLAIM TO FAME:** Part of New Zealand's A-Team alliance

Magog

- **ESTABLISHED:** 1974
- **PLACE OF ORIGIN:** New Plymouth, Taranaki, New Zealand
- **FOUNDER(S):** Unknown
- **CHAPTER LOCATIONS:** New Zealand
- **CLUB COLORS:** Gold, Red, and Black
- **CENTER PATCH:** A cross
- **CLAIM TO FAME:** Producers of the large biannual National Motorcycle Expo

MAD DOG - Established in 1994 in the garage of Tom Leber and "some close friends" in the Philippines; now the "Premier MC in Asia." The club has had a rabid Asian expansion into Thailand, Singapore, Japan, Hong Kong, "and further, creating the standard for Motorcycle Clubs in South East Asia. . . . It takes much more than a tattoo and a Harley or big cruiser to become a Dog." Mad Dog is a "brotherhood bounded by principles instead of borders."

MAGOG - Established in 1974 in New Plymouth, Taranaki, New Zealand. The early "purposes and aims" of the members were reasonably simple—"enjoy themselves, ride motorcycles, and be generally anti-social—the norm for the times." In 1982 they began to produce the successful biannual National Motorcycle Expo in 1982. Three of the club's founding members celebrated their thirty-seventh anniversary in January 2011.

✠

MERCENARIES - Established "more than a half decade ago in the capital city of Estonia, Tallin." They are now a hangaround chapter of the Red and Gold.

✠

✠

MESSENGERS - A Hells Angels support club in Serbia.

✠

MALOS HOMBRES - These "Bad Men" are a good part of Germany's group of Bandidos support clubs.

✠

MARKET STREET COMMANDOS - One of our "pioneer" clubs that is always mentioned right along with P.O.B.O.B.s and the Boozefighters as having been in Hollister 1947, at the "birth of the American Biker." In *Hell's Angel*, Sonny Barger credits the Commandos as being the origin of the San Francisco Hells Angels, eventually merging with the Fontana Hells Angels.

𝕸arket 𝕾treet 𝕮ommandos

- ◆ ESTABLISHED: In the WWII years
- ◆ PLACE OF ORIGIN: San Francisco, California
- ◆ FOUNDER(S): Unknown
- ◆ CHAPTER LOCATIONS: Now defunct
- ◆ CLAIM TO FAME: One of the true "pioneer" clubs, present at Hollister 1947 and mentioned by Sonny Barger as having been the origin of the San Francisco Hells Angels

MC CHE - Established in 1990 in Germany, a club with an obvious homage to the famous revolutionary. It would be interesting to see their center patch and Klan MC's together.

MERCILESS SOULS - A Red and White support club that made the law enforcement map in Virginia.

✠

MESCALEROS - A three-piece-patch club in Barcelona, Spain.

✠

MEXHETEXOS - X-cellently named motorcycle club that made the law enforcement map in Tejas.

✠

MEXICAN SYNDICATE - We're adding to the list of Red and Gold supporters in Germany.

✠

MIDNITE RIDERS - This back-patch MC out of Southern California's San Gabriel Valley prides itself on its extensive charity work and involvement in bikers' rights issues.

𝕸idnite 𝕽iders

- ◆ WHERE: San Gabriel Valley, California
- ◆ FOUNDERS NAMES: Mountain Bob, Old Buzzard, and Slopoke
- ◆ COLORS: Purple, black and silver.

Mid-West

- ◆ **ESTABLISHED:** 1923
- ◆ **PLACE OF ORIGIN:** Indianapolis, Indiana
- ◆ **FOUNDER(S):** Ralph Moore
- ◆ **CHAPTER LOCATIONS:** Indiana
- ◆ **CLUB COLORS:** Red, Black, and Gold
- ◆ **CENTER PATCH:** Single patch with the state of Indiana
- ◆ **CLAIM TO FAME:** One of the ten oldest clubs in the United States

MID-WEST - Established in 1923 in the basement of John Morgan's Harley-Davidson Motorcycle Shop in Indianapolis. Mid-West MC is the oldest motorcycle club in Indiana and one of the ten oldest in the United States. According to the club, the founder, Ralph Moore, was an active member until his death in 1977.

✠

MIDWEST DRIFTERS - This Galloping Goose MC support club made the law enforcement map in Missouri.

✠

MILFORD & CO. - M&C made the law enforcement map in New Hampshire. They also made the news in April 2010 when a slight scuffle occurred at a pizza joint. The *Londonderry News* was all over it:

> *The investigation into the shooting at Luigi's Pizza, located at 712 Valley Street, has resulted in the arrest of a Londonderry man. The Manchester Police were called to Luigi's Pizza on Friday, April 16th at approximately 8:40 PM for a reported fight inside the establishment. Prior to the officers' arrival, they were informed that gunshots were now being reported from that area. Upon the arrival of the officers, they located a victim who had been shot. Upon further examination of the victim, the officers were able to determine that he had sustained numerous injuries from a shotgun round. . . . During the course of the investigation, three groups were identified as being involved in the fight inside Luigi's Pizza. They were the Outlaws Motorcycle Club, Hells Angels Motorcycle Club and Milford and Company Motorcycle Club. The three motorcycle clubs involved were observed wearing insignia representing each club.*

✠

MILITARY MISFITS - The MMMC made the law enforcement map in California and they also made it into that long ATF document that—complete with surveillance photos—links servicemen with "OMGs" that they just might be associating with.

> *ATF (U) OMGs and the Military 2010 Update According to multiple law enforcement agencies, along with the Green Machine, the Military Misfits are visible at many Vagos functions, to include parties in Nevada and northern California.*

✠

Militia Riders

- ◆ **ESTABLISHED:** In the 1990s
- ◆ **PLACE OF ORIGIN:** Singapore
- ◆ **FOUNDER(S):** Unknown
- ◆ **CHAPTER LOCATIONS:** Malaysia and a probationary chapter in South Carolina, U.S.
- ◆ **CLUB COLORS:** Red, Silver, and Black
- ◆ **CENTER PATCH:** A flaming iron cross on wings
- ◆ **MOTTO:** *Live with honor, ride with pride*
- ◆ **CLAIM TO FAME:** One of just two "traditional clubs" in Singapore

MILITIA RIDERS - Established "in the '90s" in Singapore, this motorcycle club is one of the two "original traditional" clubs there. They have chapters in Malaysia and a probationary chapter in the U.S. in South Carolina. These guys seem to be genuine hardbutts, too, when it comes to riding: "Our members are true motorcycle enthusiasts and make their motorcycles as a main means of transportation, rain or shine. Prospecting is not easy. Shortest is one year and longest was three years. Our full-members never leave so you can also ask them about how to survive in MRMC. . . . Militia Riders Motorcycle Club has always been a way of life, not a weekend hobby or alternative lifestyle where you can impress your friends or play dress-up and action with your loud motorcycle exhausts for a few hours with your biker buddies. Don't judge what you don't understand.

Don't assume what you don't know. Don't believe what you don't see. Go your own way. To each his own...Live with Honor, Ride with Pride."

✠

MINOTAUR, MINOTAURI, MINOTAUROS, MINOTAURS, MINOTAURUS, MINOTAVROI - This is no bull—let's work our way through the maze of Minotaurs charging around.

Minotaurs MC Downside was founded by "ten good friends from Harloesa in Sweden." Their first clubhouse was in an old movie theater. Another motorcycle club that took protocol seriously, "The club was seeking in to the Swedish biker community called SBM and did what was necessary to be a full patched motorcycle club."

Minotaur MC is a three-piece-patch club in Norway.

Minotaurus MC is a Bandidos support club in Germany.

And there's the Minotauri MC, Chiavari, Italy; Minotauros MC, Toledo, Spain; and Minotavroi MC, Crete, Greece.

✠

MISFITS - Toys! I sort of hate to begin this list of Misfits MCs with this particular club but it's just too wacky to pass up. This "MC" is composed of toys!—21st Century Toys–marketed action figures!—and they are a band of, well, misfits who have complete histories, names, and everything else given to them by whoever spent a whole lot of time on a very different kind of website. And I thought that the large chat rooms and forums for the *Sons of Anarchy* were somewhat bent:

The Misfits are a violent group comprised of out-law bikers and survivalists, with several of them being ex-military personnel. Falkirk employs the gang as his henchmen. Members include the skull faced Doyle Von Alister; a.k.a "Monster", the Neo-Nazi Jerry Wessler; a.k.a "Chainz", James Blackfoot; a.k.a "Chief", the bounty-killer Tim Gore; a.k.a "T-Gore", AJ McLeod; a.k.a. "Krayzee Gyrl", Frank Rook; a.k.a "Kaiser", the masked man who goes by the name "Slayer"; real name unknown, "Dirty" Dick & Bobbie Jo Rollins, Cain Jenicek; a.k.a "Kane". They are led by the notorious criminal, The Sandman.

Each has a rap sheet a mile long. All are to be considered armed & highly dangerous.

Only a dozen or so Misfits have been encountered thus far, but it is speculated that there are other members.

As far as a *real* Misfits MC goes, there is a non-one-percent club in Mississippi, established in 1999, and some folks remember a "classic" one percent motorcycle club out of Northern California with the Misfits patch.

✠

MIXTECAS - This club made it onto the law enforcement map in Wisconsin. They are also in Chicago and in 2009 were reportedly in attendance at the funeral for one of the founders of the club, "Chile."

✠

Mofos

◆ **ESTABLISHED:** 1950s

◆ **PLACE OF ORIGIN:** California

◆ **FOUNDER(S):** Unknown

◆ **CHAPTER LOCATIONS:** Unknown, presumed defunct

◆ **CLAIM TO FAME:** The club is mentioned in a lot of historical nods to the California biker culture, especially noting the club's presence at the famous "1%er summit" with all the top Northern California clubs in 1960

MOFOS - A "classic" and historical club mentioned a lot in ancient literature. In George Wethern's 1978 book, *A Wayward Angel: The Full Story of the Hells Angels*, Wethern states that in 1960 the Mofos were a big part of a huge club summit held at the home of Frank Sadilek, "P" of the SF HAMC. The original purpose of the meeting was to discuss police harassment but the discussion turned toward the AMA and the one percent label. Wethern notes that at that "summit" the clubs decided to accept the one percent label as a "tribute" to identify themselves as "righteous outlaws," and reportedly, Wethern and Sonny Barger were the first to get "1%" tattoos.

There's another piece of recorded history that has made a lot of rounds, burying its origin. But it does mention a lot of the "pioneer" and "classic" clubs—including the Mofos:

The Pagans, by 1965, originally clad in white denim jackets and riding Triumphs, had begun to evolve along the lines of the California stereotype generated by such famous motorcycle clubs as the Booze Fighters, Cavaliers, Coffin Cheaters, Comancheros, Crossmen, Defiants, Devil's Henchmen, El Diablos, Falcons, Galloping Gooses, Gladiators, Gypsy Jokers, Gypsy Outlaws, Hangmen, Hells Angels, Iron Horsemen, Journeymen, Marauders, Mofos, Night Riders, Outlaws, Presidents, Road Rats, Satan's Slaves, Stray Satans, Thunderbirds, Thunder Riders, etc. Most of these were eventually merged with the Hells Angels.

Molochs

- ◆ **ESTABLISHED:** 1968
- ◆ **PLACE OF ORIGIN:** California
- ◆ **FOUNDER(S):** Unknown
- ◆ **CHAPTER LOCATIONS:** Throughout California
- ◆ **CLUB COLORS:** Black and Gold
- ◆ **CENTER PATCH:** A "reptile deity" on wheels
- ◆ **CLAIM TO FAME:** One of California's true "classic" clubs

MOLOCHS - Established in 1968, a "classic" club that was founded in California, permanently settling into the Central Coast in 1972. With chapters throughout Cali, they definitely made the law enforcement map there.

Mongols

- ◆ **ESTABLISHED:** 1969
- ◆ **PLACE OF ORIGIN:** Montebello, California
- ◆ **FOUNDER(S):** A starting core of fifteen members
- ◆ **CHAPTER LOCATIONS:** The Mongols Nation is worldwide
- ◆ **CLUB COLORS:** Black and White
- ◆ **CENTER PATCH:** A Mongol
- ◆ **CLAIM TO FAME:** The Mongols were at the heart of a 2008 U.S. government attempt to confiscate club colors—a legal case that had a major impact on motorcycle clubs worldwide.

MONGOLS - Established in 1969 in Montebello, California, in the badlands area known as East L.A. With a starting core of just fifteen members, the Mongols have become an international club and are mentioned in the same categories and acknowledgments as the Big Five and clubs like the Vagos and the Warlocks. The year of 2008 was a big one for the Mongols—their then-president, Ruben "Doc" Cavasos, released his book, *Honor Few, Fear None*. Much to HarperCollins' commercial dismay, the book became obsolete and not-so-relevant in a hurry when Cavasos and the club split ways soon after, as Operation Black Rain and the feds took aim on the club and put Doc away. The result was one of the most complex legal-leaps ever taken by the authorities as they attempted to take away not only the Mongols' name, logo, and

virtually everything else belonging to the club but also to set a precedent that could—and would—do it to every other MC out there as well. Thankfully, it didn't work and the Mongols are flying proud once again.

MONGREL - Established in 1993, a three-piece-patch club out of Oulu, Finland.

⚜

⚜

Mongrel Mob

- ◆ ESTABLISHED: 1968
- ◆ PLACE OF ORIGIN: Hastings, New Zealand
- ◆ FOUNDER(S): Unknown
- ◆ CHAPTER LOCATIONS: New Zealand
- ◆ CLUB COLORS: Red and Black
- ◆ CENTER PATCH: A bulldog in a German army helmet
- ◆ CLAIM TO FAME: Considered one of the biggest "gangs" in New Zealand, according to law enforcement; distinguishable by their tattooed faces and red bandanas

Monks

- ◆ ESTABLISHED: Late 1950s/early 1960s
- ◆ PLACE OF ORIGIN: San Gabriel Valley, California
- ◆ FOUNDER(S): A group of bikers associated with the "Tikis" club
- ◆ CHAPTER LOCATIONS: "A Monk can be found where you see him."
- ◆ CLUB COLORS: Black and White
- ◆ CENTER PATCH: Fittingly, a monk with a staff
- ◆ CLAIM TO FAME: Credited with several "firsts" in the motorcycle club community, including the switch from denim to leather cuts and the use of the word "church" for regular meetings

MONGREL MOB - Back to New Zealand for another of the major Kiwi clubs on all the lists. The Mongrel Mob originally formed in Hastings in the 1960s/early 1970s. Their members are predominantly from New Zealand's Maori or other Polynesian ethnic groups. Their chapters include Mongrel Mob Hastings, Mongrel Mob Porirua, and Mongrel Mob Notorious.

Part of the Mongrel Mob charm is their tattooed faces and red bandanas.

Legends point to their name's origin being from a District Court Judge in the Hawkes Bay in the late 1960s, referring to a group of men before him as "nothing but a pack of mongrels."

MONKS - Established in "in the late '50s/early '60s," in California's San Gabriel Valley by "a group of bikers that hung out with a club called the Tikis." They're a lock as a "classic" club—they are credited as being one of the first clubs to have a black leather cut.

"At the time, the police were washing and ruining the cut offs every time they arrested a biker," they explained, "so the club switched to leather."

The term "church" for a club meeting also goes back to the Monks and the clubs of their era and area.

This is history; *this* is patented-old school stuff.

Mortal Skulls

- **ESTABLISHED:** Unknown
- **PLACE OF ORIGIN:** Bohemia, Long Island, New York
- **FOUNDER(S):** Unknown
- **CHAPTER LOCATIONS:** New York
- **CLUB COLORS:** Black and Gold
- **CENTER PATCH:** A skull
- **CLUB AFFILIATION:** The "81"

Mount Baker

- **ESTABLISHED:** 1925
- **PLACE OF ORIGIN:** Washington State
- **FOUNDER(S):** E. L. "Pop" Place
- **CHAPTER LOCATIONS:** Washington State
- **CLUB COLORS:** Black and Gold
- **CENTER PATCH:** A skull
- **CLAIM TO FAME:** One of the ten oldest clubs in the U.S.; started the Cow Bell Enduro

MORTAL SKULLS - Based out of Bohemia on Long Island, New York, this is a tall-order, diamond-patch 1% motorcycle club. These guys made the law enforcement map in the Empire State and are Red and White supporters.

✠

MOST ENVIED - A club out of NorCal with three chapters that made the law enforcement map in Cali.

✠

MOTHERS - Out of Palmerston North, New Zealand, this is another of the clubs to make all the "lists" down there.

MOUNT BAKER - Established in 1925 in Washington State by the late E. L. "Pop" Place. Of course the Mount Baker MC is one of our "pioneer" clubs— and it is listed as one of the ten oldest motorcycle clubs in the U.S. and the second oldest on the Pacific Coast.

The club first met above the N.W. Cycle Shop at D and Dupont Street, but began meeting at Pop's converted chicken house starting in 1927. The club became an affiliated club, Charter Number 260, with the American Motorcycle Association.

In 1931, the organization started the now-famous Cow Bell Enduro patterned after the famous Jack Pine Run in Lansing, Michigan. The Cow Bell is held the first Sunday after Armistice Day (Veterans Day of old), and has been held every year since.

✠

Mountain Men

- ◆ **ESTABLISHED:** 1973
- ◆ **PLACE OF ORIGIN:** Northern mountains of Vermont
- ◆ **FOUNDER(S):** Pete and "a group of independent thinking bikers"
- ◆ **CHAPTER LOCATIONS:** New Hampshire, Vermont
- ◆ **CLUB COLORS:** Gold and Brown
- ◆ **CENTER PATCH:** A bearded "mountain man"
- ◆ **CLAIM TO FAME:** Their longevity and consistent travel throughout the New England area

Mumiah

- ◆ **ESTABLISHED:** 2007
- ◆ **PLACE OF ORIGIN:** Brazil
- ◆ **FOUNDER(S):** "Speed"
- ◆ **CHAPTER LOCATIONS:** Brazil
- ◆ **CLUB COLORS:** Red and White
- ◆ **CENTER PATCH:** A Brazilian Grim Reaper
- ◆ **MOTTO:** *Respect to be respected*
- ◆ **CLAIM TO FAME:** Possibly the only MC with a name that was taken from the Kabbalah

MOUNTAIN MEN - Established in 1973 in the "northern mountains of Vermont." Proud one percenters with chapters in New Hampshire and Vermont—and they made the law enforcement map listing in both states!

MUMIAH - Established in 2007 at the house of their president, "Speed," this three-piece-patch motorcycle club out of Brazil really makes you think—about a lot of things.

First, there's the name.

"With so many MC names often repeated with many variations, we wanted a strong name," the club says, "which had a meaning, not just any name, any design."

Naturally, the Kabbalah came up.

"We found that its name comes from the Kabbalah. Many of us wonder why the number seventy-two. This number is what governs the Mumiah angel. He is the last of the angels; each of the seventy-two angels has a meaning."

Okay.

And their overall philosophy has punch: "Battle for an ideal, it works magnificently, reserving special attention to the study of law. It has a tremendous knowledge of the macrocosm and microcosm. Angel is one of renewal, transformation, arrives to change everything that is in disagreement."

MYSTIC SEVEN - A Florida "affiliate" club of the OMC. And, yep, coming out of Pompano Beach, they made a sunny showing on the law enforcement map listing down there.

✠

MYSTERIOUS - It's really no mystery that this motorcycle club out of Thailand is a Bandidos support club!

✠

Mystery's

- ♦ **ESTABLISHED:** Unknown
- ♦ **PLACE OF ORIGIN:** Bohemia, Long Island, New York
- ♦ **FOUNDER(S):** Unknown
- ♦ **CHAPTER LOCATIONS:** New York
- ♦ **CLUB COLORS:** Black and Gold
- ♦ **CENTER PATCH:** A skull
- ♦ **CLUB AFFILIATION:** The "81"

MYSTERY'S - Established in 1980, a three-piece-patch club out of Bavaria founded by "Ali, Manni, Kreidler, and Sniff." And, yes, the apostrophe is supposed to be there! And as far as their allegiances go: "We support only one club, Mysterys MC Würzburg, Bavaria."

✠

CHAPTER 6

Na Kua Anna-Psycho Mental Sluts

NA KUA ANA - One of that small "Ocean's Eleven" of motorcycle clubs to make it onto the law enforcement map in the Hawaiian Islands.

✠

NEW ATTITUDES - A national clean and sober three-piece-patch motorcycle club that *did* make it onto the law enforcement map in Michigan. Also "Outlaws M/C Affiliated."

✠

NEW BREED - Established in 1970, a three-piece patch motorcycle club in Rochester, New York. A "classic" club that talks about the good ol' days "when you pulled up to a hotel or restaurant and they would close or call the cops."

New Breed is also a clean and sober motorcycle club out of Missouri.

✠

NEW ZEALAND NOMADS - Another of the clubs from "The Gangs in New Zealand" list. Reportedly they "split" from Black Power in 1977.

✠

NIGHT RIDERS - Established in 1975, a three-piece-patch club with chapters throughout Germany.

✠

Night Wolves

- ◆ **ESTABLISHED:** 1983
- ◆ **PLACE OF ORIGIN:** Russia
- ◆ **FOUNDER(S):** "A group of people, cultivating a philosophy of men of freedom"
- ◆ **CHAPTER LOCATIONS:** Russia, Latvia, and beyond
- ◆ **CENTER COLORS:** Black and Red
- ◆ **CENTER PATCH:** Surprise! A wolf!
- ◆ **CLAIM TO FAME:** Were very integral in the rock 'n' roll scene in the 1990s, protecting performers against government forces that weren't exactly fond of the music or the "rebellious attitude" it spawned

NIGHT WOLVES - Established in 1983, a massive motorcycle club with chapters in Russia, Latvia, and beyond. This club was established right in the middle of Soviet oppression of the lifestyle. At that same time, illegal rock concerts began that the government regarded as "anti-Soviet," with mass fights following most of the events. On one side was the militia, "directed by the System," on the other side were the bikers protecting the musicians—the Night Wolves were there.

✠

NISKA - A Scandinavian club that was right smack dab in the middle of the Great Nordic Biker wars.

✠

NOMADEN - Established in 1983, our first Nomaden MC is a three-piece-patch club out of Germany. And then there is a U.S. Nomaden MC that made the law enforcement map in Arizona.

✠

NOMADS - The name "nomad" has some very cutting meanings within the motorcycle club culture. A nomad in any club is often considered an "enforcer"—one who has the time, energy, and desire to be constantly mobile, checking things out throughout the family. Making sure everything is cool. It's one of those names—one of those words and/or phrases, like Filthy Few—that can be a club name or a very specific designation.

In terms of a name, there are a few Nomads:

In Australia, among the scooter-stew that is the crazed collection of Down Under clubs, the Nomads may not be the biggest but they do command a presence.

Established in 1983, there is a Nomads MC in Germany (with a totally different patch than the Nomadens, also founded in Germany the same year).

There is an Asian Nomad MC in Thailand and Norway.

Established in 1966 in South Africa, there is a club that is "the largest and longest established motorcycle club in Cape Town, if not the Republic. . . . the past and present members have reason to be proud of the Club's record, and hopefully the 'Winged Boot' will continue as the symbol of all that Nomads has stood for in the past—for yet another 44 years—and beyond."

No Name

- ◆ ESTABLISHED: 1972
- ◆ PLACE OF ORIGIN: Gladsaxe, Denmark
- ◆ FOUNDER(S): Unknown
- ◆ CHAPTER LOCATIONS: Denmark, Finland, Germany, Sweden, and Poland, along with support clubs
- ◆ CENTER COLORS: Orange, Black, and White
- ◆ CENTER PATCH: A warrior in a battle helmet
- ◆ CLAIM TO FAME: A huge, long-lived club; began under the name of Satan's Slaves

NO NAME - Established in 1972 in Gladsaxe, Denmark, under the celebrated name Satan's Slaves. "We changed the name to NNMC as a contrast to all the other clubs with colorful names."

This really is a big club with chapters throughout Denmark, Finland, Germany, Sweden, and Poland, along with support clubs.

✠

NORSEMEN - More Viking influence sails into clubs. One is a motorcycle club in Northern California.

There is a long, long-lived racing club of that name out of Minnesota that was founded back when Kennedy was president.

The Norsemen Motorcycle Club in Drammen, Norway, is a "hangaround" club for the Red and White.

✠

NO SPEED LIMIT - Another of the Scandinavian MCs caught up in the *complexity* that was the Great Nordic Biker Wars of the 1990s.

✠

Notorious

- **ESTABLISHED:** 2007
- **PLACE OF ORIGIN:** Sydney, Australia
- **FOUNDER(S):** Senior members and associates of the Nomads after their Parramatta Nomads branch was disbanded
- **CHAPTER LOCATIONS:** Australia
- **CENTER PATCH:** Turbaned skull brandishing twin pistols with "Original Gangster" beneath it
- **MOTTO:** *Only the dead see the end of war.*
- **CLAIM TO FAME:** Labeled by law enforcement as "one of Australia's most dangerous gangs"; and members don't have to own motorcycles

NOTORIOUS - We just finished the Nomads part of this list but we can add one more piece. First off, Notorious is an MC based in Sydney, Australia. They're an MC, but not all members ride motorcycles. Their patch is a "turbaned skull brandishing twin pistols with 'Original Gangster' beneath it, with the motto 'Only the dead see the end of war.'"

They are considered by law enforcement to be "one of Australia's most dangerous gangs" and have had a scuffle or two with the Angels and the Bandidos.

Here's where Australia's Nomads come in: Notorious was established in 2007 "by senior members and associates of the Nomads after their Parramatta Nomads branch was disbanded."

According to police, Notorious members are "sometimes called 'Nike bikies,' for wearing expensive sneakers, fashionable t-shirts, being clean shaven, and listening to RnB, Hip Hop, and Rap music, in contrast to the traditional bikie image of dirty jackets, leather boots, and beards." Police have also named "John Ibrahim, a celebrity Nightclub entrepreneur, and his three brothers Sam, Fadi, and Michael Ibrahim as senior members of Notorious. Allan Sarkis has been named as the president of Notorious but Police believe Sam Ibrahim formed the gang and is the driving force behind it. Ibrahim denies creating Notorious but admits knowing its members."

Nuggets

- **ESTABLISHED:** 1962
- **PLACE OF ORIGIN:** Buena Park, California
- **FOUNDER(S):** Unknown
- **CHAPTER LOCATIONS:** California, Iowa, and Oregon
- **CENTER COLORS:** Gold and Black
- **CENTER PATCH:** A beer-drinking rabbit on a motorcycle
- **MOTTO:** *Three things Nuggets like to do: fuck like a rabbit, drink beer, & ride motorcycles*
- **CLAIM TO FAME:** Their ability to throw a party, including their legendary "beer truck"

NUGGETS - Established in 1962, the Nuggets are indeed a "classic" club. They were founded at the Nugget Bar in Buena Park, California. Their patch (originally worn on a serape) is a beer-drinking rabbit on a motorcycle and it was representative, in a festively graphic way, of the "three things Nuggets like to do—fuck like a rabbit, drink beer & ride motorcycles." In the early 1970s, North Iowa and Grants Pass, Oregon, chapters were started.

The club has always been known for its' ability to throw a party! Its "beer truck" became more than legendary.

They express certain laments about the changing times: "Now the 'new generation' biker is among us. New clubs starting every day; women clubs, Christian clubs, sober clubs, military clubs, union clubs, cop clubs, hell...there might even be a gay cop club. . . . but the Nuggets still maintain the same values and traditions they had when the club was started."

They are just celebrating their forty-seventh anniversary!

✠

NUMBER THREE - A three-piece-patch club out of Austria. Their diamond patch carries a "#3."

✠

Oakland Panthers

- ◆ **ESTABLISHED:** Unknown (pre-1956)
- ◆ **PLACE OF ORIGIN:** Oakland, California
- ◆ **FOUNDER(S):** Unknown
- ◆ **CHAPTER LOCATIONS:** Oakland, California
- ◆ **CLAIM TO FAME:** The first motorcycle club that Sonny Barger joined
- ◆ **CLUB ASSOCIATIONS:** Sonny started the Oakland Angels to get more from a club.

OAKLAND PANTHERS - While not exactly an everyday name in the motorcycle club world, this club has a mark in history that is carved in deep. It was the first motorcycle club that Sonny Barger joined. And more than that, the lack of a true brotherhood among the "bunch of kids" in the Oakland Panthers proved to be the fire that would help temper this entire lifestyle into the hard house that it is. Sonny wanted much more from any club that he was in—and he got it.

✠

ODIN'S WARRIORS - Australia's Odin's Warriors MC is another piece in the huge puzzle that is the "Island Continent's" biker culture. Besides making most of the "lists" of "gangs in Australia," the club had to do battle in court in 2010 to try and save their clubhouse and property from demolition for the $8.2 billion Cross River Rail project.

The trial, once again, brought up a separate litigious issue in Australia—the government's enactment of laws designed to outlaw motorcycle clubs altogether.

✠

OLD BONE - A club created to preserve the legacy of Bones MC, Germany, after it merged with the Hells Angels.

✠

OLD COYOTES - Established in 2002 in Finland. Members' rides are limited to Harley-Davidson and Triumph.

✠

OLD SCHOOL RIDERS - The term "old school" may not be up there in the biker leather-lexicon like *Nomads* and *Filthy Few*, but it does apply to the vintage elements of a lot of our "classic" clubs. Ironically, a couple of clubs that have taken that historical handle for a name are not quite in that seasoned sector.

There is an Old School Riders MC in Chicago.

And then there is the Old School Riders in Southern California. We all know that from time to time this lifestyle has produced its share of issues and even some hard violence at times, but in June 2009 at a charity event being held by the Old School Riders a real head-shaker occurred. The *Pasadena Star-News* saw it like this:

Detectives tried to make sense Sunday of a pizza parlor shooting that left three men dead & seven people wounded during a charity fund-raiser. The names of those killed were not released Sunday evening pending notification of family members, coroner's officials said. Two of the dead men were cousins. The attack occurred about 6:45 p.m. on Saturday in front of Falcone's Pizza. . . . Officials believe the Old School Riders MC was holding a charity event in the eatery's parking lot when a male Hispanic adult opened fire. . . . About a dozen children were present when the shooting occurred, Sheehy said. "It was very lucky no kids were hit". . . he Old School Riders has no gang affiliation, & Falcone's Pizza is not a gang hangout. . . . [Old School Riders] described its members as "ordinary people who enjoy the freedom of riding"..."We are just friends & family who gather together & ride."

✠

OLD SHARPERS - The Melnä un Sudraba (Black and Silver), established in 2002, is a three-piece-patch one percent motorcycle club in Kevaka, Latvia.

✠

OMERTA - Another of the German support clubs for the Red and Gold.

✠

Oshkosh Aces

- ♦ **ESTABLISHED**: 1928
- ♦ **PLACE OF ORIGIN**: Oshkosh, Wisconsin
- ♦ **FOUNDER(S)**: Clarence Robl and Carl Reigh
- ♦ **CHAPTER LOCATIONS**: Oshkosh, Wisconsin
- ♦ **CENTER COLORS**: Red and Gold
- ♦ **CENTER PATCH**: A card hand of four aces
- ♦ **MOTTO**: *We ride for any positive reason.*
- ♦ **CLAIM TO FAME**: One of the oldest of the pioneer clubs.

OSHKOSH ACES - Established in 1928 in Oshkosh, Wisconsin, at National Cycle—an Oshkosh Harley-Davidson dealership—by Clarence Robl and Carl Reigh. One of our "pioneer" clubs, the Aces had a bit of a lull in "activity" between the late 1950s and 2000, when it enjoyed a resurgence, restart, and regrouping by four friends, one of whom found an early period club shirt at a rummage sale. They managed to find one of the originals and even though he has aged just a little, "he still rides with the best."

✠

OUTCAST - Established in 1969 in Detroit, Michigan—a "classic" club. This "all Black male" motorcycle club made the law enforcement map in Michigan and Illinois. They have a very somber mission statement: "This Motorcycle Club was founded by strong black men who actively participated and served their communities during the riots that had taken place during the Civil Rights Movement. Like many other historically black organizations, our founding members realized the importance for men of African descent to be able to stand together and unite as one. For this we take great pride and we offer no apologies."

The club made the law enforcement map in Michigan and Wisconsin and has other chapters nationally.

✠

OUTCASTS - Established in 1989, the Outcasts in France were founded by three former members of the Alabama Riders MC Bordeaux.

There was also a UK Outcasts club that was patched over to the Outlaws MC many years ago.

And there is a New Zealand Outcasts MC in Hamilton.

✠

Outlaws

- ◆ **ESTABLISHED:** 1935
- ◆ **PLACE OF ORIGIN:** McCook, Illinois
- ◆ **FOUNDER(S):** Unknown
- ◆ **CHAPTER LOCATIONS:** Worldwide
- ◆ **CENTER COLORS:** Black and White
- ◆ **CENTER PATCH:** Skull and crossed pistons—inspired by Brando's leather in *The Wild One*
- ◆ **MOTTO:** *God forgives, Outlaws don't.*
- ◆ **CLAIM TO FAME:** The oldest of the Big Five
- ◆ **CLUB ASSOCIATIONS:** Support clubs worldwide

OUTLAWS - Established in 1935 as the McCook Outlaws Motorcycle Club in McCook, Illinois, near Chicago. They are the oldest of the Big Four, Big Five, "top ten," or any other list that anyone may stick them on. And they have their own lists—like a list of the influence they have had on the biker world. Their back patch alone—a design of a skull and crossed pistons—was inspired in the 1950s by Brando's leather in *The Wild One* and is one of the purest biker images seen in this lifestyle. They designed the AMA parody patch, a similar design to the AMA's logo but with a hand flipping the bird and the letters "AOA" (American Outlaws Association) instead of "AMA."

In 1963, they became "the first true 1%er club east of the Mississippi" by becoming "an official member of the 1%er Brotherhood of Clubs."

For one of the big dogs, they have been a bit like the Pagans in that their media exposure has not been near what the Red and White or the Red and Gold has been. There haven't been the shelves and shelves of infiltration books and exposés. But the main media that has touched the Outlaws has all been good. There have been four books of vintage and contemporary photographs, three of which have not only chronicled the Outlaws specifically, but have really served as an overall time capsule for the "classic" era in the lifestyle—the 1960s.

Danny Lyon's *The Bikeriders*, with photos that would make James Dean look like a square and period text that's even hipper, is a gold—I mean, black and white—mine of the way it was. It's an exercise in "FTW" long before that patch and axiom were diluted by a bit too much mainstream exposure. First published in 1968 and re-released in 2003, this book may actually *scare* some people. This stuff is so, so real.

Michael H. Upright's 1999 release, *One Percent*, pays homage to Lyon's laying of a groundwork and seems to take up where he left off—several decades and a few generations later.

Beverly Roberts' collections of her Outlaws father's photos from the 1960s are right up there with Lyon's as pure treasures of this lifestyle's history. Her *Portraits of American Bikers* book series, using the original large-format negatives from the brilliant work of Jim "Flash" Miteff, are more of the "good" media enjoyed by the Outlaws and examples of what can be done by simply showing the truth—without having to build media projects on entrapment operations and disgruntled, pissed-off ex-club members.

✠

OUTSIDER(S) - We're going to bring some of the clubs with the Outsiders name *inside* where we can take a quick look at their histories:

First are the Outsiders up in the Pacific Northwest. A "classic" club, established in 1968. They made it onto the law enforcement map in Oregon and Washington.

They, too, have become a club very active in bikers' rights politics. Outsider "Double D" was instrumental in getting the state of Washington to enact an anti-profiling law that just may protect us from those all-too-familiar you-must-be-doing-something-wrong-because-you're-bearded-and-in-leather-and-on-a-Harley hits.

Their *serape*-style cuts set them a bit outside the norm, too!

Second is a huge international club, established 1973. This diamond-patch, full 1% Outsider MC stretches from Austria to Germany to the Philippines to Thailand.

There's an Outsiders MC in Pennsylvania.

And an Outsiders MC, "official support club for the 81," in Holland.

✠

OVERKILL - With its place in the history of the Great Nordic Biker Wars, Overkill was also a player in the foundation of the Black Heads MC when, in 1991, seven former Overkill members began the BHMC. There is also a three-piece-patch motorcycle club out of Brazil with the Overkill name, established in 2009.

✠

OVERNUKE - A Scandinavian motorcycle club highly involved in the Great Nordic Biker Wars.

✠

OZARK RIDERS - Established in 2001 in Arkansas, this Bandidos support club made the law enforcement map in the Natural State.

✠

PACOTEROS - The Pacoteros MC is a Bandidos support club out of New Mexico. They made it onto the law enforcement map in the land of Enchantment!

✠

Pagans

- ◆ **ESTABLISHED:** 1959
- ◆ **PLACE OF ORIGIN:** Prince George's County, Maryland
- ◆ **FOUNDER(S):** Lou Dobkin
- ◆ **CHAPTER LOCATIONS:** U.S. East Coast
- ◆ **CENTER PATCH:** The Norse fire-giant Surtr sitting on the sun, wielding a sword
- ◆ **CLAIM TO FAME:** One of the Big Five

PAGANS - The nuts and bolts of the Pagans is that they were established in 1959 by Lou Dobkins in Prince George's County, Maryland. And they have been one of the Big Five (and the Big Four before that) for as long as there have been lists. The chrome washers behind the nuts and bolts see the Pagans as the most low-profile of the major-leaguers. Their expanse—and expansion—is minimal, especially internationally where they are the only one of the Big Five without an outside-the-U.S. presence. Their denim cuts (without a traditional bottom territory rocker, but with a center patch of the Norse fire-giant, Surtr or "Surt") are seen up and down the East Coast.

Thirty-two years ago, the Pagans, rode into Ohio. My friend who prefers to remain anonymous ("for a number of reasons," according to him and his sometimes well-founded paranoia). It's his story, and stories like it, that are just never forgotten. They're the tales-over-a-beer that anyone who has been riding any amount of time has. Especially anyone who has ridden with a club:

I was heading to Youngstown, Ohio, for a brother's wake with about ninety Pagans. Being the Road Captain, I was told to "get to Youngstown and give a call for directions." It was seven a.m. when we rolled in, and it had been a long night! We made three hundred miles, stopping to pick up five chapters on the way.

We pulled off the highway for gas and I made the call. "Fat Cat" asked, of course, where we were. I told him I was at a phone booth (there were no cells in those days, for all of you too young to remember that!) near the Boron gas station, at exit such-and-such. There was silence on the other end. Finally he asked if there was a three-story building across the street.

Gypsy Raoul

"Yes," I told him.

"Does it have twelve-foot walls and barbed wire all around?" he inquired further.

"Yes…"

"I guess you don't know that that's the Outlaws' clubhouse…"

At the same time, we both said, "We need to get the hell outta here!"

He gave me some real quick directions and it turned out we were only about thirty miles from where we needed to be. I ran back to the gas station screaming that we had only thirty miles to go…we can make it! Let's go! We're late!

When we showed up, Fat Cat came up to me and asked, "Well?"

I told him we got out fast and I was sure phones were ringing all over Ohio. We agreed to keep this little issue between us, and we've done just that—until now! That was thirty-two years ago when there was a disagreement or two going on between the clubs!

Other than *Gangland*'s hit on the Pagans in their 2009 "Devil's Fire" episode, the main media reach into Pagan's history has been John Hall's 2008 book *Riding On the Edge: A Motorcycle Outlaw's Tale*. Like the vintage photo books centered on the Outlaws that make a statement far beyond that of just one club, Hall's book is a look into so many parts of this culture, not just the Pagans—again in the never-dull 1960s.

✠

PAN HANDLERS - Established in 1978, the Pan Handlers are just one of five motorcycle clubs to make the law enforcement map in Alaska! They sponsor a big toy run every year (a toy run in Alaska…in December?).

✠

PARA DICE RIDERS - Another of the clubs shuffled into the long history of motorcycle clubs—and their conflicts—in Canada. Reportedly, the club was absorbed by the Hells Angels in 2001.

✠

Pariah

- ◆ **ESTABLISHED:** 1984
- ◆ **PLACE OF ORIGIN:** Leicester, England
- ◆ **FOUNDER(S):** Eight men "tired of what the motorcycling scene in Leicester had to offer"
- ◆ **CHAPTER LOCATIONS:** Leicester, England
- ◆ **CLUB COLORS:** Black and White
- ◆ **CENTER PATCH:** A Viking's head
- ◆ **CLAIM TO FAME:** In 1992, nine former members and one prospect of Pariah became the Leicester chapter of the Outlaws MC.

club has a lineage that includes being integral to the establishment of the Outlaws MC Midlands in 1992, as nine former members and one prospect became the Outlaws Leicester chapter.

There is also a Pariah Nomad MC, established in 2004 in Texas.

✠

PATRIOT LEGION - A three-piece-patch club out of Tartu, Estonia.

✠

Patriots

- ◆ **ESTABLISHED:** 1995
- ◆ **PLACE OF ORIGIN:** UK
- ◆ **FOUNDER(S):** Three military friends
- ◆ **CHAPTER LOCATIONS:** UK
- ◆ **CLUB COLORS:** Green and White
- ◆ **CENTER PATCH:** The blood red and black swords from the Army, the royal blue from the Royal Air Force's eagle and the navy blue anchor from the Navy
- ◆ **CLAIM TO FAME:** A UK motorcycle club for British military veterans only

PATRIOTS - Established in 1995 (with the permission of a club with the same name in Australia). This is a serious motorcycle club for "veteran and current members of Her Majesty's Armed Forces MC throughout the UK." The club does not allow law enforcement officers, as opposed to a U.S. club with the same name out of the Midwest that *does* allow them.

✠

PAWNEES - "The White and Black," a monster three-piece-patch motorcycle club throughout Spain and beyond.

✠

PEACEMAKERS - There are a few motorcycle clubs keeping the peace out there.

One is a three-piece-patch motorcycle club out of Northern California in the Hayward area (or "Nickel and Dime, CA" as they call it).

There's a family club out of Rochester, New York.

And a club out of Tennessee.

✠

PECKERWOODS - A familiar motorcycle club throughout the San Diego area that made the law enforcement map in California.

✠

PHANTOM LORDS - An East Coast motorcycle club that made it onto the law enforcement map in Massachusetts and Connecticuit. Back in 2003 there was another law enforcement hurdle they had to deal with. The *Outsider News* reported:

It's a bad time to be a biker in a motorcycle club.

The Phantom Lords in Enfield are temporarily out of a clubhouse. The Nordic Lords were pushed out of Manchester because of a zoning violation. The Hartford Hells Angels had to move their spring party from Suffield to East Hartford and then finally held it in East Windsor.

And the Viet Nam Vets Motorcycle Club in South Windsor, which state law enforcement officers agree has no criminal element to it, has been ordered to cease its clubhouse activities.

As the spring and summer riding season commences, state and local law enforcement agencies are sharing information and making it difficult for these clubs to operate.

Members of some of the state's 20 or so small clubs are crying foul, arguing that law enforcement is erring on the side of enforcement, leaving the law behind.

What's worse, they say, is that while they're used to what they call "nuisance stops" by police, they're not used to being hounded by building and zoning officials.

✛

Phantoms

- ◆ **ESTABLISHED:** 1962
- ◆ **PLACE OF ORIGIN:** Virginia
- ◆ **FOUNDER(S):** Unknown
- ◆ **CHAPTER LOCATIONS:** Virginia
- ◆ **CLUB COLORS:** Black and White with a red center patch
- ◆ **CENTER PATCH:** A skull in a warrior helmet
- ◆ **MOTTO:** *We have done so much with so little, we can do almost anything with nothing.*

PHANTOMS - Began as a car club in the 1950s, switching to a 1%, diamond-patch motorcycle club in 1962; a "classic" club from the 1960s that has "survived the bad times, along with the good times and will continue to do so."

There are two Phantoms in the shadows.

One is a Bandidos support motorcycle club throughout Texas.

Another is a three-piece-patch club out of Russia.

There have also been other clubs using the name "Phantoms" as seen in the vintage cut above.

✛

✠

PIRATES - Established in 2003, this is a full-on diamond-patch 1% club out of Slovakia.

✠

PIT BULLS - Established in 1994, this is a three-piece-patch club taking bites out of the Czech Republic.

✠

PISTOLEROS - This Bandidos support club made the law enforcement map in Mississippi and Alabama.

(There are three Pistoleros, Bandidos support clubs in France, and there is a law enforcement motorcycle club, Los Pistoleros, established in 1972, in Texas.)

✠

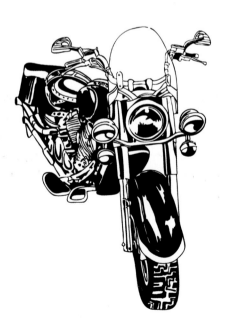

P.O.B.O.B.

- ◆ **ESTABLISHED:** 1945
- ◆ **PLACE OF ORIGIN:** Southern California
- ◆ **FOUNDER(S):** Otto Friedl and Arvid Olsen, among others
- ◆ **CHAPTER LOCATIONS:** Southern California
- ◆ **CLUB COLORS:** Red and Blue
- ◆ **CENTER PATCH:** A skull in a WWII military aviator's helmet
- ◆ **CLAIM TO FAME:** This club was present at Hollister in 1947 and is credited as being the founding roots of the Hells Angels.

P.O.B.O.B. - The Pissed-Off Bastards of Bloomington (Southern California) is one of our "pioneer" clubs that's always mentioned right along with the Market Street Commandos and the Boozefighters as having been in Hollister in 1947 at the "birth of the American Biker." And beyond that, their "pioneer" rank intensifies in that they are the recognized roots of the Hells Angels Motorcycle Club. As the club disbanded, former members of the P.O.B.O.B.s—Arvid Olsen, Otto Friedl, and others—went on to form the HAMC in 1948. Now known as the Pissed-Off Bastards of Berdoo, the club has chapters in Southern California and Northern Nevada.

✠

POPEYES - Another of those clubs in the mix of the maelstrom that was the club shuffles in the formative years of Canada's motorcycle club growth. Reportedly, the Popeyes were the club that essentially became the HAMC Quebec.

✠

POTFAT - Established in 1998 in Gevgelija County, Macedonia. Their first "P" was Lazar. Potfat is "the first backpatch club and the only MC in Macedonia."

At the beginning, there were two chapters in Potfat MC, one in Skopje, and one in Gevgelija. Today, Skopje is the city that most of the members are from, and stays as a hometown of Potfat.

✠

PRAIRIE RATTLERS - A Sons of Silence support club based out of Williston, North Dakota.

✠

PREDADORES - A Bandidos support club in Thailand.

✠

PREDATORS - We've tracked down at least three Predators MCs.

There is a diamond-patch 1% club in Sedgemoor in the UK.

There are Predators in Norway.

And there is a "Predators Motorcycle Association" in Alabama.

✠

PRIVATEERS - Established in 2001, a one percent motorcycle club out of the Caribbean with a great center patch—Cap'n Jack Sparrow meets Captain America.

✠

PROMETHEUS - Established in 1985 in North Dakota. This motorcycle club turns a curve when it comes to the usual types of charities most motorcycle clubs support—this club chose not to support the standard causes against disease and for those less fortunate. No. Prometheus supports charities that focus on animal protection.

✠

PROSCRITOS - A three-piece-patch, diamond-patch 1% motorcycle club out of Spain. Supporters of Forajidos MC.

✠

PSYCHO MENTAL SLUTS - Okay, we're going to mention one more all-female motorcycle club. These babes are out of the UK and they have a couple of compelling mottos: *"My liver is evil, I must kill it"* and *"P.M.S.F.T.W."* (Psycho Mental Sluts Fuck The World).

✠

Ramblers-Run Post Rustlers

NOTE - Before we begin the rambling "R" road, we need to mention that there simply weren't any "Q" entries for this encyclopedia. Now, we *did* find the Quick Quacks Motorcycle Club—"a club for doctors, dentists and medical students who ride motorbikes" out of the UK, but seeing how they have a small blue patch with a helmeted duck wielding a stethoscope and they have T-shirts that say, "Duck, here come the Quick Quacks!" we all felt that they just might be a little on the bubble when it comes to being in a one percenter encyclopedia.

RAMBLERS - A three-piece-patch out of Switzerland: "Rock hard…ride free."

⸸

RAPIDOS - Another of the Germanic Bandidos support clubs.

⸸

RAPPERS - We don't know if they're rapping about it, but this club made it onto the law enforcement map in Georgia.

⸸

RAPTORZ - They made the law enforcement map in Iowa although they do say that they are not a one percent club—they are a brotherhood. They are also Sons of Silence supporters.

⸸

RARE BREED - A couple of clubs share in the rareness of this breed:

One was a UK club that was patched over to the Outlaws MC many years ago.

A second is a primarily African-American motorcycle club established in 1989 in Southern California with chapters there and in Georgia. The club's pride is so evident in its bikes: "Rare Breed members have built some of the most beautiful Harleys in the world and have logged thousands of miles riding them across America. Our bikes, often referred to as 'Cali-Style,' have been in movies and graced the pages of many magazines."

RATS - Established in 1980, this German club has a center patch that's not for anyone with muriphobia!

⸸

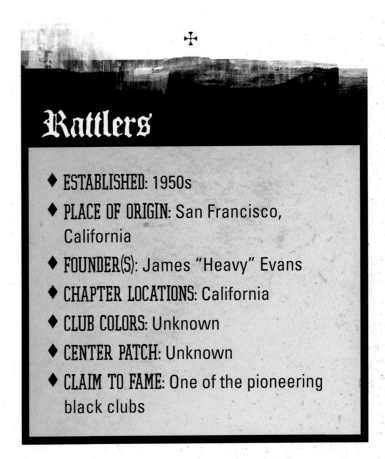

Rattlers

♦ **ESTABLISHED:** 1950s
♦ **PLACE OF ORIGIN:** San Francisco, California
♦ **FOUNDER(S):** James "Heavy" Evans
♦ **CHAPTER LOCATIONS:** California
♦ **CLUB COLORS:** Unknown
♦ **CENTER PATCH:** Unknown
♦ **CLAIM TO FAME:** One of the pioneering black clubs

RATTLERS - Established back in the 1950s by James "Heavy" Evans, this is a "classic," mixed-race motorcycle club out of the Bay area. The Rattlers are described by East Bay Dragons' founder Tobie Gene Levingston in his book, *Soul on Bikes: The East Bay Dragons MC and the Black Biker Set:*

Then, of course, there were the Rattlers in San Francisco. The Rattlers were a mixed club, though mostly Black, who had chapters up and running in Frisco and Los Angeles. By mixed, I mean they had a couple of white boys as members. They rode Harley choppers and full dressers. James "Heavy" Evans, the motorcycle-racing king of California joined the Rattlers as a founding member on Christmas Eve 1955. . . . In San Francisco, the three clubs that mixed it up were the Hells Angels, the Gypsy Jokers, and the Rattlers. The Rattlers' turf was the Fillmore district. Like Oakland's Seventh and Market, the Fillmore at night in San Francisco was brimming with pimps, whores, card sharks, thieves, and murderers. The rattlers kept a hole-in-the-wall clubhouse right on the corner of Ellis and Fillmore Streets. If you could handle yourself on the streets of the Fillmore, you were tough enough.

✠

RAVEN - A three-piece-patch motorcycle club out of Coastland, Germany, celebrating their fifteenth year.

✠

RAVENHEAD - Established with roots going back to 1971, this three-piece patch motorcycle club in the UK evolved from the Vikings MC and Lupus MC, becoming Ravenhead MC in 2003. "Ride Hard, Ride Free!"

✠

RAZORBACK, RAZORBACKS - There are three Razorback(s) MCs.

Our first is a Razorback MC in Germany that began life as a "sleeve patch" club in 1993 but evolved into a three-piece-patch club in 1999.

Next is the three-piece-patch, diamond-patch Razorbacks MC in Singapore: "We are not affiliated to any clubs. We are who we are."

Then there is the Razorbacks MC in Switzerland, a powerful HAMC (Hells Angels Motorcycle Club) support club.

"Razor" is their "P" and his understanding of the MC scene in Switzerland definitely comes from the inside:

The Razorbacks and a look at Motorcycle Clubs in Switzerland

Switzerland with its roughly eight million inhabitants is a relatively small country. Still, the density of population is one of the highest in the world because only around seven percent of the land is actually populated. This fact and the wealth of its inhabitants may be two of the reasons many people in Switzerland search out their freedom on the road—very often on a Harley Davidson motorcycle. Switzerland has a relatively high rate of Harley bikers. Since this country has a militia army, most of the bikers are actually members of the Swiss Army or are veterans.

Today, there are twenty-three official back-patch clubs, of which two are currently on probationary status, and some of the clubs are represented in different chapters. In addition, we have the so-called front-patch clubs. Currently there are twelve of those clubs but none of them have spread out with different chapters.

You can find a list of the official Swiss Clubs on the web (www.bike-time.ch).

Starting up a new MC requires getting approval by the Confederation of all back-patch MC's, including approval of turf and design and color of the patches. For more than twenty-five years now we live by this system of peaceful coexistence based on mutual respect and it is maintained by many shared activities like runs, parties, and other events. The friendly and respectful relations are also upheld to MCs and chapters abroad. Clubs and lone riders are warmly welcomed in our community as friends, as long as they show due respect and proper compliance to our rules. They can move freely and unchallenged throughout Switzerland and the regions, where MCs are residing. And most festivals and parties are open to the public.

Of the American Big Four only the Hells Angels Motorcycle Club runs chapters in Switzerland. HAMC is without any doubt the largest back-patch club in this country. The charter of Liechtenstein included, HAMC is one of the

172

three international clubs in Switzerland and is represented by eight charters spread all over the country. Broncos MC and Hurricanes MC are likewise running chapters in the neighboring countries of Europe.

✠

REBEL ROUSERS - Established in 1965, "the oldest North Carolina–based club" is an HAMC support motorcycle club.

✠

REBELLIONS - A three-piece club out of Estonia.

𝕽𝖊𝖇𝖊𝖑𝖘

- ♦ **ESTABLISHED:** 1969
- ♦ **PLACE OF ORIGIN:** Brisbane, Australia
- ♦ **FOUNDER(S):** Clint Jacks
- ♦ **CHAPTER LOCATIONS:** Australia, Sweden, U.S., Malta, and Thailand
- ♦ **CLUB COLORS:** Blue and White
- ♦ **CENTER PATCH:** A skull in a U.S. Confederate Civil War cap on a Confederate flag
- ♦ **MOTTO:** *Like us or hate us, you better get used to us.*
- ♦ **CLAIM TO FAME:** One of, if not the biggest, motorcycle clubs in Australia; their national "P" is former boxer Alex Vella.

REBELS - Established in 1969 in Brisbane, Queensland, Australia, by Clint Jacks, their motto says it all: "Like us or hate us, you better get used to us." In the strength-flexing dynamic of Australian motorcycle clubs, they are the biggest. Their original name was the Confederates and their national "P" is former boxer Alex Vella.

In 2000, author Daniel Wolf's book *The Rebels: A Brotherhood of Outlaw Bikers* was released, detailing life with the Canadian Rebels MC in the 1970s and early 1980s.

The Name "Rebels" has been used by many, many clubs around the world, including in the U.S., as seen in the cut above.

Red Devils

- ◆ ESTABLISHED: Unknown
- ◆ PLACE OF ORIGIN: Unknown
- ◆ FOUNDER(S): Unknown
- ◆ CHAPTER LOCATIONS: Worldwide
- ◆ CLUB COLORS: Red and Black
- ◆ CENTER PATCH: A red devil!
- ◆ CLAIM TO FAME: Canada's oldest one percent club and the major HAMC support club throughout the world

RED DEVILS - Now we turn red—and it's perfect that our first motorcycle club in the crimson corner of this encyclopedia is "Canada's Oldest 1% Motorcycle club" and more. The Red Devils MC is worldwide, a major support club for the HAMC.

✠

RED EMERALDS - Established in 1964 and a "classic" club on the East Coast. The Red Emeralds are "Boston's oldest continually running motorcycle club."

✠

RED INDIANS - Established in 2001, this motorcycle club in Poland is an HAMC support club.

RED KNIGHT'S - Established in 2004, diamond-patch 1%ers out of Portugal.

✠

RED LION'S - Established in 1988, a full-out one percent club out of Sud Tirol, Italy.

✠

RED NATION - A one percent motorcycle club out of Northern California that made the law enforcement map out there. The motorcycle club specifically notes that "we are no longer a Native American motorcycle club."

There is, however, a Red Nations American Indian Motorcycle Council that calls itself a "100%'er Club."

✠

REDNECKS - A three-piece-patch club from, no, not below the Mason-Dixon, but Denmark!

✠

RED RIDERS - Established in 2008, with ex-members of The Riders MC in Bulgaria. They are an HAMC support club.

✠

RED SCORPIONS - Yet another of the motorcycle clubs mentioned on one of the strangest (and never-ending) "anti gang" websites in the universe, as an associate club of the HAMC in Canada.

✠

RED THUNDER - "A motorcycle club only for Native Americans and their Descendants" in Washington State. In their diamond patch is stitched "1st."

✠

RED WARRIORS - Another of the "red" Euro HAMC support clubs—this one is in Poland.

✠

RED WOLVES - A three-piece-patch, diamond-patch 1% club out of Turkey. Another of the Eurasian "official support clubs of the 81 world."

✠

RENEGADE, RENEGADES, RENEGADE'S - As we leave the red road, we begin our ride with some renegades:

These Renegades made it onto the law enforcement map in Virginia and were another of the clubs cited in the aforementioned Alexandria, Virginia, Grand Jury June 2010 indictment of the Outlaws MC (see *Desperados*).

There is a Detroit Renegades MC that dates back to the 1960s.

Renegades

- ◆ **ESTABLISHED:** 1960s
- ◆ **PLACE OF ORIGIN:** Detroit, Michigan
- ◆ **FOUNDER(S):** Joe Weiner, Herbie Lewis, Art Kurgin, Pete and Danny Carroll, and Ishmael Fugat (Curly)
- ◆ **CHAPTER LOCATIONS:** Three chapters in Michigan
- ◆ **CLUB COLORS:** Black and Gold
- ◆ **CENTER PATCH:** "A rider on a motorcycle with a fairing"
- ◆ **CLAIM TO FAME:** A "pioneer" club from the 1960s

RENEGADES - A Renegade MC in England has put on the big "Pissed Indian Rally" for many years.

There's a Renegade's MC in South Africa also with roots back to the 1960s.

And one more Renegades becomes yet another of the motorcycle clubs mentioned on what we now lovingly call "one of the strangest (and never-ending) 'anti-gang' websites in the universe," as an associate club of the HAMC in Canada.

✠

REINDEERSHIT - Established in 1993, in Finland, this is one of those back patches that wearing on a regular basis might take a little getting used to. Their center patch always generates a bit of a Pavlovian reaction—it looks a lot like the Jägermeister label (if the deer had been dead awhile, of course).

RESERVOIR DOGS - One Reservoir Dogs MC made the law enforcement map in Connecticut. There is also a family club on the other coast with the name.

RESURRECTION - This motorcycle club made it onto the law enforcement map in Washington State. And in 2000, a Resurrection MC received a "special thanks" in the monumental movie *Girl Gone Bad* featuring Gail Chambers, Giggles, and other top-level stars.

RIGHTEOUS & UNRULY - Established in 1994, they are among the motorcycle club crowd that made the law enforcement map in Connecticut—but it is primarily a drug rehab group.

RIGHTEOUS ONES - They righteously made it onto the law enforcement map in the Silver State.

RIPPERS - Established in 2007, in Italy, they are another of the tough throng of Bandidos Support Clubs.

ROAD CAT'S - With these cats, we start down the long path of road-named clubs. Established in 1998 in Maru, France, the Road Cat's are an HAMC Support Club.

ROAD DEMONS - A diamond-patch 1% HAMC Support Club in Spain.

ROAD HOGS - Established in 1987, a three-piece-patch motorcycle club in Denmark.

ROAD KNIGHTS - The Road Knights Motorcycle Club make all of the "gang" lists in New Zealand. They are based in the South Island of New Zealand with chapters in Invercargill, Dunedin, and Timaru.

ROAD RATS - Established "back in the 1960s" in England, this club seems to have an admirable degree of self-awareness: "At one time or another the Road Rats have pissed off nearly every major club in this country and many abroad. . ."

Road Reapers

- ◆ **ESTABLISHED:** 2001
- ◆ **PLACE OF ORIGIN:** Gravesend, Brooklyn, New York
- ◆ **FOUNDER(S):** Mike "Steel"
- ◆ **CHAPTER LOCATIONS:** Virginia, Minnesota, and prospect clubs in Maryland and Florida
- ◆ **CLUB COLORS:** Red and Black
- ◆ **CENTER PATCH:** A Reaper skull!
- ◆ **CLUB ASSOCIATIONS:** "All chapters support 81 World Wide"

⊹

ROAD REAPERS - Established in 2001 by Mike "Steel" in Gravesend (pronounced Grave's End!), Brooklyn, New York. The club has chapters in Virginia and Minnesota, and prospect clubs in Maryland and Florida. "All chapters support 81 World Wide."

⊹

ROAD REBELS - Established in 1985, a motorcycle club in Munich, Germany.

⊹

ROAD RUNNER, ROAD RUNNERS, ROADRUNNERS
We have several Road Runners speeding around the world: a Road Runner MC in Germany; one diamond-patch 1% Road Runners MC out of Poland; an AMA club in Wisconsin that dates back to 1979; a three-piece-patch Road Runners in Malaysia; a Roadrunners MC in Bern, Switzerland; and one in Denmark.

And then there is another of those clubs that you hear about in reminiscing mentions, those classic clubs of which you'd love to run into an old member. In this case, there apparently was a Road Runners around Chicago in the 1950s. The "P" was an uncle of Charley Chan, current "P" of the Boozefighters Chapter 37, but Charley's uncle left little info beyond that.

Beep, beep!

⊹

ROAD TRAMPS - Established in 1987, this diamond-patch 1% motorcycle club in Ireland evolved through the Reapers MC, Limerick.

⊹

ROAD VULTURES - Old-school stuff here—these biker buzzards were established in 1958 in New York. And they made it onto the 2010 law enforcement map there, too!

Rock Machine

- **ESTABLISHED:** Mid-1980s
- **PLACE OF ORIGIN:** Montreal, Canada
- **FOUNDER(S):** Salvatore Cazzetta
- **CHAPTER LOCATIONS:** Canada, U.S., and Australia
- **CLUB COLORS:** Black and White
- **CENTER PATCH:** A bird of prey
- **MOTTO:** *A La Vie A La Mort!*
- **CLAIM TO FAME:** One of the most storied clubs in Canada because of their "involvement" with the Hells Angels in the so-called "Quebec Biker Wars" of the 1990s
- **CLUB ASSOCIATIONS:** In 2000, the majority of the Rock Machine patched over to the Bandidos, and some went to the Angels; the original roots were revived in 2007–2008.

action, and have been the subject of an armful of books. The media and the authorities called those years the Quebec Biker War and alleged the conflict to be over competition for the drug trade. In 2000, the majority of the Rock Machine patched over to the Bandidos—some went to the Angels. In 2007–2008 the Rock Machine began to go "back to its roots" and now has Canadian, U.S., and Australian chapters.

✠

ROCKERS - Established in 1992 in Montreal, Canada. They were another of the Canadian clubs so integral to the entire "scene" that was the motorcycle club conflicts of the 1990s. In 2001, the Canadian authorities focused their Operation Springtime on the Rockers, resulting in arrests and trials of members on various charges.

✠

ROCK MACHINE - Established in the mid-1980s (some say 1986 to be exact) in Montreal, Canada, by Salvatore Cazzetta, a former friend of Red and White leader "Moms" Boucher. The issues that went on in the 1990s involving the Rock Machine, the Hells Angels, and other Canadian clubs are legendary, bloody, riddled with law enforcement

shutterstock.com

Rogues

- **ESTABLISHED:** 1979
- **PLACE OF ORIGIN:** Opmeer, the Netherlands
- **FOUNDER(S):** Unknown
- **CHAPTER LOCATIONS:** Two chapters in the Netherlands
- **CLUB COLORS:** Black and White
- **CENTER PATCH:** A "rogue" in front of a bike wheel
- **MOTTO:** Fuck Stock, Stock Sucks. All our MC members ride Harley-Davidsons. Most of our Harleys are chopped

✝

ROGUES - We have several Rogues to put into our gallery:

This first club made it onto the law enforcement map in Oklahoma and made the newspapers there in April 2010 when their clubhouse was raided by Tulsa County Sherriff's Deputies—a raid that resulted in the deputies' shooting of Russel Doza. The shooting caused a public outcry because the raid—ostensibly a drug raid—evidently brought no results.

Another interesting distinction that the club has is that it seems to be the first motorcycle club joined by the controversial author Edward Winterhalder.

There is also a Rogues MC in the Netherlands, linked to Brother Speed MC in the U.S., that just celebrated its twenty-fifth anniversary.

The Rogues in Holland were established in 1979, and are a full one percenter motorcycle club.

✝

ROGUES GALLERY - A heavy player in the Great Nordic Biker Wars in Scandinavia.

Rolling Anarchy

- **ESTABLISHED:** 2000
- **PLACE OF ORIGIN:** Belarus
- **FOUNDER(S):** "3 smart Belarusian heads": Roman Ivanovich (Volk), Andrey Romanovskiy (Ferre), Vladimir Tsesler
- **CHAPTER LOCATIONS:** Belarus, Russia, Sweden, Poland, Ireland, Slovakia, Estonia, Latvia, Lithuania, Ukraine, and U.S.
- **CLUB COLORS:** Black and Orange
- **CENTER PATCH:** Three skulls on a flag above wings
- **CLAIM TO FAME:** They have a very interesting take on "anarchy."

✝

ROLLING ANARCHY - Established in 2000. Unlike the fictional Sons of Anarchy, these guys seem to put their money where their anarchistic mouths are! As they considered a name they really put some thought into it:

"The word 'Anarchy' must be in the club's name; the club must unite individuals…individuals who didn't want anyone to rule over them."

Understood. Next was the "Rolling" part:

"The word 'Rolling,' however, was added after hot debates that required more than one day and more than one shot of tequila. It was finally agreed that the word 'Rolling' also expressed the club's essence: ride always, ride everywhere, and ride no matter what."
  —*"How about a leader for the meeting?"*
  —*"Fuck the leader!"* (Literally: stick the leader in a cunt)
  —*"How about a president?"*
  —*"Fuck the president!"* (as above)

And:

Generally, the club's regulations have only two paragraphs:

  1. Screw it all (loosely translated from some very bad words, like "FTW")
  2. Shut up and drink (also loosely translated)

There is one rule for clothing: "A denim vest, in memory of the golden age of biking in the 60s and 70s."

Rolling Wheels

- **ESTABLISHED:** 1976
- **PLACE OF ORIGIN:** Berlin, Germany
- **FOUNDER(S):** "Six young men"
- **CHAPTER LOCATIONS:** Germany and Serbia
- **CLUB COLORS:** Black and White
- **CENTER PATCH:** An iron cross
- **CLAIM TO FAME:** A huge club throughout Germany and Serbia with its own support club
- **CLUB ASSOCIATIONS:** A big support club, Dark Division, also with chapters throughout Germany

ROLLING WHEELS - Established in 1976 in Berlin, this club is *riesige* with chapters throughout Germany and a tight support club system with Dark Division.

RONDOS - Established in 1974, a three-piece patch motorcycle club in Germany.

RONINS - One of Italy's many Bandidos support clubs.

╬

ROTTEN DEAD - This three-piece patch club out of Pusan, South Korea, should be making slasher flicks in Hollywood! Their center patch is a "decayed zombie head with gaping jaws. A zombie was chosen as the club's logo and central patch because the founders were both fans of zombie movies, and as one of them put it: 'Zombies are cool.' The name Rotten Dead was chosen both to describe the zombie, as well as to signify that the motorcycle brotherhood survives beyond the grave. That sentiment, 'Brotherhood survives beyond the grave' was chosen as the club's motto. The club's colors are purple and gray, a good rotting flesh and pus color."

╬

ROUGH RIDERS - There are at least two Rough Riders: One, established in 1976, is a motorcycle club in Germany. There is also a veteran-oriented club that has been riding in Southern California for many years.

╬

RUM POT RUSTLERS - These boys made the law enforcement map in Massachusetts. They also made the April 2001 National Drug Intelligence Center's Massachusetts Drug Threat Assessment manual with some harsh, if not perhaps exaggerated and possibly presumptive comments:

The Hells Angels Motorcycle Club (HAMC) is the most significant OMG involved in drug trafficking in Massachusetts. The HAMC has established

chapters in Lowell, Lynn/Salem (headquartered in Lynn), Cape Cod (headquartered in Buzzards Bay), and Lee/Berkshire (headquartered in Lee). All but the Cape Cod chapter have been active in recent years. Other OMGs are associated with the Hells Angels as part of a "coalition," which means they pay monthly dues to the Hells Angels in exchange for the right to wear motorcycle club patches. If they fail to pay, the HAMC forces them out of existence. Noncoalition OMGs include the Devil's Disciples (in the city of Hull), Diablos (Westfield), East Coast MF (New Bedford), Nomads (Norton), Outlaws (Brockton), and Rum Pot Rustlers (Somerville). At least some of these gangs distribute drugs, but their involvement is less significant than that of the HAMC.

181

CHAPTER 8

Saints and Sinners-Syndicate

SAINTS & SINNERS - Established in 2004, this is a clean and sober motorcycle club, but they made the law enforcement map in California!

✠

SADDLEMEN - A three-piece-patch motorcycle club saddling up in Denmark.

✠

SADDLE TRAMPS - A club that made it onto the law enforcement map in Missouri.

✠

SALTEADORES - A Russian Bandidos support club, adding their red to the gold.

✠

SAMARAI'S - A three-piece motorcycle club out of Thailand.

✠

San Francisco

- ◆ **ESTABLISHED:** 1904
- ◆ **PLACE OF ORIGIN:** San Francisco, California
- ◆ **FOUNDER(S):** Twelve original charter members, including C. C. "Daddy" Hopkins, James Tormey, George Payton, Joe Holle, Harry Rockwell, and Al Freed
- ◆ **CHAPTER LOCATIONS:** San Francisco, California
- ◆ **CLAIM TO FAME:** The second oldest motorcycle club in the U.S.

SAN FRANCISCO - Another of our "pioneer" clubs, and this one is for sure in that forefather category. The San Francisco Motorcycle Club (established in 1904) is the second oldest in the U.S., just behind the Yonkers MC (established in 1903). They held their first meeting at the Thor Motorcycle shop with twelve members. They weathered the infamous 1906 'Frisco earthquake—it happened just five hours after one of their dances and destroyed their clubhouse. They rebuilt and kept going strong.

They allowed women members and gave them "the vote" before the United States government did. In 1910, their Road Captain, Volney Davis, set a new transcontinental record riding his Indian from San Francisco to New York and back.

In 1913, the true legend, Dudley Perkins, joined up. A year later he opened his own Harley-Davidson dealership, a dealership that is still putting the Bay on bikes. And this is just some of the motorcycling history that has rolled beneath the tires of the SFMC.

✠

SARACENS - This club made the law enforcement map up in Maine and it's a club with a history that goes back forty years in the Pine Tree State.

✠

SATAN SAINTS - Okay, now we begin our walk with the Satans of the motorcycle club world! This one was a 1997 club that had roots back to 1968 in South Africa. It later became the core for what is now the Syndicate MC in South Africa and the UK.

✠

SATANS BREED - A Satanic bunch out of Wales, established in early 1980s.

✠

SATAN'S CHOICE - This is one of those cases where you had to be there to know what truly went down. The Satan's Choice MC in Canada is mentioned in lore of all types—from mainstream media to barroom conversations and everything in between. They apparently were part of the 1977 expansion of the Outlaws MC beyond the U.S. borders, and somewhere along the line they were also part of the HAMC's (Hells Angels Motorcycle Club) Canadian movements in the early 2000s. It's complex and not something that makes for particularly healthy speculation.

✠

SATANS OUTCASTS - A three-piece-patch club in New Orleans, the land of the 2011 Super Bowl champions!

✠

SATANS OWN - This is another of those clubs that may—or may not have been—lost in history. It's one of those clubs you'd love to meet an old member of, in some shadowed bar somewhere. Some guy who has a closet of pictures and patches and a memory full of bits and pieces that simply had to be lived to understand. Maybe someday one of us will run into an old member of Satans Own, an early 1980s club that was a part of the never-ending 'Frisco "biker scene."

✠

SATANS SLAVES - A "classic" club that is also a part of that ageless "lore" that is swapped around among bikers on several different continents who were "there" back in the day. Satans Slaves (no apostrophe!) today are a solid, diamond-patch 1% club throughout England, Germany, and other parts of Europe. They are all linked but some have different patches.

SATANS SOLDIERS - Satans Soldiers (again, no apostrophe!) is a diamond-patch 1% motorcycle club out of New York with chapters in New Jersey and Australia. The club made the law enforcement map in New York and New Jersey.

Satudarah

- ♦ ESTABLISHED: Early 1990s
- ♦ PLACE OF ORIGIN: Moordrecht, Netherlands
- ♦ FOUNDER(S): Nine close friends mainly with a Moluccan background
- ♦ CHAPTER LOCATIONS: Chapters throughout the Netherlands
- ♦ CLUB COLORS: Black and Gold
- ♦ CENTER PATCH: Two warrior faces
- ♦ MOTTO: *Give respect and you'll get respect* (Lawamena Haulala).

SATUDARAH - Established in 1990, this club is diamond-patch 1%ers in the Netherlands with ten chapters throughout the country: "Our great grand-fathers were Moluccan warriors and they feared nobody. Their motto was: Give respect and you'll get respect ('Lawamena Haulala')."

⊹

Scorpions

- ♦ ESTABLISHED: Mid-1960s
- ♦ PLACE OF ORIGIN: Detroit, Michigan
- ♦ FOUNDER(S): "Tony"
- ♦ CHAPTER LOCATIONS: Michigan, Illinois, North Carolina, and Texas
- ♦ CLUB COLORS: Black and White
- ♦ CENTER PATCH: Yes, a scorpion!
- ♦ MOTTO: *Scorpion Forever, Forever Scorpion till death do we part a 100%er to the end*
- ♦ CLAIM TO FAME: Had a part in the 1976 major motion picture *Northville Cemetery Massacre*!

SCORPIONS - Established "around 1965 on the west side of the Motor City." A "classic" club that made the law enforcement map in Illinois and Texas. Their motto is a twist on the one percent brand: *"Scorpion Forever, Forever Scorpion till death do we part a 100%er to the end."*

They were another club that had a part in a major motion picture, 1976's *Northville Cemetery Massacre*!

⊹

SEMANON - This motorcycle club made the law enforcement map in Florida.

Set Free Soldiers

- ◆ **ESTABLISHED:** Unknown
- ◆ **PLACE OF ORIGIN:** Southern California
- ◆ **FOUNDER(S):** Emerged from the ministry of Phil Aguilar
- ◆ **CHAPTER LOCATIONS:** Southern California
- ◆ **CLUB COLORS:** Black and White
- ◆ **CENTER PATCH:** A "serious-looking" member in a German-style helmet
- ◆ **CLAIM TO FAME:** Easily the most one percent of the Christian motorcycle clubs

SET FREE SOLDIERS - I can remember watching Phil Aguilar years ago on TBN (the Trinity Broadcasting Network) and thinking—no, *knowing*—just how different he was from the orthodox suit-and-tied preachers that made up the 99% of Paul and Jan Crouch's "religious" bunch. The Set Free Soldiers that rolled out of Aguilar's ministry are also very different. Their self-assessment: "A group of men who Love Jesus and Love to Ride Hard. We are not your normal motorcycle club. Some say we are too Good for the Bad guys, and too Bad for the Good guys. We don't argue that."

Pastor Phil has said that he is "a 1%er for Jesus."

✝

SFB - Established in 2006, this North Carolina–based Special Forces motorcycle club didn't make it onto the law enforcement map in the Old North State, but they did make it in Wisconsin!

✝

SHADOW CLUB - Another of the motorcycle clubs mentioned on one of the strangest (and never-ending) "anti-gang" websites in the universe, as an associate club of the HAMC in Canada.

✝

SHARKS - Another of our "pioneer" clubs that came out of California's post-WWII years. One of the Sharks' survivors was Jack Jordan. A half-century or so later, Jack was in his eighties and tending bar in the El Dorado area above Sacramento, when in rode a customer wearing Boozefighters colors. The two began talking and the history poured out, along with the booze. A short time later Jack Jordan became the oldest known BFMC prospect and eventually became one of their senior (age-wise)—and most respected—brothers.

✝

Pioneer Sharks.

SHE DEVILS - "The hottest ride in town!" Alright, just one more mention of a female club! This three-piece-patch, all-lady motorcycle club is out of Northern California. And, really, they have a nicely provocative motto: *"A she-devil is a woman who is brave, loyal, trustworthy, intelligent, well spoken, accomplished, adventurous, and kindhearted, but also has a healthy appreciation for the perfect tattoo, a great set of pipes, thigh-hi stockings, a love of laughter, and the smell of leather, anytime..."*

She Devils "P" is Big Mama. I had the opportunity to spend a significant portion of a recent NCOM (National Coalition of Motorcyclists) convention with her. Trust me, Mama's understanding and dedication to the undeniable female factor in this lifestyle will go a long way toward establishing a permanent, non-penile club presence.

✛

SICK BASTARDS - Established in 2002, this three-piece-patch club is out of North Dakota.

✛

SIDEWINDERS - The Sidewinders made the law enforcement map in Massachusetts. They were also called "A violent motorcycle gang" by U.S. Attorney Michael Sullivan during the 2007 trial of the Sidewinders' Fall River chapter "P" on weapons and drug charges.

✛

SILENT FEW - A Sons of Silence support club out of Arkansas.

✛

SILENT REBELS - A Sons of Silence support club in Louisiana.

✛

SILENT SKULLS - Established in 1965, an international club based in Belgium: "One earth on two wheels."

✛

SILENT THUNDER - Established in 2005, this Sons of Silence support club made the law enforcement map listing in North Dakota.

Sin City Deciples

- ◆ ESTABLISHED: 1966
- ◆ PLACE OF ORIGIN: Gary, Indiana
- ◆ FOUNDER(S): Unknown
- ◆ CHAPTER LOCATIONS: Nationwide
- ◆ CLUB COLORS: Red and White on Black
- ◆ CENTER PATCH: A rider on a big chopper
- ◆ MOTTO: *Death before Dishonor*
- ◆ CLAIM TO FAME: One of the longest-running and most well-known of the Black motorcycle clubs

SIN CITY DECIPLES - Established in 1966, in Gary, Indiana. This very high-profile Black motorcycle club made the law enforcement map listing in the Hoosier State, Michigan, and Wisconsin.

SINNERS - Established in 1963 this long-running motorcycle club has been transgressing across Michigan and Indiana for a couple of generations. Ten Hail Marys, brothers! There was another club called "Sinners" that used the unusual serapé-type cut shown here, but there is no information available about this club.

SINN FEIN - Another of the clubs on all the New Zealand "lists of gangs." It was reported that in 2010 members of the Sinn Fein's Wellington chapter patched over to the Head Hunters MC. The New Zealand motorcycle club carousel never stops turning.

✠

SKELETON CREW - This three-piece-patch club in Northern California laid their bones on the law enforcement map there!

✠

SKULL MUNCHERS - A legendary, now-defunct one percent motorcycle club in Texas' DFW area.

✠

SKULL RIDERS - A three-piece-patch motorcycle club in Germany.

Also, "a group of guys tha like to ride, drink & shoot pool together" that "aren't an MC" in Missouri: "We ride every Thursday bitch—so don't ask!"

✠

SKULL SPIDER'S - Established in 1975, a three-piece-patch club out of Germany with a bitchin' center patch (unless, of course, you're an arachnophobe!).

✠

SLEEPWALKERS - Established in 2000, diamond-patch 1%ers out of Galicia, Spain.

✠

SOJOURNERS - A motorcycle club out of Illinois— they didn't make the law enforcement map there for some reason, but there is a surveillance pic of some of their members on the Genoa, Illinois, PD's Gang Information site!

✠

SOLID BROTHERHOOD - Established in 2006 in Minnesota. They're a Sons of Silence support motorcycle club with chapters there in the North Star State and in North Dakota.

✠

Solo Angeles

- ◆ ESTABLISHED: 1959
- ◆ PLACE OF ORIGIN: Tijuana, Mexico
- ◆ FOUNDER(S): Unknown
- ◆ CHAPTER LOCATIONS: Mexico and the Southwest U.S.
- ◆ CLUB COLORS: Orange and Black
- ◆ CENTER PATCH: A vintage chopper
- ◆ CLAIM TO FAME: Their annual toy run and the "stealing" of their name by ATF agents during the feds' infiltration of the Arizona HAMC

Sons of Hell

- ◆ ESTABLISHED: 1970
- ◆ PLACE OF ORIGIN: Sheffield, England
- ◆ FOUNDER(S): Unknown
- ◆ CHAPTER LOCATIONS: Sheffield, England
- ◆ CLUB COLORS: Orange and Black
- ◆ CENTER PATCH: A winged skull
- ◆ CLAIM TO FAME: A long-running one percent club in the UK

SOLO ANGELES - Established in 1959 in Tijuana, Mexico, the Solo Angeles are considered the first motorcycle club founded in Mexico. Their annual toy run is a solid part of the Cali-Mex biker scene. The club gained a bit of infamy in the exposé/infiltration book *No Angel* by ATF Special Agent Jay Dobyns. Dobyns describes in the book how the ATF set up a phony nomads chapter of the Solo Angeles to try and get inner circle access to the Arizona Hells Angels. It really is a weird and complex story.

✠

SONS OF HAWAII - A legendary club in the islands that didn't make the law enforcement map there but did make it in California.

SONS OF HELL - Established in 1970 in Sheffield, England, this is a diamond-patch 1% motorcycle club that has "stayed true to its values...over the years many things have changed...but, Brotherhood, Motorcycles and Having a good time, all the time is still the best way to be."

There is also a Sons of Hell Southwest three-piece-patch motorcycle club in the sometimes Hades-like temperatures of Tucson, Arizona. They are supporters of the Red and White.

✠

SONS OF SATAN - A Pennsylvania motorcycle club that spent a lot of 2003 wrangling with city officials in Rapho Township to be able to rebuild the clubhouse that they had since 1966. The property had apparently been destroyed by a pipe bomb.

Road Capt.
Minahuni
Buddha
WHITE
RED
FOUL
HARLEY-DAVIDSON
CHICKEN
Sons of Hawaii
M. C.
Frisco

Sons of Silence

- **ESTABLISHED:** 1966
- **PLACE OF ORIGIN:** Niwot, Colorado
- **FOUNDER(S):** Bruce "Dude" Richardson
- **CHAPTER LOCATIONS:** Worldwide
- **CLUB COLORS:** Red and White
- **CENTER PATCH:** An eagle superimposed over an "A"
- **CLAIM TO FAME:** The newest member of the Big Five clubs

Soul Brothers

- **ESTABLISHED:** 1967
- **PLACE OF ORIGIN:** Palo Alto, California
- **FOUNDER(S):** A group of close friends
- **CHAPTER LOCATIONS:** California, Arizona, and Nevada
- **CLUB COLORS:** Red and Black
- **CENTER PATCH:** Black and white arms clasped in "unity" in front of a "U"
- **CLAIM TO FAME:** A racially mixed motorcycle club: "This club was making history. In the 1960s there were far and few racially mixed biker organizations."

SONS OF SILENCE - The club that expanded the Big Four into the Big Five is the SOS, founded in Niwot, Colorado, in 1966 by Bruce "Dude" Richardson. In 1998, the first chapter outside of the U.S. was founded in Munich, Germany, and the club's international expanse has been strong ever since. They also have a wide web of support clubs both in the U.S. and beyond. Their patch is unique and differs from the traditional three-piece patches—one big center patch with a bottom rocker. Their motto is a bit more traditional, however: *"donec mors non separate,"* Latin for "until death separates us."

The 2009 *Gangland* episode, "Silent Slaughter," is the major media piece on the Sons to date—but with their continual growth, I expect that some hungry vicarious fans will be begging for more volume when it comes to an honest presentation of their long history.

A proud part of the Sons of Silence brotherhood is their unrestrained and active support system for their brothers behind bars.

SOUL BROTHERS - Established in 1967 in East Palo Alto, in the Bay Area of Northern California. Indeed, a "classic" club! Their patch symbolizes "unity" and the importance of "brotherhood among men regardless of race." These brothers made the law enforcement map in California and Arizona.

SOUTHERN STEELE - Established 2009, this Florida MC is a support club for the Sons of Silence. And they are *definitely* not to be confused with Southern Steel MC—a law enforcement club also in Florida.

F*t A**?

SOUTHERN VIKINGS - Another motorcycle club on the various New Zealand OMG lists. The Southern Vikings are based in Dunedin.

In 2004, their clubhouse was the subject of its second police raid in as many years. The raid resulted in one arrest of a thirty-year-old man, charged with possession of cannabis.

The prior 2002 raid resulted in the arrests of four men charged with possession of methamphetamine—the charges were later withdrawn, however, because of lack of evidence.

✠

SOUTHLAND - This Bandidos support club is certainly in the southland—the South Pacific, that is—in Indonesia.

✠

SPARTAN RIDERS - They made the law enforcement map in Arizona. And there was quite a lively discussion about them in 2008 on a law enforcement Internet forum. Now, I know that every special group or niche of people has their own unique lingo, but some things said in that discussion seemed elusive to say the least. One conversation in particular was perplexing:

Spartans are a b1tch/feeder club for HA. Not a whole lot else to tell; same rules apply as dealing with HA members. Have backup and watch your 6.

Why do they spell "bitch" as "b1tch"? Is using the "1" for the "i" some sort of code or is it to disguise the use of a rough word? Like F**K! And when a cop watches his "6," can he even see behind his

SPECIAL CREW - A *spezielle* Bandidos support club in Germany.

✠

STAHLPAKT - Established in 1996, one of the *große Hunde* in Germany with chapters throughout the country.

✠

STATE OF JEFFERSON - Established in the historic town of Happy Camp, California, with a "concept" that goes back to the late 1960s. Now, a lot of clubs are founded on many of the same principles and goals—brotherhood, riding, drinking, etc. But these guys are somewhat different. This motorcycle club is based "from the idea of the State of Jefferson movement from 1941, where Northern California and Southern Oregon wanted to secede from their States to form a separate State, the State of Jefferson."

Hmmm, it's certainly worth some thought…

✠

STATESMEN - Established in 1970 by "Chop, T-Bone, Fox, Big John, and Gary" in Belleville, Illinois. They made the law enforcement map in Missouri.

✠

STRAYS - A West Wales club that was patched over to the Outlaws MC many years ago.

✠

SUNDOWNERS - Established "in the early 1960s" in Southern California and settled in the San Fernando Valley of Los Angeles. A "classic" club that formed a bond with another of our classics, the Humpers MC.

The Sundowners made the law enforcement map listing in California and Utah.

There was a thought-provoking statement made in Utah's *Deseret Morning News* back in 2004, in an article that mentioned a few of the issues that the Sundowners had to deal with in the Beehive State. A retired cop was quoted in his obviously experience-laden description of motorcycle clubs:

"Being in a motorcycle gang is about drugs, women, and money, and not always in that order..."

With all due respect, officer, I know a lot of club brothers that don't have any of that stuff—regardless of the order you put it in!

✠

SURVIVORS - Established in 2002, a three-piece patch HAMC supporter club in Slovakia.

✠

SWORDSMEN - These guys fenced their way onto the law enforcement map in Ohio.

✠

SYNDICATE - Established in 2004 with roots back to 1968, the Syndicate's members at one time comprised the Satan Saints MC. They have chapters in South Africa and the UK. They do state that they aren't a one percent club, but in one form or another, they have a long history of two wheels on the African continent.

✠

CHAPTER 9

The Brothers-Zombie Elites

(Another quick note about our alphabetization here: We have included a few entries with **"The"** in front of club names because that's the way they seem to have it on their patches and in other forms.)

THE BROTHERS - Three-piece patch out of Belgium that is pretty vehement about the use of their name: "We, The Brothers, are on the road since more than twenty-five years. We will not tolerate that any other club in Belgium uses the name 'Brothers' in their colours. This is NOT negotiable!"

THE END - I know, this should be the last listing in this encyclopedia with echoes of Jim Morrison haunting the background, but it's not. The End here is a full diamond-patch 1% motorcycle club out of Hampshire, England.

THE JURY - A motorcycle club out of New York, bending the traditional display of the 1% patch just a tad. With them, it's included on the "heavy" side of a scales of justice in their center patch.

Themadones

- ◆ **ESTABLISHED:** 1958
- ◆ **PLACE OF ORIGIN:** Minnesota
- ◆ **FOUNDER(S):** "Carl" and two of his friends
- ◆ **CHAPTER LOCATIONS:** Minnesota
- ◆ **CLUB COLORS:** Red and Gold
- ◆ **MOTTO:** *MC does not mean My Car!*
- ◆ **CLAIM TO FAME:** Longest continuous motorcycle club in Minnesota

THEMADONES - Established in 1958 in Minnesota, this motorcycle club gets mid-twentieth century "pioneer" status. They also have a great motto: "MC does not mean My Car!" And they swam right into the law enforcement map in the Land of Ten Thousand Lakes!

The name does have all the words purposely run together: THEMADONES!

The Wheel

- ◆ ESTABLISHED: 1985
- ◆ PLACE OF ORIGIN: England
- ◆ FOUNDER(S): A lonely triker and a few "like-minded lost souls"
- ◆ CHAPTER LOCATIONS: Folkestone, Kent, in the Southeast of England
- ◆ CLUB COLORS: Black and Gold
- ◆ MOTTO: The Wheel MC; where blood is thicker than water...and colours are thicker than blood
- ◆ CLAIM TO FAME: The club evolved from the Brotherhood of the Wheel.

THE WHEEL - A "1%, traditional, back patch motorcycle club" out of England, with roots back to 1985; evolving from the Brotherhood of the Wheel MC.

✠

THROTTLELOCKERS - Another of the motorcycle clubs mentioned on one of the strangest (and neverending) "anti-gang" websites in the universe, as an associate club of the HAMC in Canada.

✠

THUNDER - Established in 1983, a German three-piece-patch club—not to be confused with a New Jersey law enforcement club ("No Justice, Just Us").

✠

THUNDERBIRD, THUNDERBIRDS - Both of these clubs have been flying for a long time. Thunderbird MC was established in 1967 in Minnesota and made it onto the law enforcement map up there. They are also friends with a German Thunderbirds MC, established in 1975. In 1985, the German 'Birds made essentially successful efforts to unify all of the Thunderbird MCs in Germany and Austria.

✠

THUNDERGUARDS - This motorcycle club made the law enforcement map in Delaware. And made the news in 2009 as covered by *The News Journal*:

Wilmington city officials shut down the social hall of the Thunderguards Motorcycle Club... after a triple shooting nearby left one man dead and two injured shortly after 3:30 a.m.

✠

THUNDERHEADS - A Bandidos support club in Little Rock, Arkansas.

✠

THORS - Established in 1995, this three-piece-patch club out of Switzerland refers to their clubhouse as "Valhalla."

TITANS - "Support the Madness" with this motorcycle club out of Baltimore, Maryland.

TOMBSTONE RATS - Established in 1981. A club out of Switzerland with a great center patch that features a skull, a cross, and, yes, their own special version of "Ben."

Top Hatters

- ◆ **ESTABLISHED:** 1947
- ◆ **PLACE OF ORIGIN:** Hollister, California
- ◆ **FOUNDER(S):** Included Jess and Joe Bravo
- ◆ **CHAPTER LOCATIONS:** Three or four chapters in Northern California
- ◆ **CLUB COLORS:** Black and Gold
- ◆ **CENTER PATCH:** A skull wearing a top hat, with wings
- ◆ **CLAIM TO FAME:** A true pioneer club that was in Hollister in 1947

TOP HATTERS - The Top Hatters have a "pioneer"-pairing similar to that of the Jackpine Gypsies. They, too, were founded right in the middle of sacred ground in the MC world. Established in 1947 in Hollister, California, in and at the "birthplace of the American biker." The Bravo brothers, Jess and Joe, were two icons of the club—"originals" who were seen for years in their top hats and cuts at all of the Hollister Rallies (before the authorities up there decided that the celebrations of the "birthplace of the American biker" were more trouble than they were worth). When Jess passed away in 2010 at the age of eighty-nine, not only were the venerable brothers separated, but the entire biker brotherhood suffered the loss of one of its most esteemed pioneers. Oh, and yes, the club did make the law enforcement map in California. I'm sure Jess is looking down and chuckling!

Ruth Erickson

199

(There is also a Top Hats MC out of Wisconsin.) THMC Chairman of the Board, "Hollywood," has a few thoughts about what the one percent label just might be:

The Top Hatters Motorcycle Club is a community-oriented Brotherhood of Bikers who strive to strengthen their bond with all those in our areas. Although, we do not wear the 1% patch, our history shows us as non-conformists, with the AMA, dating back to 1947.

Today, the LEAs [law enforcement agencies] have put a very negative interpretation on the 1% patch, creating a chilling effect with the general public—an effect opposite to the way in which we all actually live.

We love to ride with our brothers and we love that freedom of the road that is so often talked about—freedom that so many of us have earned by putting our lives on the line. From the WWII vets who were around at the beginning to the veterans of today's conflicts, we have all served our country with pride!

Perhaps, the 1% patch should really refer to the small percentage of us who have chosen to surround our lives with the brothers and sisters of our choice and to enjoy true "Life, Liberty, and the Pursuit of Happiness!"

✠

TORNADO - Established in 1992, this motorcycle club has been twisting for many years in Bulgaria.

✠

TRAMPS - A three-piece-patch motorcycle club out of Germany.

✠

TRIBE, TRIBES, TRIBESMEN - There are several organizations that have banded together under the variations of this name.

There is a family-oriented Tribe MC, established in 1992 in Ohio.

Another Tribe MC is "A Club of Jewish Bikers in the Washington D.C. Area."

And there is a Tribes MC celebrating their thirty-fifth year nearby in Maryland. (My guess is that this is the club that made the law enforcement map in the Old Line State, even though the authorities listed it as "the Tribe.") Somehow I can't see the Jewish group with their annual Tribe Family Picnic ("We are also looking for people to bring charcoal and lighter, hamburgers and hot dogs and rolls, chips and various salads. We will also need soda, water, and ice") getting law enforcement upset enough to make their "list." But you never know. . .

There is also a Tribesmen MC in Maryland—a Black club, and a Tribesmen MC in Nebraska who made the law enforcement map there!

And The Tribesmen is a prominently Maori motorcycle club formed in the 1980s in Otara, New Zealand. It is connected to the Killerbeez youth street gang.

✠

TRUE FEW - A Bandidos "sanctioned" motorcycle club out of Texas. Named for the "few" who split off from their former riding club, because they were the only ones willing to put forth the "work and effort necessary" to become who they are.

✠

Trust

- ◆ **ESTABLISHED:** Unknown
- ◆ **PLACE OF ORIGIN:** Germany
- ◆ **FOUNDER(S):** Unknown
- ◆ **CHAPTER LOCATIONS:** All over Germany, Belgium, and Romania
- ◆ **CLUB COLORS:** Black and White
- ◆ **CENTER PATCH:** Iron cross with a fist
- ◆ **CLAIM TO FAME:** Eine der größten! (One of the biggest!)

TRUST - Another heavyweight Euro one percent motorcycle club with chapters in Germany, Belgium, and Romania. *Eine der größten!*

✠

TYRANTS - There are a couple of Tyrants ruling things around the motorcycle club world.

One is actually a club from New York that got some publicity back in the mid-1990s when they were mentioned in a lengthy appeal that centered on legal action against Thomas "Tom-Tom" LaDuca, a Pagans MC member who had been facing a number of charges. The appeal really read like a script for the *Sons of Anarchy*. Cue the Tyrants:

OCTOBER 1996 INCIDENT: SEARCHING FOR CYCLE LORDS IN THE CATSKILLS

...the Pagans were having "problems" with the Cycle Lords in the Catskills. To resolve the problems, the head of the Pagan's Catskills chapter, a man known as "Timmy," organized a raid on a bar where the president of the local Cycle Lords chapter was said to live. Forty or 50 Pagans and Tyrants, some with ax handles, knives and guns, took part in this raid. No Cycle Lords were found. Undaunted, Timmy scheduled a larger raid for the following weekend.

And the Tyrants in New Zealand are another of the clubs all over their law enforcement lists down there, based out of Pahiatua.

✠

Undertakers

- ◆ **ESTABLISHED:** 1970s
- ◆ **PLACE OF ORIGIN:** Adelaide, Australia
- ◆ **FOUNDER(S):** Members of mostly Italian descent
- ◆ **CHAPTER LOCATIONS:** Australia
- ◆ **CLAIM TO FAME:** One of the early groups to come out of the now-massive Australian motorcycle club scene

UNDERTAKERS - Several clubs really dig this name!

One is an Outlaws MC support club in Lexington, Kentucky.

And then there was a club in Australia in the late 1970s called the Undertakers, according to author Arthur Veno, that had members of mostly Italian descent, based in Adelaide.

The Undertakers Scandinavia were right in the middle of the Great Nordic Biker Wars that changed their name from the Morticians to the Undertakers. And amidst all of the macabre madness is a family-oriented club, established in 2008 in Connecticut (maybe deep down, they really have some of the Fisher family traits).

╬

UNFORGIVEN - We'll have to forgive these couple of motorcycle clubs for grabbing the same name (but we might not forgive the cops we mention at the end for what they did).

Our first Unforgiven MC is out of New York and they made the law enforcement map listing there.

There is an Unforgiven Motorcycle Brotherhood in Belgium.

But now we need to go on a weird journey into undercover land back in 1999 that had some ATF agents fabricating a club—in this case the Unforgiven—trying to entrap a real club into an altercation. The *Denver Post*, in a long article about feds' attempts to indict the Sons of Silence on a variety of charges, sets up the drama:

One other case, in which [SOS] members Doug Luckett, 40, and Robert Bryant, 44, both of Colorado Springs, were charged with assaulting federal officers, was dropped and referred to the state for prosecution. Luckett and Bryant are charged with getting into a brawl in a Colorado Springs bar with three undercover ATF agents who came in wearing patches of a rival gang, The Unforgiven, which the ATF made up. Prosecutors said the case would be easier to try locally because of the number of witnesses.

╬

UNIDOS - A motorcycle club out of Arizona with an enthralling motto: *"Never Let Up, Never Let Down, Never Give In!"*

╬

UNITED - Established in 1978, a three-piece-patch club uniting in Denmark.

╬

UNRULY - A club "not for the weekend motorcyclist" that made the law enforcement map listing in New Hampshire.

╬

UNTAMED - This feral herd made the law enforcement map in Virginia and were yet another club included in that huge Alexandria, Virginia, Grand Jury June 2010 indictment of the Outlaws MC (See *Desperados*).

╬

UNTAMED REBELS - A motorcycle club in North Carolina that didn't make it onto the law enforcement map there, but did make it into an odd and random "gang awareness" flyer apparently generated by some kind of "public service" Tar-Heel safety-circle:

GANG ACTIVITY
Despite Eastern North Carolina's relative low population density and rural nature, unwanted gang activity is alive and well. A neighborhood's best protection against unwanted gang activity is knowledge of potential activity, a

vigilant watch system, and prompt reporting of suspicious activities. To that end, the CPCW is publishing the following information, training the Block Captains, and assisting with reporting suspicious activity.

There are a number of known gangs and affiliate groups operating in the general vicinity.

1. The Pagans Motorcycle Club and an affiliate group called the Untamed Rebels are operating out of local bars in the Eastern Craven County area. The Pagans are considered extremely violent and can be recognized by their black vests (called colors) with the words "Pagans M.C."

✠

VAGABONDS - There's a couple of Vagabonds drifting around out there.

One is a motorcycle club out of Belgium that is *not* a one percent club.

A club that *was* a one percent club was the Vagabonds out of Ontario, Canada, which were reportedly absorbed into the Hells Angels in 2000/2001.

But for a real pocketful of history involving the Vagabonds Motorcycle Club, we need to go back to The Toronto Rock and Roll Revival, a one-day, twelve-hour music festival held in Toronto, Ontario, Canada, on September 13, 1969.

It was originally set up as kind of an "oldies" show with artists from the 1950s and 1960s, but the thing began to grow, and an appearance by John Lennon and Yoko Ono—as the Plastic Ono Band—was scheduled, along with a performance by The Doors.

Lennon and Yoko's *Live Peace in Toronto 1969* album came out of the show, as did the D.A. Pennebaker film, *Sweet Toronto.*

Okay, so where do the Vagabonds come in? The motorcycle club wound up being the escort into Toronto for both The Doors and John and Yoko, with forty bikes in front and forty bikes in back of the rockers' limos.

Less than three months later, motorcycle club members and rock artists would interact again at Altamont.

The result would be much different than it was in Toronto.

✠

Vagos

- ◆ **ESTABLISHED:** 1966
- ◆ **PLACE OF ORIGIN:** San Bernardino
- ◆ **FOUNDER(S):** Thirteen friends
- ◆ **CHAPTER LOCATIONS:** North America
- ◆ **CLUB COLORS:** Green
- ◆ **CENTER PATCH:** Loki, the Norse god of mischief
- ◆ **MOTTO:** *We give what we get!*
- ◆ **CLAIM TO FAME:** One of the early groups to come out of the now-massive Australian motorcycle club scene

VAGOS - Established in 1966 "on the corner of Eighth and Davidson in San Bernardino" by thirteen friends, the Vagos are definitely a "classic" club and one of the motorcycle clubs bubbling just under the Big Five, having made several of the "Top Ten" lists. They are international and getting bigger. Their center patch—the red Norse god of mischief, Loki—was suggested by "Lucky," one of the thirteen originals, after he ran across a picture in *LIFE* magazine of a devil coming out of the ground in smoke with letters that said "Return From Hell." Loki was also depicted in 1966 in one of the most famous/infamous paintings of the collaborative efforts of Dave Mann and Ed "Big Daddy" Roth—a piece centered around a Bakersfield run, which shows Loki overlooking a chaotic party that features some of the most recognizable vintage and "classic" patches ever!

And it was a few decades or so back when The Vagos instituted their million-dollar-winning lawsuit against the Hawthorne, California, police department over harassment issues. That sort of stuff isn't new in the MC community, and the Vagos took a serious stand early on.

Their brotherhood was also serious early on—from the beginning. And for forty years or so, Vago "Dizzy" was there. We spent an afternoon at the clubhouse of his chapter, out in the high desert, in a free and remote atmosphere that made you forget about urban harassment and looks over your shoulder. It was kingdom-like, where the club had control and the outside was literally and figuratively locked out. It's always a good feeling in a place like this. We talked amidst brothers and beer:

Our bylaws were simple. They were about brotherhood and respect.

When I came in, in '68 or '69, there was already about a dozen Vagos from San Bernardino. There was no other charters—nothing. Me and a homeboy from Norco were the first ones outside of Berdoo.

I was living in Corona, and me and my homeboy, we were just loners.

Then we met the Vagos…

The first time was when me and my homeboy were at this bar drinking. There was this bar out on this dirt road behind the house, a block from where I lived.

The bar was empty except for me and him, and we heard all kinds of scooters coming in. There were ten or twelve Vagos. We got together; we got to know each other. They talked us into going to Berdoo with them and I became a prospect that same night.

I was running back and forth from Corona, 'til I split up with my old lady and then I moved to Berdoo, and I lived in the clubhouse, a brother's house, wherever I could. My high school sweetheart—I sent her down the road for the Vagos. And we'd been married just five years.

Then I was getting a divorce; it was just me and the bike.

Things have changed since then in a lot of ways. Prospecting now is a lot different. When I came in, we had guns; the sentries had guns. We were always at war. We did at least six months of hard prospecting.

The club was growing. Pluto was in charge. He lived on 16th Street right out of Mount Vernon; we used to line up in front of his house, twenty-five to thirty bikes, one chapter. Like everything else, the club has its peaks and it has its downfalls, but you always go back up.

I've been here forty years, and I've had no regrets. But I've been lucky, too.

At that time in San Bernardino, there were Amigos and there were Psychos. They were like low-riding biker clubs. And their members were related to some of our club brothers—blood-related cousins and brothers.

There was a guy named Hank; he was a Psycho. One time, we were barhopping, and we went to a bar at 5th street and Mt. Vernon, which is now a liquor store—there was about ten of us. We went in there, and they didn't like me from the gate. I was the "outside" one. I wasn't from Berdoo with all the other homeboys.

They told us to leave. Now, whenever we had to leave anyplace, I always made sure I was the last one to go. And that's just what I did that time, too. I was pretty fucked up on tequila; we were all drinking—because we were barhopping! When everybody else left, they jumped on me. I'm on the floor next to the pool table; I'm just kicking.

Then they all backed off for some reason—a reason I'd soon find out. I just wanted to get the fuck out. So I got up and went out to the sidewalk and started my bike. Then I felt something really hot. So I walked over to another brother's bike and that's when we realized that I'd got stabbed! So he throws me into some car, and that's the last thing I remember.

I woke up about two weeks later.

They took me to St. Bernadine's in Berdoo. And that doctor told me, "You know what, I worked on you for fourteen hours. You were dead when you got here." That was the Psychos!

It took us about two years to straighten all that out, because of all the blood relations amongst the clubs. That made it hard to get to people sometimes. They would say, "Oh man, it's family. I'll take care of it."

We had a good time at all our runs. We'd go to the Indio Festival every year. That was a regular thing.

The way we expanded, we were looking for biker brothers: not if you were white, brown, black, or whatever. We were looking for righteous fucking brothers.

When I came into the club, there was already a guy called Deputy Paul; he was a Black guy.

And there was "Whitey," a real good mechanic; he just died a little while back. He would do all of our wrenching. He would love to do it. He worked on dirt bikes and Harleys; he had to work on bikes—otherwise he wasn't happy. That motherfucker taught me a lot about putting engines together. He says when all else fails, you have a hammer.

We all went to the L.A. Zoo one time, and Crazy Jack was fucking with this lion. Whitey walked up and punched the lion right in the nose. No wait, that was up at that big game preserve up off of the 14 in Aqua Dulce!

Another brother now joined the conversation: Knuckles. Like Dizzy, Knuckles has been around— he has been a proud Vago for a long time.

Knuckles: *Whitey gave me my first Vagos tattoo and he pierced my ears.*

Dizzy: *That same weekend that CJ punched the lion, we were having those hill climbs, and a whole bunch of guys broke their legs. We were all trying to see who could get to the top of the hill. We had to put a lot of those bikes on trucks, because they broke up a lot of stuff.*

Knuckles: *I had an old knucklehead with a twenty-two-inch girder on it—you don't see that anymore!*

Dizzy: *We would all go out to Lake Elsinore and race go-carts too. And Steve McQueen had a bar out there. And he would be out dirt racing all the time.*

We never had a problem in Elsinore.

I was living in Chino. Every morning I would go to work at four or five o'clock in the morning, and in Chino it gets foggy like a bitch; you can't even see in front of you. I noticed there was this bike sitting in front of these apartments. It had been there forever. It's got leaves on it; full of dirt. I saw that thing for over a month. No one ever moved it.

I told my old lady, the next time it gets foggy, we ought to take that motherfucker. And I did.

We had a bar, The Shack, in Corona. We were coming back from there, and it was foggier than a motherfucker. And that bike was sittin' there, and we were feeling pretty good. We were fucked up. About three o'clock in the morning and it was just me and her. We pulled up to it, and it was locked. I had to turn it to face the right way, toward the back of our pick-up truck.

You could only see maybe two blocks in that fog. But two blocks from there was the Chino Police Department, and we could see these guys going back and forth, these cops.

Me and her lifted the front of the bike onto the tailgate. Then we pulled it around the corner, where the cops couldn't see us. She's driving; I'm sitting back there holding onto the bike with the front tire on the tailgate. Around the corner, we muscled that thing all the way into the back of the pickup. It was a '79 low-rider. I took it apart, fixed it, changed everything.

I rode that bike for two years.

And then me and my old lady were coming back on the I-10, and we got stopped by the highway patrol. I'll never forget that officer's name; his name was Talbot. He pulls me over. I got my patch on, my ol' lady's got her ol' lady patch on. We're on the side of the road. The bike was green. And this motherfucker cop—he's about

6'5"—he starts checking me out, checking numbers on the bike.

"Where'd you get this bike?" he asked.

I said, "Well you know what, I'm trying it out because I might want to buy it. Me and my ol' lady got it for the weekend."

The pink slip and the paperwork had an address in Lake Elsinore. I told the cop, "I gave the guy a deposit, so I'm riding it." Well the cop didn't question it but we're sittin' there and he's still checking things out. Then he gets on the radio.

He comes back to me and says, "You know what—I don't like the way the numbers are stamped on this bike."

So he calls the tow truck to take the bike!

The cop dropped us at the next exit at a Denny's. As we're getting out he says to us, "That's what I specialize in with the highway patrol: vehicle theft. Don't feel so bad, I already took a boat today, and another motorcycle."

He called me toward the end of the week and said, "If you have any interest in this bike, you need to come down and claim it."

And I thought, This is a setup.

The address on the paperwork was an empty field, so I said, "They're not gonna go for that!" So I had to just let it go.

✠

Spike from the Hessians

Jeff "EZJ" Kraus

Jeff "EZJ" Kraus

VALHALLAS - Making the law enforcement map in the Cornhusker State, this motorcycle club is a supporter of the Red and White.

✠

VALIANT'S - Making the law enforcement map in the Centennial State, "This Motorcycle Club is for Life…"

✠

VALLEY COMMANDOS - A three-piece-patch club with chapters in west Wales and south Wales. An "affiliate" club to the Outlaws MC.

✠

VANDALOS - Established in 1992 in Argentina—a three-piece-patch motorcycle club out of the Land of Perón.

✠

VANGUARD - A three-piece-patch club in Deutschland with a "22" in their diamond.

✠

VATOS LOCOS - Okay, as we near the end of this list we have learned many things. One of those glimmering gems of reality grasps is that the Bandidos have—I mean *really* have—a lot of Euro support clubs. So, as we begin to roll home, we are going to allow even more international savoring to enter into our list, especially when it comes to the sheer number of SYLB (Support Your Local Bandidos) clubs. So, with all that in mind, the Vatos Locos are a *Deutsche Unterstützung Club für Bandidos Motorradclub!*

✠

VENGATOR - *Ein weiterer Deutsche Unterstützung Club für Bandidos Motorradclub!* (You get the idea!)

✠

Veterans

- ♦ **ESTABLISHED:** Unknown
- ♦ **PLACE OF ORIGIN:** Netherlands
- ♦ **FOUNDER(S):** Unknown
- ♦ **CHAPTER LOCATIONS:** Netherlands
- ♦ **CLUB COLORS:** Green and White
- ♦ **CENTER PATCH:** Skull wearing a beret, in front of crossed swords
- ♦ **MOTTO:** *We give what we get!*
- ♦ **CLAIM TO FAME:** The only military motorcycle club in the Netherlands

VETERANS - A name and an honor that is close to the heart of most true bikers—whether they've been in the military or not. Echoes of the armed forces are all around this lifestyle; from the American WWII and Vietnam eras that produced so many of the "pioneer" and "classic" clubs to the current engagements throughout the world to the international veterans who have fought and died on every inch of this globe. There is a "toughness" bond and a freedom-lust camaraderie that brings the two continually together.

Our first Veterans MC is a three-piece, diamond-patch 1%er club in the Netherlands: "The Only Military MC in the Netherlands."

There is a Veterans MC in Canada, established in 2006, with similar colors and with links to the Netherlands club.

There's a Veterans MC, established in 1982, out of North Carolina that made the law enforcement map listing.

A Veterans Brotherhood VMC is in Alabama.

An Australian Veterans MC is pretty vehement about their impact and influence Down Under: Veterans MC Australia still believes that CASPER (the skull and slouch hat patch) should be available to all ex-servicemen. Significant changes to existing clubs need to be made to achieve this. This requires commitment and effort that may result in conflict. Unfortunately prospective members who are not "Vietnam Veterans" have been taking the soft and easy option of starting new breast patch clubs instead of forcing the change. In line with this, the Veterans MC has and will continue to stop any new or existing Military Motorcycle Clubs from operating in Western Australia. To date Western Australia is the only state running "Veterans MC" on the top rocker. V.F.F.V.

✠

Viet Nam Vets

- ◆ **ESTABLISHED:** 1984
- ◆ **PLACE OF ORIGIN:** New York
- ◆ **FOUNDER(S):** Brother Frenchie and a group of other Vietnam War veterans
- ◆ **CHAPTER LOCATIONS:** U.S. (all 50 states), Canada, and Europe
- ◆ **CLUB COLORS:** Red and Black
- ◆ **CENTER PATCH:** An eagle flying over Vietnam, carrying in its beak the bomb that "we didn't drop"
- ◆ **CLAIM TO FAME:** Considered by some law enforcement sources to be the sixth largest one percent club! Membership strictly limited to those who served in the U.S. military during the Vietnam War era
- ◆ **CLUB ASSOCIATIONS:** The Legacy Vets MC, a branch of the club founded to continue the VNVMC's "principles, traditions, and vision" after all the Vietnam-era veterans have passed on

VIET NAM VETS - Everything that has been written about the Vietnam War; every movie and television production that has focused on it; all of the social commentary, laments, speculation, opinionating, condemnation, congratulating, and politicizing about our "police action" in Southeast Asia can't even touch the emotional level that permeates this brotherhood—a brotherhood with a very special common bond. A bond that is a war and a period of social explosiveness unlike anything else ever experienced in American history.

Established in 1984, the VNVMC has chapters in all fifty states, Canada, and Europe. And they made the law enforcement map in most all of the states—and in fact, they are considered (on that particular list, at least) to be the sixth of the "Largest 1% Clubs."

"Ringo," the "P" of the VNVMC's "F" Troop explains some of the emotion behind the founding of the club:

We came home from 'Nam and we were treated so poorly. We figured since we were being treated like that, we'd go ahead and establish our own family, our own brotherhood. The club started in many forms; it actually started off as a patch club that you could buy into, but then it turned into a regular motorcycle club back in '84.

It's definitely an outlaw club.

We enjoy each other's company and all the other clubs' company.

It's a brotherhood—a tight brotherhood with many, many people involved worldwide and we look forward to being around for a lot longer. We also have a branch called the Legacy Vets now that's going to take our club over when we're all gone—and that's happening a lot nowadays. When the Viet Nam Vets are gone the Legacy Vets will still be here running the Red & Black!

✠

VIGILANTES - Established in 1967, "101%ers." A high-profile, "classic," and well-known motorcycle club out of Michigan.

✠

VIKINGS - In his book, *One Percenter: The Legend of the Outlaw Biker, Easyriders* magazine editor Dave Nichols tethers the Vikings to bikers with some pretty thick leather:

Few groups spur the fearful imagination of the general public more than a tribe of screaming, axe-wielding Vikings. In fact, the modern image of the outlaw bikers shares many similarities with this famous group of hell raisers. Yes, the Vikings were seafaring warriors and robbers (making them pirates), but they were also farmers, traders, and craftspeople from countries that are today known as Sweden, Norway, Denmark, and Iceland. Their wild appearance and love of freedom are hallmarks of the outlaw biker.

And he's right. Maybe that why the Vikings name is so popular.

Established in 1975 is the Vikings MC Ireland. "The 1% club with the right attitude!" Originally known as Vikings MC Nomads, the club's bottom rocker was changed to "Ireland" in 1997 with colours of blue and white. The club is one of the oldest back patch clubs in Ireland and is proud to be members of the Alliance Ireland group of combined Irish one percent clubs "who are united to keep the Irish bike scene free of international biker politics." They also have chapters in England.

There is a Vikings family club celebrating their thirty-eighth anniversary in Hayward, California.

And there is a long-running (established in 1983) AMA/racing-type Vikings MC also out of California.

✠

VIOLATORS - A three-piece-patch motorcycle club out of Northern California.

✠

VIP - *Bandidos støtte klubben i Danmark!*

✠

VIPERS - Established in 1997, a three-piece-patch club coiling around Austria.

✠

VITUSCANS - Made the law enforcement map in California! And in another of those off-beat little public documents that can be acquired with the right digging, it was noted that at a civic meeting of sorts in the NorCal community of Citrus Heights, the Vituscans were mentioned in conjunction with local "gang warnings:"

"Vituscan Riders MC – motorcycle club they are associated with Hells Angels."

✠

VORAI - Established in 1998, the Vorai (meaning "spiders") is a diamond-patch 1% motorcycle club spinning its web in Lithuania.

✠

WARHEADS - *Deutsche Unterstützung Club für Bandidos Motorradclub!*

✠

WARHORSE BROTHERHOOD - Veterans three-piece-patch motorcycle club in South Carolina.

✠

Warlocks

- **ESTABLISHED**: Roots going back to 1967
- **PLACE OF ORIGIN**: Orlando, Florida
- **FOUNDER(S)**: "Grub," a sailor on the U.S.S. Shangri-La
- **CHAPTER LOCATIONS**: U.S., England, and Germany
- **CLUB COLORS**: Red and Gold
- **CENTER PATCH**: A "blazing-style" eagle
- **MOTTO**: *To find us…you must be good. To catch us…you must be fast. To beat us…you must be kidding!*
- **CLAIM TO FAME**: Often mentioned in the "top lists" of motorcycle clubs
- **CLUB ASSOCIATIONS**: Has its own support clubs

WARLOCKS - With roots going back to 1967, the Warlocks MC is included on many of the "top ten" motorcycle club lists (along with the Big Five and clubs like the Mongols, the Vagos, the Highwaymen, and Free Souls). This is also another club that began with the lucky number of thirteen originals. All were sailors on the U.S.S. Shangri-La. While all thirteen were behind the idea of forming a motorcycle club after their discharges, one guy in particular really took the commitment seriously. "Grub" from Lockhart, Florida, founded the mother chapter in Orlando, where it still remains. The club now has chapters in the U.S., England, and Germany.

As always, the best information and insight comes from within. Billy Warlock takes us inside:

The Warlocks MC, like a lot of the early motorcycle clubs, found its roots coming from the U.S. military. But unlike other MCs who were basically formed by returning servicemen, the creation of the Warlocks MC was actually developed while its founders were still in the military.

In February, 1967, an aircraft carrier, the U.S.S. Shangri-La, was cruising the Mediterranean Sea on an eight month deployment with the Navy's entire 6th Fleet. The deployment was to show our country's readiness to stand against the Russian Navy, as well as the new and escalating conflict in Vietnam. Aboard this carrier—which was like a floating city of over four thousand military personnel—were thirteen young sailors who had bonded together through their love for motorcycles. As their friendship grew, they decided they would create their own motorcycle club.

They chose a name, designed their patch, and using the "Shang's" onboard post office, they ordered and received their new colors while still at sea.

Their original intentions were not to be just one chapter of the new club, but individual founders. Each of the thirteen were to return to their hometowns as each of their enlistments ended and establish their own chapters of Warlocks MC. Two of these original thirteen did form chapters—one in Jacksonville, Florida, in July 1967 and the other in Louisville, Kentucky, in 1970—but, for whatever the reasons, neither of these two chapters managed to survive for more than a few years.

In 1971, another of these Navy founders, Grub Freeland, after having returned home to Florida from his transferred tour to Vietnam, befriended and gathered together several new young bikers; most were transplants from various northern states. Many of these young men never had any intentions of becoming members of a motorcycle club. They simply enjoyed their new riding camaraderie in the Sunshine State. But when they were confronted by a club that was threatening to no longer allow them to ride together as a group, these young bikers—most barely out of their teens—refused to disband or be pushed around. Instead, following Grub's lead, they fought back by forming the Warlocks Motorcycle Club of Orlando, Florida.

Their defiant move certainly caused some issues—for the better part of two decades—but in the end, those original Orlando Warlocks not only managed to stand their ground, but have continued to grow in numbers and in chapters.

Today, that original mother chapter that Grub founded still rides proudly in Orlando. Through the decades, the chapter has evolved into an international motorcycle club, with chapters and nomad brothers scattered throughout the United States, Canada, and Europe.

The Warlocks MC, who still pride themselves on their club's original values and their undying love and respect for their brotherhood, can boast an ongoing membership of brothers still active from the '60s, '70s, and '80s, as well as the '90s and the present-day millennium.

In spite of their violent past, today they manage to peacefully and respectfully co-exist with other major clubs in the world, including their former rivals. In fact, the only real hostilities they must face today are the same hostilities all the major one percent clubs are having to face—that of various law enforcement agencies who use their power and the media to try and paint all one percenter clubs as criminal organizations. Nonetheless, the Warlocks Motorcycle Club continues to support not only its own brothers in need, but also the communities where they live and organizations like the Big Brothers, Big Sisters, and the Shriner's.

Florida brothers have raised tens of thousands of dollars over the last several years for charities. West Virginia's Crabfeast Party has continued to put coats on needy children every winter. South Carolina's benefit parties donate proceeds to a local children's home.

The Warlocks still continue to love the life they live, and just want to live the life they love—as a respected one percenter motorcycle club that is pledged to their own brotherhood.

—Billy Warlock, Warlocks MC

WARLORDS - Diamond-patch, 1%, three-piece-patch motorcycle club out of Thailand. They also have chapters in Malaysia, Japan, and the United Arab Emirates. "Respect all, support none."

Variations of the rare War Lords has been used by other clubs, as seen in the vintage cut below.

✠

WARRIORS - There are many Warriors marauding around the world.

Established in 1999 in the middle of Harstad Fjordgata is a three-piece-patch club in Norway.

In Sweden, a Warriors MC was formed by the merger of No Clue MC and Stone MC. Their patch is a "symbiosis in which the skull from Stone Head MC donned No Clue MC's Celtic war mask."

There's a three-piece-patch club out of the Czech Republic.

Also one in Portugal.

And a Warriors MC "social club" in Thailand.

✠

WEEKEND MONSTERS - Established in 2003 in Zagreb, Croatia. This motorcycle club has a very cool, neo-modernish spider for a center patch.

✠

WEREWOLVES - A hairy three-piece-patch club out of Russia. They call their clubhouse a "lair," but this lair is a hotel, restaurant, concert hall, Harley museum, sauna, and more!

✠

WEST COAST OG RIDERZ - Established in 2005 in Stockton, California, this motorcycle club made the law enforcement map in the Golden State.

✠

WESTWALL - *Deutsche Unterstützung Club für Bandidos Motorradclub!*

Wheels of Soul

- ♦ ESTABLISHED: 1967
- ♦ PLACE OF ORIGIN: Philadelphia, Pennsylvania
- ♦ FOUNDER(S): Cliff English, T.K. Hall, Dino, Boneyard
- ♦ CHAPTER LOCATIONS: Nationwide U.S.
- ♦ CLUB COLORS: Red and Black
- ♦ CENTER PATCH: A wheel with wings.
- ♦ MOTTO: *God forgives, Wheels don't*
- ♦ CLAIM TO FAME: Touted as "the only racially mixed 1% outlaw club in America"; the subject of the award-winning 2002 *Wheels of Soul* documentary

WHEELS OF SOUL - Established in 1967 in Philadelphia, this is without a doubt a "classic" club. The Wheels of Soul MC is touted as "the only racially mixed 1% outlaw club in America." They were the subject of the 2002 film documentary *Wheels of Soul*, winner of Best Documentary at the Berlin Black International Cinema. And Wheels of Soul made the law enforcement map in Pennsylvania, Maryland, Delaware, and New Jersey.

✠

WHEELS OF STEEL - Established in 1984, a three-piece-patch club in Bavaria.

WHISKEY DRIVERS - Established in 1989, a three-piece-patch club out of Opoeteren, Belgium.

✠

WHITE BIKERS - A motorcycle club out of Clarksville, Tennessee. In 2007, the local authorities listed the club on their "Gangs in Clarksville" site: "White Bikers Motorcycle Club—Serves as a support group for the Outlaws."

✠

WILD BUNCH - The Wild Bunch MC out of Nevada made the law enforcement map there. There is also a Black co-ed Wild Bunch out of North Carolina.

✠

WILD HEROES - Established in 1978, a *heroisch* three-piece-patch club in Coburg, Germany.

✠

WILD HORDE - Established in 1994, another *voln* three-piece-patch motorcycle club of the Czech Republic.

✠

WILD VIKINGS - Established in 2006 in Germany, this *sehr große* one percent club is a supporter of Born to be Wild MC.

Wingmen

- ◆ ESTABLISHED: 1976
- ◆ PLACE OF ORIGIN: Boscomantico, Italy
- ◆ FOUNDER(S): A member of the Fort Lewis Freedom Riders
- ◆ CHAPTER LOCATIONS: Italy, Germany, and U.S.
- ◆ CLUB COLORS: Black and White
- ◆ CENTER PATCH: An eagle
- ◆ MOTTO: *Good times, good friends, fast bikes, and baaad women*

WINGMEN - Established with roots back to 1976 "at the base of Boscomantico near Verona, Italy, the home of the Combat Support Company, 1st Battalion, of the 509th Airborne Combat Team."

This motorcycle club spread its wings from its U.S. military origin in Italy to soar into a truly international motorcycle club.

✠

WOLF BROTHERS - A three-piece-patch motorcycle club prowling around Moscow, Russia.

✠

WOLFMEN - Established in 2008. A three-piece -patch club in Leutershausen, Germany, with their "23" in the diamond.

WOLF PACK, WOLFPACK - This den of wolves is getting just a little crowded.

There is a three-piece Wolf Pack MC in Florida with chapters throughout the state. And they are Warlocks MC supporters.

And a three-piece-patch Wolfpack in Germany "L.H.R.—Loyalty, Honor, Respect"

A Wolf Pack MC in the U.S. was established in 1994, with chapters in Wisconsin, Illinois, and Arkansas.

There's an African-American Wolf Pack in Atlanta.

And a male-female, all-brands-of-bikes-accepted-into-the-pack group in California.

✠

WOLVES - Established in 1995, a one percent motorcycle club in Germany with their "23" in the diamond.

✠

WOLVERINES - Two Wolverines MCs are scratching around.

One, established in 2000, is a motorcycle club out of Rockwall, Texas.

The other, established in 1986, is a three-piece patch club out of Austria: "25 years on the road, respect all fear none."

✠

X-TEAM - The X-Team is a worldwide support club for the Bandidos—with chapters all over Europe and into Australia.

✠

YANKTON - Established in 1985, this *un pour cent club de moto* is based out of Beauvais, France.

Yellow Jackets

- ◆ **ESTABLISHED:** 1938
- ◆ **PLACE OF ORIGIN:** Gardena, California
- ◆ **FOUNDER(S):** Unknown
- ◆ **CHAPTER LOCATIONS:** California
- ◆ **CLUB COLORS:** Yellow and Black
- ◆ **CENTER PATCH:** A yellow-jacket bee
- ◆ **CLAIM TO FAME:** A "pioneer" club with a true "original" left
- ◆ **CLUB ASSOCIATIONS:** The founder of the Boozefighters MC, "Wino Willie" Forkner, flew Yellow Jackets colors when he was racing.

"We'd also set up a race course and every lap you had to swig down a beer and the last guy who could stand up was the winner. It was a real fun place!"

—Bob McMillen, one of the early Yellow Jackets

YELLOW JACKETS - Established in 1938 (some sources say even before) in Gardena, California, we have one of the last (alphabetically, of course) "pioneer" clubs—and it's well worthy of the distinction. Like the rest of the California "pioneers," the Yellow Jackets had their favorite "hang out" bar. In this case it was the Crash Inn. And they weren't the only club to frequent the joint—over the years the Crash Inn served up hooch to Sharks, 13 Rebels, Boozefighters, Hounds, Hells Angels, Galloping Gooses, and more. And some founding chapter members of the Yellow Jackets were also in Hollister 1947.

The founder of the Boozefighters, "Wino Willie" Forkner, also flew Yellow Jackets colors when he was racing—the AMA didn't want anything to do with the Boozefighters!

Felicia Morgan

Felicia Morgan

Yonkers

- ◆ **ESTABLISHED:** 1903
- ◆ **PLACE OF ORIGIN:** Yonkers, New York
- ◆ **FOUNDER(S):** George Eller
- ◆ **CHAPTER LOCATIONS:** New York
- ◆ **CLUB COLORS:** Blue and White
- ◆ **CENTER PATCH:** A shield with "YMC"
- ◆ **MOTTO:** *I.Y.C.P.G.T.F.H.: If Ya Can't Party, Go The Fuck Home!*
- ◆ **CLAIM TO FAME:** The Oldest Motorcycle Club in the World!

Y-ROHIRRIN - Established in 1988, the "only independent Welch 1% MC"—with chapters in Abertawe, Dyfed, and Pen Y Bont.

☩

Zapata

- ◆ **ESTABLISHED:** 1963
- ◆ **PLACE OF ORIGIN:** Brazil
- ◆ **FOUNDER(S):** Seven boys with bicycles and a political heart for their hero, Emiliano Zapata
- ◆ **CHAPTER LOCATIONS:** Brazil
- ◆ **CLUB COLORS:** Red and Gold
- ◆ **CENTER PATCH:** A sombreroed Emiliano Zapata wearing a sarape
- ◆ **MOTTO:** *101% 26 Hasta la Muerte!*
- ◆ **CLAIM TO FAME:** A motorcycle club that is dedicated to a political leader

YONKERS - Established in 1903! Yes, here we are, near the end of this encyclopedic list and just now we introduce the "Oldest Motorcycle Club in the World"! The Yonkers MC was indeed born in the same year that Harley-Davidson started to produce a motorized conveyance that would also enjoy a certain degree of longevity. This pioneer-of-all-pioneer clubs was founded by George Eller when George decided to go modern and motorized by converting his Yonkers Bicycle Club to the Yonkers Motorcycle Club. In 1927 the club received AMA Charter #6.

Long after ol' George passed away, another (and unfortunately also departed) brother in the club, "Joe Cool," came up with a motto that really gets to the heart of just what it takes to have a long and happy existence: "If Ya Can't Party, Go The Fuck Home!"

Amen!

ZAPATA - There are two motorcycle clubs that carry the name and cache of the Mexican revolutionary, Emiliano Zapata.

One is the last—alphabetically—in our extensive enumeration of German Bandidos support clubs, Zapata MC: *Deutsche Unterstützung Club für Bandidos Motorradclub!*

The second is a pretty damn cerebral bunch down in Brazil. This club was established in 1963 by seven boys with bicycles and a political heart for their hero, Emiliano Zapata. Their passion remained: *"101% 26 Hasta la Muerte!"*

☩

✠

ZEALOTS - Okay, I said I wasn't going to do this, but now that we're coming down to the end of this massive list of a super-sampling of the outlaw, three-piece, one percent motorcycle club world, I feel that I have to mention—just for the hell of it and maybe even a smile—that "Zealots MC" was reportedly one of the alternate titles suggested for the *Sons of Anarchy* series…

✠

ZIG ZAG CREW - A legendary club out of Canada that was right there in the middle of the entire Rock Machine–HAMC "experience" and our final club—alphabetically—that is listed on that strange (and never-ending) "anti-gang" website, as an associate club of the HAMC in Canada (pretty much everyone from the Sisters of Mercy to the Jonas Brothers are in some way defamed on that list!).

✠

Zombies Elite

- ♦ **ESTABLISHED:** 1974
- ♦ **PLACE OF ORIGIN:** Germany
- ♦ **FOUNDER(S):** The "rowdies" in the Angels of Freedom MC and the "hardcore" of MC Neuremburg
- ♦ **CHAPTER LOCATIONS:** NA
- ♦ **CLUB COLORS:** Black and Gold
- ♦ **CENTER PATCH:** A green zombie head, with a bolt of red lightning emblazoned on the forehead

ZOMBIES ELITE - A very colorful way to end this list is with Germany's Zombies Elite MC and their zombie-head patch. The club goes back to 1969 with the "rowdies" that were in the Angels of Freedom MC. In 1974, the "hardcore" of MC Neuremberg would be the founders of Zombies Elite.

✠

Okay.

That's it.

Sort of.

Have we covered *every* motorcycle club on the planet? Every one percenter? Every outlaw? Every three-piece-patch, diamond-patch-wearing, bat-outta-hell MC that there is?

No.

Hell, no!

There are simply too many clubs, too many roads to roll down, and too many shadow towns where a few good ol' boys can get together at their favorite bar, forge some sort of working relationship with the local power club, slap a patch on the back of their cuts, a support patch on the front, and call it a club—for a few years or so, anyway. And that happens in essentially every country on earth.

Ultimately, that's good. The lifestyle stays alive, vibrant, and in constant motion.

But we have tried to cover all the big guns. The clubs that aren't going anywhere anytime soon. The ones who have made a sledgehammer impact on their territory, on this entire way of life, and the world. And we have attempted to surround them with a pretty fair sampling of everyone else. Like the "pioneer" clubs that blasted out of the near-prehistoric, no-helmet, rigid frame, let 'er rip generations. And the "classic" clubs that powered

out of the angry Vietnam War years and the years just before and after. Years that witnessed a damn serious build-up of three-piece-patch clubs that knew just how powerful this lifestyle is, was, and would become.

We tried to list "established dates" whenever we could. That's important. How many clubs had "est. in 2000-something"? That proves just how alive, vibrant, and in motion "all of this" is. How many had "birth dates" in the 1950s and 1960s and even fifty years before that? There's your longevity. There's your impact. And there's more proof. Proof that this whole biker thing—this whole badass, freedom-loving, high-caliber, FTW, we-push-back look at the other 99% means something.

And to all those on this list, it means everything.

Huguette Roe/shutterstock.com

221

A Final Definition

"IT'S THE CATALYST FOR WILLING HELP FOR ANYTHING AT THREE A.M."

"PROMISES MADE TO BROTHERS MUST BE KEPT."

—Dr. Stephen "Skinz" Kinzey, Devils Diciples Motorcycle Club

When you put on that cut the world changes. You look in the rearview mirror a bit more and at the staring eyes all around you a bit less. You go to different public places. And you *never* go to the ones with *the sign*—even if you had been a regular.

Even your friends change; even those non-club—maybe even *non-biker*—friends that you felt would have no problem simply being in the mix.

"It's funny. One of the things I remember so clearly is that the perception people had of me—even those who really knew me—immediately changed as soon as I embraced that lifestyle. They were pensive. They seemed like they didn't know me. They were cautious with what they said around me—how they acted around me. Friends, family, even other motorcycle riders acted like that."

—George Christie,
Hells Angels Motorcycle Club, retired

When you're not on that bike and your colors are hanging up or draped over a chair, you look at them. Even a casual or passing glance is never a taken-for-granted *blink*. You see that cut and remember that day when you were patched in—even if it was forty years ago. You remember who was there. Who is dead. Who has gone on to another club—or another life altogether. Who is still there, riding next to you like this all began yesterday. And if it did, you think of all the years to come.

You think of the prospects and the hangarounds who welcome the indenture that will add grease to their acceptance.

Nothing in this way of life is thrown in the closet like seasonal sports-team jerseys. You wear those colors—in one form or another—*every* day.

Every day.

The world changes and the cautious looks in the rear-view mirror expand well into everyday life—well beyond the bike.

✠

I was in a remote, high-desert clubhouse of an exceptionally high-profile club, and I got into a conversation with an *exceptionally* clean-cut member.

"I'm an officer in the military," he told me, "and I'm very close to retirement.

"I'm loyal to both of these *brotherhoods*. My dream someday is to write a book about my parallel life over all these years; it's been more than *interesting!* But I can't do it now, of course, because it might affect my status and retirement."

That's affirmative.

Right after I spoke with him, I came upon an ATF publication, *OMGs and the Military: 2010 Update*. There, with plenty of surveillance photos, were fifty-one pages of names of military personnel along with descriptions of their "OMG" ties.

Working with fellow colleagues in the law enforcement community, it is ATF OSII's [ATF Office of Strategic Intelligence and Information] goal to identify and report on all active-duty, reservists, and National Guard military members, DOD contractors, and State and Federal employees who are associates, hangarounds, prospects, or members of a documented 1% OMG or support club in the United States and abroad.

—ATF OMGs and the Military 2010 Update

That mirror just gets bigger. But so does the circle of brotherhood that will eventually eclipse those "pensive" peripheral friends and report-prone employers.

When you put on that cut and enter a clubhouse, ride in a pack, roll into an event, *produce* an event, drink in a bar, or eat together at a restaurant, it's not just about the "uniform." If it was just about the uniform, then every group and organization from the Cub Scouts to the Ohio State Marching Band would know this feeling.

They don't.

This "uniform"—this patch—is so earned. It isn't *given*. And everyone—inside and out—knows it. It's power and it's pride. And that's the catalyst for the debates, the love, the respect, the occasional fight, and even the occasional "war." It's the catalyst for miles-long stretches of bikes at funerals, answered phone calls at midnight, and willing help for *anything* at three a.m.

✠

Dr. Stephen "Skinz" Kinzey is an Associate Professor at California State University, San Bernardino. He is also a proud brother in the legendary Devils Diciples Motorcycle Club.

Skinz turns the letters of the word *patchholder* into an explanation of just what this feeling beyond the "uniform" means. He gives you an understanding of this lifestyle if you're *worlds away*—and tells you what is required if ever you enter the *worlds within*.

The explanation actually becomes an oath of sorts—an oath that just might have a positive effect if the other 99% of humanity will get on board:

PATCHHOLDER

When someone asks you what it means or what it takes to be a patchholder and you're searching for the right words—or for the times when you yourself need a little refresher on the subject:

P Promises made to Brothers must be kept.
A Always be accountable to your Brothers.
T Trust the Brotherhood.
C Come readily when called upon by a Brother.
H Hold the tenets of the club sacred and close.
H Help those who are new and excited to learn about the club.
O Open your doors and heart to your Brothers.
L Learn something beneficial to you and the

Brotherhood from every situation.

D Drive toward personal and Brotherhood goals.

E Extend your hand to Brothers when they are down.

R Ride your motorcycle with skill and passion.

—Skinz

Skinz' "oath" may also add yet *another square* to the patchwork of definitions that *is* the patchholder and the one percenter. But that, too, is how it should be. Nothing that is truly alive, moving, and vital can really be burdened with a simple, one-dimensional classification.

And *nothing* screams with social-sway and machines-in-motion across this entire planet like the one percenter.

The rank-and-file who take the risks.

The ones who push back.

The tribes.

The "rowdy," living by their own rules.

The outlaws.

The *committed*.

Manual

Judging by the text throughout this manual and the clubs it discusses, this particular "law enforcement guide to the world of outlaw motorcycle gangs" was published in the early- to mid-1970s. The sad and especially distressing aspect to this "learning instrument," however, is that the materials accepted as gospel in this workbook aren't currently seen as archaic and lame (like the Carpenters' songs and Bread tunes that were probably playing out of a background, light-rock-tuned radio as someone typed all this up). Just as some folks out there are still jamming to "Close to You" and "Baby I'm-a Want You," a lot of people—especially those with badges and guns—are *still* looking at similar manuals like this and *still* thinking, "Yep, we need to see if those handlebars are really a shotgun!" They're *still* making citation careers and red-light-stop excuses out of equipment violations. And they're *still*

doing a fine and relentless job of making "these persons feel that they are not wanted in [their] area" (see rule #10 on the "Field Contacts" page). . . regardless of all the discussion lately about profiling and other non-politically correct actions.

This "manual" is presented in the interest of examining outlaw and one-percenter history, of course. It should be in the same campy, fun class that includes old reruns of *Dragnet* with the over-dramatic and hippie-hating Sergeant Joe Friday—but it's not. It just can't be. It still hits too close to home and modern reality in its sentiments and the actions it produces.

Not everyone is still rockin' out to Karen and Richard, but a fair number of 1970s tunes *were* well worth some immortality. Like, say, "I Shot the Sheriff."

Rule #4. Use good interrogation techniques. . .

OUTLAW MOTORCYCLE GANGS

WEAPONS COMMON TO OUTLAW MOTORCYCLISTS:

                    BUCK KNIVES
                    MOTORCYCLE CHAINS
                    RAZORS
                    BAYONETS
                    HATCHETS
                    ALL TYPES OF CLUBS
                    ALL TYPES OF GUNS

THERE HAVE BEEN REPORTS OF OUTLAW BIKERS CARRYING KNIVES AND GUNS RESEMBLING

FOUNTAIN PENS. HOMEMADE SHOTGUNS RESEMBLING ROAD FLARES. HOMEMADE SHOTGUNS THAT

ARE MOUNTED WITHIN THE MOTORCYCLE HANDLE BARS AND THE FOOT PEGS.

SEARCH THE ENTIRE SUBJECT AND HIS MOTORCYCLE FOR YOUR OWN SAFETY. BIKERS ARE KNOWN

TO CARRY WEAPONS IN SPECIAL ZIPPERED TYPE SEATS, IN THE GAS TANK, UNDER THE FENDERS,

IN THE HEAD LIGHT ASSEMBLY, ETC.

> NOTE: DON'T OVERLOOK THE GIRL FRIEND OF THE SUBJECT, SHE MAY BE CARRYING THE
>
> GUN OR KNIFE. THE BROAD OF A BIKER CAN PROBABLY BESTOW NO HIGHER HONOR
>
> ON THE CLUB THAN KNIFING OR SHOOTING A COP TO SAVE HER OLD MAN.

IDENTIFICATION OF MOTORCYCLES, TRUCKS, OR AUTOS.

BE COMPLETE

FULL READABLE LICENSE NUMBER

COLORS OF THE VEHICLE

ANY AND ALL ODDITIES

YEAR AND MAKE IF AT ALL POSSIBLE

-11-

OUTLAW MOTORCYCLE GANGS

JARGON:

THE JARGON USED BY OUTLAW MOTORCYCLISTS IS VERY SIMILAR TO THAT USED BY THE
HIPPIE AND NARCOTIC USER. THIS IS MOST LIKELY DUE TO THE CLOSE ASSOCIATION
OF THESE PERSONS.

EXAMPLES PERTAINING TO OUTLAW BIKERS:

APE HANGERS: MOTORCYCLE HANDLE BARS.

ANGEL WEDDING: HELL'S ANGEL WEDDING USING THE HARLEY DAVIDSON MOTORCYCLE REPAIR
    MANUAL INSTEAD OF THE HOLY BIBLE. DIVORCE IS OBTAINED BY MERELY
    TEARING UP THE MANUAL.

BIBLE: HARLEY DAVIDSON REPAIR MANUAL.

BROTHERS: FELLOW MEMBERS OF EITHER THEIR OWN CLUB OR ANOTHER FRIENDLY CLUB.

CHOPPER: CUSTOMIZED MOTORCYCLE.

CLASS OR SHOW CLASS: ANYTHING OUT OF THE ORDINARY, SNAP THE CITIZENS MIND,
    WILD AND BIZARRE BEHAVIOR, IMMORAL ACTS, VICIOUS ACTS.

COLORS: USUALLY A LEVI TYPE JACKET WITH SLEEVES CUT OFF AT SHOULDER WITH THE
    CLUB EMBLEM ON THE BACK SIDE. MAY BE A LEATHER JACKET, SWEATER, ETC.
    JACKET USUALLY CONTAINS OTHER PATCHES, EMBLEMS SCATTERED ALL OVER
    THE FRONT AND SIDES OF THE JACKET.

CRASH: TO FIND A PLACE TO REST, SLEEP, GET DRUGGED, PASS OUT FROM DRUNKENESS, ETC.

FLASH: TO VOMIT.

FLYING COLORS: TO BE WEARING HIS JACKET CONTAINING THE CLUB EMBLEM, MAY OR MAY
    NOT BE ON HIS MOTORCYCLE.

GARBAGE WAGON: STOCK MOTORCYCLE.

-12-

JARGON CONTINUED:

HOG: CHOPPED DOWN MOTORCYCLE, UNLIKE THE CHOPPER WHICH IS ALSO CHOPPED
      DOWN BUT CUSTOMIZED.

MAMA: FEMALE THAT IS AVAILABLE TO ALL MEMBERS OF THE CLUB FOR WHATEVER
       PURPOSE THEY SO DESIRE, SEXUAL GRATIFICATION, SERVANT, ETC.

OLD LADY: GIRL FRIEND OR WIFE (LEGAL OR COMMON LAW).

PATCH: ANY TYPE OF EMBLEM THAT IS WORN ON THE JACKET (COLORS).

SCOOTER: MERELY MEANS A TWO WHEEL MOTORCYCLE.

SCOOTER PEOPLE: PERSONS WHO RIDE OR ASSOCIATE WITH MOTORCYCLISTS.

SHEEP: TERM SOMETIMES USED FOR MAMA'S.

SISSY BAR: BAR THAT IS ATTACHED AT THE BACK OF THE MOTORCYCLE SEAT.

TRIKE: THREE WHEEL MOTORCYCLE.

RUN: A MOTORCYCLE RALLY, MAJOR OUTING TO A CERTAIN LOCATION, USUALLY WITH
      OTHER CLUBS.

SNUFF: TO KILL A PERSON.

PULL A TRAIN: HAVING INTERCOURSE IN A LINE WITH ONE GIRL EITHER BY USING
               FORCE OR OTHERWISE.

TURNOUT: A GANG RAPE.

COMMON MOTORCYCLE EQUIPMENT VIOLATIONS

1. HANDLEBAR HEIGHT - Maximum height is 15" above the seat when depressed by the rider's weight. 27801 (b) CVC.

2. MIRROR - One required and be able to see 200' to the rear. 26709 (a) CVC.

3. MUFFLERS REQUIRED - Not loud or with a bypass. 27150 CVC. Directed to the side between 2' and 11'. 27152 CVC. Flame, smoke, oil, or gas. 27153 CVC.

4. ODOMETER - Not required, but if there is one, it may not be disconnected. 28051 CVC.

5. GAS CAP - If parked or moving, it must be covered, and with non-combustible material. 27155 CVC.

6. PASSENGER EQUIPMENT - Passenger must sit to the rear; seat and foot pegs securely attached; rider must have feet on the pegs (no side saddle). 27800 CVC. Passenger may not ride, and driver may not allow passenger to ride, on part of vehicle not intended for passengers. 21712 (a) CVC.

7. LICENSE PLATE - One required and attached to the rear. 5200 CVC. Securely attached, clean and visible; attached from 12" to 60" on the rear. 5201 CVC. License plate light, white, and visible from 50'. 24601 CVC.

8. HORN - Required, and may not be harsh, but must be audible from 200'. 27000 CVC. Unnecessary use of the horn. 27001 CVC.

9. TOO LOW - Vehicle modified as to make any part of the vehicle lower than rim heighth. 24008 CVC.

10. CONTENTS LEAKING - Sifting, dropping, or otherwise escaping and falling to the pavement. 23114 CVC.

11. BRAKES - One required for motorcycles prior to June, 1966. 26311 (a) CVC. Defective condition or defective components. 26453 CVC. If the person refuses to submit to brake inspection, he may be arrested. 2800 CVC.

12. REGROOVED TIRE - A tire, in which the tread has been burned or cut. 27461 CVC.

13. HEAD LIGHT - One required during darkness, two permitted and must meet requirements of Division 12 - 25650 CVC. Except prior to January, 1930, mounted between 24" to 54". 24400 CVC.

    SINGLE BEAM - Vehicles sold prior to September, 1940, may have single beam, must reveal persons at 200'. 24410 (b) CVC.

    MULTI-BEAM - All after September, 1940, must be multi-beam, different beams selected at will. 24406 CVC. High beam reveal persons at 350'. 24407 (a) CVC. Low beam reveal persons at 100' and no glare. 24407 (b) CVC.

14. HIGH BEAM INDICATOR - New vehicle after January, 1940, have indicator, red or amber and no glare, shall not show to front or side. 24408 (b) CVC.

15. <u>TAIL LIGHT</u> – Red and visible 500' to the rear. 24600 CVC.

    <u>STOP LIGHT</u> – Red or amber, visible 300', night or day. 24603 CVC.

    <u>REFLECTOR</u> – Required; red and visible 50' to 300', mounted between <u>16" and 60"</u>. 24607 (a) CVC.

16. <u>REGISTRATION</u> – Need not be displayed, but must be presented. 4454 CVC.

17. <u>FAILURE TO MAINTAIN LIGHTING EQUIPMENT</u> – General catch all for lighting violations. 24252 CVC.

18. <u>LIGHTING DEVICES NOT PROPERLY MOUNTED</u> – 25953 CVC.

19. <u>UNSAFE VEHICLE</u> – Condition of vehicle, load or equipment. 24002 CVC.

20. <u>OPERATION AFTER NOTICE BY TRAFFIC OFFICER</u> – Citation or warning re: equipment violation, must take it: HOME – <u>PLACE TO HAVE IT REPAIRED</u> – <u>PLACE OF EMPLOYMENT — IMMEDIATELY.</u> 24004 CVC.

21. <u>ORDER BY TRAFFIC OFFICER</u> – If the driver refuses to submit to brake or light inspection, the driver can be arrested. 2800 CVC.

-15-

UNSAFE VEHICLE

24002 CVC

1. When the front suspension is modified to extend it and lift the front, often the handlebar height is raised and becomes in violation or the rider may be thrown so far back that he cannot hold onto them when the front wheel is rotated to the left and right.

2. Check the clamp holding the handlebars to ascertain if it is loose; often the rider will leave it loose so the handlebars (which are too high) can be pulled down if he is stopped.

3. Check the clamps attaching the front forks to the "goose-neck." They may be modified to extend the front forks. Pay particular attention to the lower clamp - it should have "stops" to prevent the front wheel from being rotated 90° from center.

4. Check the "goose-neck." This is often cut and re-welded to extend the front forks. The temper of the metal is affected by too much weldings and it is not subjected to the same inspection processes used at the factory. Pay particular attention to the frame number - all motorcycles, other than some years of Harley Davidson, have frame numbers, and they are usually located in this area. If they are altered or covered the motorcycle should be impounded under 10751 CVC. (A rider lost a $900 motorcycle via the court, after it was impounded for this very same reason.)

5. Check the front forks for modified extension of the front wheel.

6. Check for shock action in the front fork; even if it has a shock, ascertain if it is operable under normal conditions.

Why is front fork extension unsafe?

1. Changes the wheel base the factory determined was best for that particular motorcycle.

2. Changes the center of gravity and basic handling characteristics.

3. Places unusual stress on the front end, that the fork and goose-neck was not designed for - shock action is designed to absorb the impact without torque action on the fork member, clamp and goose-neck. When the forks are extended, the torque could cause metal fatigue and fracture the welds.

4. The factory has teams of engineers and metalurgists who tested and designed the frame extensively prior to releasing it for sale. IF IT WAS SAFER, THE FACTORY WOULD HAVE SOLD IT THAT WAY.

FIELD CONTACTS

Past experiences have indicated that when dealing with these outlaws, certain steps should be taken in the field, so that we may safeguard ourselves from danger, prosecute violators successfully, and maintain good records and intelligence.

1. When approaching a large group of outlaw motorcycle people, you should have one officer to every three members.

2. Pull over quickly and advise occupants to remain on motorcycles.

3. Watch for hidden weapons. There have been cases where a 12-gauge single shotgun has been built into handlebars of motorcycles.

4. Use good interrogation techniques. Separate and question.

5. Fill out a field interrogation card and use all of his identification. Check all numbers on motorcycles, with registrations. Listen for use of nicknames and place on F.I. cards. If using temporary drivers license, obtain number, as well as alphabetical letter in front of numbers. List what office issued, and the date issued on the F.I. card.

6. Check license plate to see if all tabs for previous years are on. Check draft card.

7. Check motorcycle engine number background to see if it is the same rough surface that is on the rest of the case.

8. These gang members have been known to have hidden compartments in the gas tank and/or seat where weapons or narcotics are hidden.

9. Run a record check through LASD and LAPD.

10. Again, stress a strong enforcement approach. Cite for all violations. Make these persons feel they are not wanted in your area. Do this in a professional and firm manner. Be aware of who and where these members are located in your area.

The "creed" of most outlaw gangs calls for a "one for all, all for one" attitude, along with complete disregard for law and order.

1. Law enforcement officers represent all they dislike and in many gangs, assault on a peace officer is part of the initiation rite.

2. Due to the rigid enforcement effected by the L.A.S.D. obtaining the shoulder patch or badge through violent means is the quickest means of attaining status in the gang.

Stopping Motorcycle Gangs

1. Due to the superior maneuverability, it is best to be as close as possible before activating the lights and siren.

2. If attempting to stop a group, ask for assistance.

3. Do not allow yourself to be drawn into an alley or house. Example: Lakewood incident.

4. Don't be "conned."

-27-

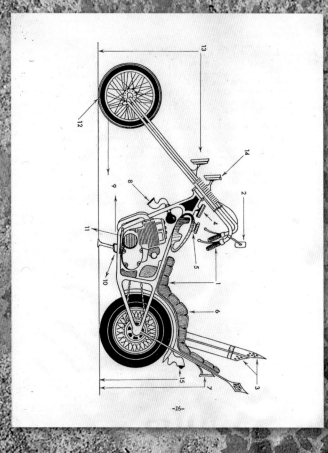

Bibliography & Literature Review

BY GYPSY RAOUL

(with a few comments thrown in by the author!)

The first book I read on one percent motorcycle clubs was Hunter Thompson's *Hells Angels: The Strange and Terrible Saga of the Outlaw Motorcycle Gangs*. I wasn't the only one. An entire generation—or two—had their senses pierced by a power and a back-patched underworld that had come into the light with an emotional weaponry and a societal-slapping panache unlike any other. *This* stuff was different. *This* stuff was the true answer to "how to never get sand kicked in your face." It was real, and a lot of us wanted to be a part of it—some in the bloody-muddy trenches; others just in the daydreams of the safe and unfulfilled.

Then there was a gap. Thompson's magic—and the Angel's magic—would be strong enough to float over, under, around, and through the POS movies and the tabloid trash of a variety of "men's magazines" and other newsstand hits. But then things got serious again.

The next book I read on one percenters was Yves Lavigne's *Three Can Keep a Secret If Two Are Dead*. I then read Lavigne's follow-up, *Hell's Angels: Into the Abyss*, in 1996.

Something was happening. Both of these books were exploitations that showed MCs in the worst possible light. Where was someone to defend the one percenters with a book that portrayed the *other* side of this lifestyle—the side that I'd seen while living in the San Francisco Bay Area for nearly twenty years?

The scales began to tip in 2001, when Sonny Barger published *Hell's Angel: The Life and Times of Sonny Barger and the Hells Angels Motorcycle Club*. People also began to revisit earlier publications that were released a bit under the reading-riding radar, but were still a part of the written and lived history of this lifestyle—for good or ill.

Books written about MC life *tend* to fall into two basic categories. The first are those written by investigative reporters, professional snitches, and ex-members who've turned state's evidence and depict club members as brazen criminals. The second are those written by unbiased authors and members in good standing that offer a balanced perspective of what club life is all about.

A couple of minutes standing in line at the grocery store will tell you which category prevails. People love the sensational. It's human nature. They'll buy the rag with the headlines about their favorite star's latest Botox-in-the-cheeks exposé before they'll buy the newest issue of *TIME. And* club members have a tendency to be tight-lipped about their world, which has given police reporters an advantage in their effort to sway public opinion against motorcyclists in general and one percenters specifically.

In all honesty, when clubs shun *any* kind of publicity—"We just want to be left alone!"—like the occasional biker magazine article or interview, they may be guarding their privacy, of course, but they really are missing a chance for some preemptive shots at unwanted heat and negative attention. And that's the stuff that will *really* put a dent in that "just leave us alone" wish. Because the sensation-driven—and often money-driven—authors and producers are always ready to come up with *something.* And if they can't get a voice from the "inside" to substantiate that *something,* they'll make *something* up.

With that said, *finding* books on one percent MCs is not the real dilemma; the challenge is how to separate the wild wheat from the cheap-suited chaff.

This bibliography lists over a hundred thirty titles. Reviews of *all* of the books referenced here aren't included, but many are—more than enough to offer an overview of the genre and a good sample of what's out there.

⊹

Literature for this review was divided into the following subcategories:

AUTOBIOGRAPHICAL - The author actually lived the story and wrote the book.

OBSERVATIONAL - The author witnessed the story or researched it, but may not have lived it him- or herself.

PHOTOGRAPHY AND ART - The author or artist tells the story through their photos and art.

INVESTIGATIVE AND POLICE REPORTING - The author uses law enforcement resources to tell the story.

FICTION - The author tells a story in which one or more MCs play a major role.

MISCELLANEOUS - Entries that don't fit into any of the above categories.

WIKIPEDIA BOOKS - Available print-on-demand summaries of entries in the Internet Wikipedia dictionary.

⊹

AUTOBIOGRAPHICAL

Barger, Sonny, with Keith and Kent Zimmerman. *Hell's Angel: The Life and Times of Sonny Barger and the Hell's Angels Motorcycle Club.* Harper Paperbacks, 2001.

Barger, Sonny. *Freedom: Credos from the Road.* William Morrow, 2005.

Barger, Sonny, and Darwin Holmstrom. *Let's Ride: Sonny Barger's Guide to Motorcycling.* New York: William Morrow, 2010.

Cavazos, Ruben. *Honor Few, Fear None: The Life and Times of a Mongol.* It Books, 2009.

DeLeone, Arturo Rossenaldo Romero (Alias "Cat Daddy"). *Motorcycle Gangster "PURO VIDA": Stories & Poetry of Life, True Love, Champagne and Rock & Roll.* Red Lead Press, 2010.

Desolate, Angelina and Jimmy Trotta (authors) Elizabeth Plastina and Nicole Plastina (editors). *Ice Cream Man From Hell You're Next.* D.T.W. Press, 2006.

Hall, John. *Riding on the Edge: A Motorcycle Outlaw's Tale.* Motorbooks, 2008.

Hayes, Bill, and Jim Quattlebaum, with a foreword by Dave Nichols. *The Original Wild Ones: Tales of the Boozefighters Motorcycle Club.* Motorbooks, 2009.

Hayes, Richard. *Outlaw Biker: My Life at Full Throttle.* John Blake, 2009.

Levingston, Tobie Gene, and Keith & Kent Zimmerman. *Soul on Bikes: The East Bay Dragons MC and the Black Biker Set.* Motorbooks, 2004.

Martineau, Pierre, and Jean-Paul Murray. *I Was a Killer for the Hells Angels: The Story of Serge Quesnal.* McClelland & Stewart, 2003.

McCusker, Michael Patrick, A.K.A.: Irish Mike. *A Road Without End: The JUS BROTHERS Motorcycle Club, 1990–2007.* PublishAmerica, 2008.

Menginie, Anthony "LT," and Kerrie Droban. *Prodigal Father, Pagan Son: Growing Up Inside the Dangerous World of the Pagans Motorcycle Club.* Thomas Dunne Books, 2011.

Reynolds, Frank, as told to Michael McClure. *Freewheelin Frank: Secretary of the Angels.* Grove Press, 1967. Out of Print.

DeLeone, Arturo Rossenaldo Romero (Alias "Cat Daddy"). *Motorcycle Gangster "PURO VIDA": Stories & Poetry of Life, True Love, Champagne and Rock & Roll.* Red Lead Press, 2010.

Sadgirl, *The Other Side of the Fence: Love, Loyalty, Respect, Betrayal: A Woman in the Motorcycle Club World.* Outskirts Press, 2010.

Saxon, Kurt. *Wheels of Rage: The True Story of the Iron Cross Motorcycle Club.* Atlan Formularies, 1974.

Senia, Parco. *Blessed with Evil: A Story of the Hells Angels and the Evil Spirits Motorcycle Clubs.* iUniverse, Inc., 2007.

Wethern, George, and Vincent Colnett. *A Wayward Angel: The Full Story of the Hells Angels.* 1978. 2nd edition, The Lyons Press, 2008.

Winterhalder, Edward. *Out in Bad Standings: Inside the Bandidos Motorcycle Club—The Making of a Worldwide Dynasty.* Blockhead City Press/Seven Locks, 2005.

Winterhalder, Edward, and Wil De Clercq. *The Assimilation: Rock Machine Become Bandidos—Bikers United Against the Hells Angels.* ECW Press, 2008.

Wolf, Daniel R. *The Rebels: A Brotherhood of Outlaw Bikers.* University of Toronto Press, Scholarly Publishing Division, 1991.

Zito, Chuck, and Joe Layden. *Street Justice.* St. Martin's Griffin, 2003.

The earliest story in this category is George Wethern's *A Wayward Angel*, written by a former Oakland Hells Angels vice president. Wethern's story begins as he joins the club shortly after the Oakland chapter was established in 1957 and concludes with events following his arrest and incarceration in 1972. What began with a young man's interest in motorcycles, adventure, and the lure of brotherhood offered in MC life transitioned into major drug trafficking and a murder that finally forced Wethern to choose between a life behind bars or betraying his club. He chose betrayal: he went into a witness protection program and wrote his story— the first, but certainly not the last, in a long series of "befriend and betray" scenarios.

Frank Reynolds told his more positive story in *Freewheelin Frank: Secretary of the Angels*. Reynolds became a member of the 'Frisco Hells Angels in 1961. His story gives the reader a realistic account of what it was like to have been a one percenter during the early years of the Hells Angels. Reynolds captures the essence of the lifestyle that has lured young men and women away from stable and boring society into the devil-may-care world of bikes, booze, and broads.

One of the best autobiographies written on MC life is Sonny Barger's *Hell's Angel: The Life and Times of Sonny Barger and the Hell's Angels Motorcycle Club*. Barger may not have been the first to use the term "1%er," but he certainly solidified the *mark* as applied to outlaw motorcycle clubs. In contrast to Thompson's *Hell's Angels*, which offers only a thin chronological slice of the long HAMC history, Barger's book spans several decades and provides a perspective of how this one percent MC evolved. Reviews of this book are a mixed bag, not so much about the story that's told, but as to whether the club's members are choir boys or villains. As Sonny has explained on several occasions, the HAMC is not a criminal organization. Even though every member wears the same patch, each member has his own life and makes his own choices. At least Barger's *Life and Times* offers a counterpoint to the investigative and police reporting titles of authors like Yves Lavigne.

Sonny has written several other books that may not have the impact of his autobiography but are still worthwhile reads. *Freedom: Credos from the Road* and *Let's Ride* are more philosophy than autobiography. The charm in these books is their liberal doses of Barger's views on life and riding. My favorite *credos* from *Freedom* are: "Early is on time; on time is late," "If you want to travel fast, travel light," and the best, "Treat me good, I'll treat you better. Treat me bad, I'll treat you worse." *Let's Ride* contains Sonny's philosophy on motorcycles and safety. This book should be required reading for a novice rider serious about learning to survive the kamikaze sorties that cagers continually direct toward motorcyclists.

Many other clubs are represented in the autobiographical section by its members: John Hall's *Riding on the Edge*, chronicling Hall's life with the Pagans MC in the 1960s, is well written and paints an excellent picture of the early rough-and-tumble lives of one percenters. Bill Hayes' *The Original Wild Ones: Tales of the Boozefighters Motorcycle Club*; Tobie Gene Levingston's *Soul on Bikes*; Kurt Saxon's *Wheels of Rage: The Story of the Iron Cross Motorcycle Club*; and Michael Patrick McCusker's *A Road Without End: The Jus Brothers Motorcycle Club* are all books that present a good cross-section of club life in very different eras.

And we can throw *Street Justice*, an autobiography from Chuck Zito, a former very high-profile member of the Hells Angels, in there, too. Hayes' *Tales of the Boozefighters MC* has been routinely well-reviewed and has become very popular. This book is not so much a history of the Boozefighters MC as a compilation of stories about the early days of this legendary club. The early days, in this case, are 1946 through the early 1950s. The Boozefighters' book focuses on the members and their motorcycle adventures and provides an excellent accounting of the 1947 Hollister "riot" that got the whole biker thing started.

Tobie Gene's *Soul on Bikes* describes his life as President of the East Bay Dragons, a Black MC with the same geographic roots as the Oakland Hells Angels. The Dragons built and rode chopped Harleys alongside the Oakland Hells Angels; they rode the same "mean streets" and always seemed to maintain good relationships with other clubs.

For a glimpse at Hells Angels club life on the East Coast, Zito's book comes well recommended. Originally a member of the Ching-a-Ling MC, Zito joined the HAMC, fought in the New York Golden Gloves, and was a bodyguard to Liza Minnelli and Mickey Rourke. Zito left the Angels after twenty-five years to focus on his acting career. He had a continuing role in the HBO prison drama *Oz*.

Daniel Wolf's *The Rebels: A Brotherhood of Outlaw Bikers* is a Thompson-esque approach at doing a study from more-or-less the inside. But Thompson was up-front with the Angels back in the 1960s—he was writing a book about them. Wolf was doing the same, but he tried to come in "undercover," by prospecting for the Canadian Rebels (or "striking" as they say way up north). He eventually told the truth and interestingly enough was allowed to stay and actually finish the book.

Two final authors listed in the autobiographical section are Ruben "Doc" Cavazos with *Honor Few, Fear None: The Life and Times of a Mongol* and Edward "Connecticut Ed" Winterhalder with two books: the first, *Out in Bad Standings: Inside the Bandidos Motorcycle Club—The Making of a Worldwide Dynasty*; and the second, *The Assimilation: Rock Machine Becomes Bandidos—Bikers United Against the Hells Angels*. These authors have at least one thing in common: They were both high-ranking officers within their respective clubs and they both left their clubs in bad standing.

Cavazos' story describes his rise to power in the Mongols MC following the Laughlin River Run incident in April 2002. As the International President of the Mongols MC, Doc was responsible for recruiting "street gang members" into the Mongols. He was voted out of the club in 2008 with allegations that he was stealing from the club and provoking a war with the Mexican Mafia. Less than two months later, Doc was arrested and convicted of racketeering charges. He currently faces up to twenty years in federal prison.

Winterhalder was a member of the Rogues MC before he joined the Bandidos and established a chapter in Oklahoma. He quickly rose through the ranks of the Bandidos and was heavily involved in the assimilation of the Rock Machine MC into the Bandidos in 2001. The two books cited in this section focus on his time with the Bandidos and his involvement with the Canadian Bandidos chapters. After leaving the Bandidos in bad standing, Winterhalder wrote several books about life in one percent MCs and is credited with being the executive producer of a television series, *Biker Chicz*. The series began shooting in June 2010 and, according to Winterhalder, will offer a far different perspective than shows like *Sons of Anarchy* and *Gangland*. *Biker Chicz* is intended "to capture the true nature of bikers, their spirit, and the Harley lifestyle" (yeah, right!).

✝

OBSERVATIONAL

Barker, Thomas. *Biker Gangs and Organized Crime*. Anderson, 2007.

Bowe, Barry, *Born to Be Wild*. Grand Central Publishing, 1994.

Detroit, Michael. *Chain of Evidence: A True Story of Law Enforcement and One Woman's Bravery*. Dutton Books, 1994.

Dicks, Shirley. *Road Angels: Women Who Ride Motorcycles*. Writers Club Press, 2002.

Gauss, James F. *Bond Slaves: Confessions of Hard Core Bikers*. CreateSpace, 2010.

Hamma, Doug. *The Motorcycle Mamas—uncensored first-person stories of the outlaw cycle-club chicks and their wild, wild ride along the razor's edge of unbridled sex and savagery!* Venice Publishing Company, 1967.

Hayes, Bill. *American Biker: The History, The Clubs, The Lifestyle, The Truth*. Flash Productions, LLC, 2010.

Klancher, Lee, Kevin Cameron, Jack Lewis, and Hunter S. Thompson. *The Devil Can Ride: The World's Best Motorcycle Writing*. Motorbooks, 2010.

Langton, Jerry. *Showdown: How the Outlaws, Hells Angels and Cops Fought for Control of the Streets*. Wiley, 2010.

Major, Zephyros. *The Shovel Revival: A Motorcycle Manifesto*. iUniverse, Inc., 2007.

McDonald-Walker, Suzanne. *Bikers: Culture, Politics & Power*. Berg Publishers, 2000.

Nichols, Dave, and Kim Peterson. *One Percenter: The Legend of the Outlaw Biker*. Motorbooks, 2007.

Remsberg, Rich. *Riders for God: The Story of a Christian Motorcycle Gang*. University of Illinois, 2000.

Reynolds, Tom. *Wild Ride*. TV Books, 2001.

Thompson, Hunter S. *Hell's Angels: A Strange and Terrible Saga*. 1966. Revised edition, Modern Library, 1999.

Veno, Arthur. *The Brotherhoods: Inside the Outlaw Motorcycle Clubs*. 2002. Revised edition, Allen & Unwin, 2010.

Veno, Arthur. *The Mammoth Book of Bikers*. Running Press, 2007.

Winterhalder, Edward, and Arthur Veno. *Biker Chicks: The Magnetic Attraction of Women to Bad Boys and Motorbikes*. Allen & Unwin, 2009.

Zanetti, Geno. *She's a Bad Motorcycle: Writers on Riding*. 2001. Reprint, Da Capo Press, 2002.

The earliest book on this list is still one of the most epic and well known. Thompson's *Hell's Angels: A Strange and Terrible Saga*, first published in 1966, was preceded by an article he wrote, published in *The Nation* magazine in May 1965, entitled "Motorcycle Clubs: Losers and Outsiders." These two pieces not only helped launch Thompson's career, but set the bar for sensationalism that would define the world of one percent MCs for all eternity. With some arguable exceptions and his special brand of literary license thrown in, Thompson presented a fairly accurate account of the social climate—including the Angels—in the 1960s. The Bay Area pioneers of the Red and White were portrayed as quick-tempered but fun-loving, freeloading men whose central focus was building motorcycles and riding to the next big party. As strange as it might sound, this was the age of innocence for one percent MCs. The international heaviness to come was still a ways off.

One Percenter: The Legend of the Outlaw Biker by Dave Nichols focuses on the variety of roots in outlaw genealogy.

Arthur Veno's *The Mammoth Book of Bikers* is a compilation of over forty stories contributed by nearly an equal number of writers. This book would be an excellent starting place for a study of the biker culture with a focus on bike clubs. Most of the legitimate authors listed in this chapter's bibliography have contributed a chapter to the book, and Dr. Veno has done a nice job of selecting material for the book and arranging the chapters to create continuity for the reader. This author should be applauded for his attempt to portray the biker lifestyle in an unbiased manner. *The Mammoth Book* begins with chapters on the Birth of the Outlaw Biker and the Outlaw Biker Lifestyle and transitions to Old Ladies, Mammas, and Broads, before dealing with Bikers and Crime, Infamous Biker Wars and Rats, Snitches, Dogs, and Undercover Cops. Dr. Veno's *Mammoth Book of Bikers* is a volume you can keep on your nightstand and dredge out for that end-of-the-day read before you nod off for the night.

A second compilation, *The Devil Can Ride: The World's Best Motorcycle Writing* by Lee Klancher, et. al., contains several stories intended to offer the reader the very best motorcycle-related stories ever written. Although this book shouldn't be advertised as a study of one percent MCs, it does contain several chapters that describe the genre. Authors whose work is contained in the review bibliography as well as in Veno's *Mammoth Book* include: Hunter S. Thompson, Dave Nichols, John Hall, and Bill Hayes. Adele Kubin's contribution, "Grease Under the Angel's Wings," previously published in the *International Journal of Motorcycle Studies*, contains her personal account of scenes from Thompson's *Hells Angels* in which her recollection is at odds with the great Dr. Gonzo. Kubin's parting statement, made in 1979, to the one percenter family that took her in when she was eleven and treated her like their own proved to be true: *"Times were changing. On the margins, the club was being pulled down into organized crime, to drug dealing and violence directed by outsiders. Money was replacing loyalty; fear was replacing respect."* The *Devil Can Ride* is a book that will remain in my permanent collection.

The final title in this review section is Bill Hayes' *American Biker: The History, The Clubs, The Lifestyle, The Truth.* Hayes provides an intelligent and insightful look into a phenomenon that's been over a hundred years in the making. The American biker—the species not the book—wouldn't have been possible without the American motorcycle, and that's where Bill's story begins. The focus of this book is not the motorcycle itself, but how the biker lifestyle evolved out of a primordial ooze of fifty-weight oil, leaded gasoline, and the men who tinkered incessantly to maintain these mechanical beasts. This story tracks the American biker from his birth in the 1940s to where he is today. Make no mistake, being a biker in the 1940s required a much greater commitment and a lot less money than it does now.

Bill describes the evolution of the American biker using a forester's metaphor, dendrochronology, the scientific method of determining a tree's age and evaluating the good years and the bad based on the analysis of tree-ring patterns. He uses the growth ring analogy to describe four distinct periods and the influences that impacted each one. He tells the truth (*again* and quickly; the "one beer version") about the 1947 Hollister "riot" and credits the motorcycle clubs that first drew attention to the difference between bikers and motorcycle enthusiasts. He acknowledges the role that media, Hollywood, and law enforcement have had in propagating what might have been a passing fad into an American legend.

From the American biker's creation following World War II through the 1950s and 1960s, the Vietnam era, and into the twenty-first century, the reader is taken on a ride that took the original bikers a lifetime to complete.

✠

PHOTOGRAPHY AND ART

Lyon, Danny. *The Bikeriders*. Chronicle Books, 2003.

Dixon, Martin, and Greg Tate. *Brooklyn Kings: New York City's Black Bikers*. PowerHouse Books, 2000.

Mann, David. *50 Magnificent Works of Motorcycle Art from Easyriders*. Paisano Publications, 1987. (Out of Print)

Mann, David. *The Artist's Choice Collection of David Mann's Motorcycle Art*, Paisano Publications, 1993. (Out of Print)

Mann, David. *David Mann's Motorcycle Masterpieces*. 2009. Available at www.davidmannart.com, limited supply.

Roberts, Beverly V. *Portraits of American Bikers: Life in the 1960s*. Flash Productions, LLC, 2008.

Roberts, Beverly V. *Portraits of American Bikers: Inside Looking Out*. Flash Productions, LLC, 2010.

Shaylor, Andrew, with a foreword by Sonny Barger. *Hells Angels Motorcycle Club*. 2005. Revised edition, Merrell, 2007.

Upright, Michael H. *One Percent*. Action Publishing, LLC, 1999.

This section provides a true change of pace, represented by a group of books that portray one percenter MCs and biker culture in its most romantic and idyllic setting.

Danny Lyon was a photographer before he joined the Outlaws MC in 1965. The *Bikeriders* is the story of his time with the Outlaws between 1965 and 1967. The book was first published in 1968 and was reissued in 2003. The majority of photographs are black and white, and a portion of the book contains interviews with several of Lyon's club brothers. Photographs presented in *The Bikeriders* accurately reflect the 1960s style in much the same way as the narrative; for example: "Anyhow, while he's sniveling down there, I'm salty, see, and I injected a shell into the chamber; I got one in the chamber now. And I said, 'You move, you dirty motherfucker, and I'll blow your cap off...'"

Photo documentaries of the Outlaws MC continue with Beverly V. Roberts' *Portraits of American Bikers: Life in the 1960s and Portraits of American Bikers: Inside Looking Out* (the first two of an eventual three-book series called The Flash Collection), as well as Michael H. Upright's *One Percent*. Both books contain only black-and-white photos.

Upright's photos were all taken between 1992 and 1995.

Robert's photos, like Lyon's, are from the 1960s. Photos in Roberts' book were shot by her father, Outlaw MC member Jim "Flash "1%" Miteff. The photo collection was kept private until after Miteff's death; a promise he made to his Outlaw club brothers. Therefore, the book contains never-before-seen images taken from original negatives that had been in storage for over forty years. . . a virtual time capsule preserved for this generation.

Martin Dixon (photos) and Greg Tate's (essay) book, *Brooklyn Kings: New York City's Black Bikers* is the only selection in this section that focuses on Black MCs. The title doesn't reflect a specific club, but refers to a group of clubs. This photo-essay provides a true-life, what-you-see-is-what-you-get view of Black bike clubs in and around New York City.

Hells Angels Motorcycle Club by Andrew Shaylor contains photos of members from Great Britain and European chapters. Sonny Barger offers the foreword; the book contains over three hundred photographs; and, as you'd expect, is a quality publication. The book is truly impressive, but you may be a little disappointed that it doesn't focus on members of the U.S. HAMC chapters. To my knowledge, no such book currently exists, leaving those of us looking for high-quality photos of Hells Angels to collect yearly calendars containing the work of New York member Steve Bonge.

No review of photography and biker art would be complete without a reference to the contributions of David Mann. Mann spent the majority of his life producing paintings that reflect scenes that bikers can relate to in their own lives. Rides, parties, breakdowns, women, and how custom bike styles changed through the years—Dave Mann captured it all. Three books containing his art are included in this review. The two out-of-print books by Paisano Publications were large-format coffee table books with a paper cover that contained the centerfold art published in *Easyriders* magazine beginning in about 1972. Dave's monthly contributions to *Easyriders* continued through the decades until his death in 2004. A third collection of his work is still available, although in limited supply, through the David Mann Art website. Dave was inducted into the Motorcycle Hall of Fame in Pickering, Ohio, the same year as his death.

✠

INVESTIGATIVE AND POLICE REPORTING

Anonymous. *An Inside Look At Outlaw Motorcycle Gangs*. Paladin Press, 1992.

BackgroundNow Staff. *USA V The Mongols Outlaw Motorcycle Gang: Two Federal Indictments And Dozens Arrested, The USA's Efforts To Dismantle The Mongols*. CreateSpace, 2008.

Caine, Alex. *Befriend and Betray: Infiltrating the Hells Angels, Bandidos, and Other Criminal Brotherhoods*. Thomas Dunne Books, 2009.

Caine, Alex. *The Fat Mexican: The Bloody Rise of the Bandidos Motorcycle Club*. 2009. Reprint edition, Vintage Canada, 2010.

Coulthart, Ross, and Duncan McNab. *Dead Man Running: An Insider's Story on One of the World's Most Feared Outlaw Motorcycle Gangs...The Bandidos*. Allen & Unwin, 2008.

Dobyns, Jay, and Nils Johnson-Shelton. *No Angel: My Harrowing Undercover Journey to the Inner Circle of the Hells Angels*. Crown, 2009.

Droban, Kerrie, *Running with the Devil: The True Story of the ATF's Infiltration of the Hells Angels*. The Lyons Press, 2008.

Langton, Jerry. *Fallen Angel: The Unlikely Rise of Walter Stadnick and the Canadian Hells Angels*. Wiley, 2006.

Lavigne, Yves. *Hell's Angels: Three Can Keep a Secret If Two Are Dead*. 1987. Carol Publishing Group Edition, Lyle Stuart, 2000.

Lavigne, Yves. *Good Guy, Bad Guy*. 1991. 11th edition, Ballantine Books, 1993.

Lavigne, Yves. *Hell's Angels: Into the Abyss*. HarperTorch, 1996.

Lavigne, Yves. *Death Dealers: A Witness to the Drug Wars That Are Bleeding America*. HarperCollins Publishers, 1999.

Lavigne, Yves. *Hell's Angels: Taking Care of Business*. Seal Books, 2000.

Lavigne, Yves. *Hells Angels at War*. HarperCollins, 2004.

Mallory, Stephen L. *Understanding Organized Crime (Criminal Justice Illuminated)*. Jones & Bartlett Publishers, 2007.

Miller, Frederic P., Agnes F. Vandome, and John McBrewster. *Highwaymen Motorcycle Club*. Alphascript Publishing, 2011.

Miller, Frederic P., Agnes F. Vandome, and John McBrewster, *Mongols Motorcycle Club*. Alphascript Publishing, 2011.

Miller, Frederic P., Agnes F. Vandome, and John McBrewster, *Rebels Motorcycle Club*. Alphascript Publishing, 2011.

Miller, Frederic P., Agnes F. Vandome, and John McBrewster, *The Breed Motorcycle Club*. Alphascript Publishing, 2011.

O'Deanne, Matthew. *Gang Investigator's Handbook: A Law-Enforcement Guide to Identifying and Combating Violent Street Gangs*. Paladin Press, 2008.

Queen, William. *Under and Alone: The True Story of the Undercover Agent Who Infiltrated America's Most Violent Outlaw Motorcycle Gang*. Ballantine Books, 2007.

Sher, Julian, and William Marsden. *Angels of Death: Inside the Biker Gangs' Crime Empire*. 2006. Illustrated edition, Da Capo Press, 2007.

Sher, Julian, and William Marsden. *The Road to Hell: How the Biker Gangs Are Conquering Canada*. Seal Books, 2005.

Timpledon, Lambert M., Miriam T. Markseken, and Susan F. Surhone. *Outlaws Motorcycle Club*. Betascript Publishing, 2010.

Timpledon, Lambert M., Miriam T. Markseken, and Susan F. Surhone. *Sons of Anarchy Motorcycle Club.* Betascript Publishing, 2010.

Timpledon, Lambert M., Miriam T. Markseken, and Susan F. Surhone. *Warlocks Motorcycle Club.* Alphascript Publishing, 2010.

Valentine, Bill. *Gang Intelligence Manual: Identifying and Understanding Modern-Day Violent Gangs in the United States.* Paladin Press, 1995.

Vandome, Frederic P., Agnes F. McBrewster, and John Miller. *List of Outlaw Motorcycle Clubs.* Alphascript Publishing, 2010.

Law enforcement's view of one percent MCs comprise the largest number of entries in this review. These books are contained in two bibliography sections: the first, Investigative and Police Reporting and the second, Wikipedia Summaries.

The Investigative and Police Reporting section contains the real meat of law enforcements view of one percent MCs. These titles run the gamut from the ridiculous "manual," *An Inside Look at Outlaw Motorcycle Gangs* by Paladin Press to Yves Lavigne's early exposé directed primarily towards the Hells Angels; William Queen's infiltration of the Mongols; Alex Caine's infiltration of organizations ranging from the Ku Klux Klan to the Russian Mafia to the Hells Angels and the Bandidos; and Jay Dobyns infiltration of the Arizona Hells Angels.

And there's a lot of commonality within so many of the plot lines. It's almost template-like, as the stories begin with supposedly upstanding cops or citizens who befriend a group of alleged bad guys with the intentions of single-handedly bringing their entire organization down. In the course of the investigation, millions in taxpayer dollars are spent, and the infiltrators live underground long enough for their allegiances to shift toward who they're trying to bust. Generally, the case handlers pull the plug on the investigation when they suspect they're losing control of the infiltrators and bust as many members as they can. The media makes a big to-do over the busts, lawyers bail out the bad guys, and sooner or later, the bad guys go to trial. Most of the cases are thrown out because law enforcement has bungled the evidence or has entrapped the bad guys. The cops or rats or professional snitches lose their families, move to B.F. Egypt, and sleep with a pistol under their pillow, knowing it's just a matter of time before the bad guys hunt them down and exact their revenge. That's the theme.

But each does possess its own unique twists.

And some are very well written from a purely technical standpoint.

But then again, some aren't...

An Inside Look at Outlaw Motorcycle Gangs is a law-enforcement training manual used in a course called Dangerous Motorcycle Gangs. It contains an opening statement by the late Republican Senator Strom Thurmond, made before the committee on the judiciary referencing organized crime hearings. The Honorable Senator from South Carolina concluded that outlaw gangs were using a portion of their profits from criminal activities to invest in legal businesses that included ice cream shops. Ice cream shops, indeed—my reaction exactly. No wonder an old Hells Angel told me the feds always seemed to him like they were fifty-one cards short of a deck.

The most prolific contributor to the investigative and police reporting genre is Canadian author Yves Lavigne. *Hell's Angels: Into the Abyss* is probably Lavigne's best work. He tells Anthony Tait's story, from his childhood (he was definitely a product of poor parenting) through his voluntary decision to become an FBI informant.

Tait stumbles onto the Anchorage chapter of the Hells Angels and is recruited into the club, even though he's never ridden a motorcycle. Shortly after earning his patch in 1982, following what must have been a cake-walk prospect period, he decides to become an informant. His handlers finance his activities and he begins traveling on taxpayer dollars doing things for the club that ingratiate him and enhance his standing.

He gains the trust of the West Coast Hells Angels and turns that trust into entrapment. His efforts continue through 1987 when the feds finally issue warrants and arrest members in several states. Charges ranged from conspiracy to commit murder to drug manufacturing and sales to possession of illegal weapons.

Sonny Barger did fifty-nine months in federal correction facilities for his alleged murder conspiracy. Kenny Owens was sentenced to forty-one years in custody and fined over two million bucks. But if the intent was to break the back of the Hells Angels, it didn't work. Sonny was released from prison in 1993 to a hero's homecoming, and even during his absence life went on within the Hells Angels. Tait disappeared with a quarter-million dollars in bonus money (again from U.S. taxpayers) but still shows up occasionally as an expert on the TV series *Gangland*.

None of the remaining titles written by Lavigne come near to the story of Tony Tait, so buyer beware.

Alex Caine has two titles in the investigative reporting category: *Befriend* and *Betray and The Fat Mexican*. Alex Caine, if that's his real name, must be one of the best professional rats of all time. He successfully worked his way into several organizations and lived to tell about it.

Now that his career as an infiltrator has come to an end, he's transitioned to a writer. In *Befriend and Betray*, Alex offers a first-person account of an ambush orchestrated by the feds just before the 2002 Laughlin River Run. He describes a gun battle between the feds, who are disguised as members of the Mongols MC, and a pack of Hells Angels. If this account is true, it suggests that the feds were actually responsible for stirring the pot between the two clubs just prior to the late-night melee in Harrah's Casino.

It's quite an interesting suspicion.

Alex Caine's writing can only be recommended to readers who have a particular interest in the organizations he claims to have infiltrated.

William Queen's story, *Under and Alone*, describes events beginning in 1998 that unfolded during a two-year infiltration and investigation of the Mongols MC.

Queen, an ATF agent, used a local snitch to gain an introduction to the Mongols and parlayed that introduction into a long hangaround and prospect process before gaining membership in the club. Throughout the investigation, the club's Sergeant at Arms, Red Dog, had strong suspicions that Queen was a cop. The undercover agent held his ground every time Red Dog confronted him and, eventually, against Red Dog's counsel, earned his patch.

Once inside the club, Queen was privy to the criminal comings and goings of not only his chapter but the entire Mongols Nation. Unlike the work of Yves Lavigne and Alex Caine, Queen avoids over-dramatizing the actual events or making moral judgments about the men he was investigating. He maintained his professionalism and seldom wavered from his duty as an ATF agent, even though he had become friends with many of his club "brothers."

A total of fifty Mongols were prosecuted as a result of Queen's infiltration. He became an immediate hero within the law enforcement community and was awarded, among other honors, the 2001 Federal Bar Association's Medal of Valor.

The consequences of Queen's life undercover included loss of the friendships he'd established with Mongols members who *weren't* associated with criminal activities, separation from his children, and retirement from the ATF.

He relocated from California in an effort to protect his identity from Mongol retaliation. Although the Mongol organization was damaged by these arrests and subsequent convictions, the club remained much the same as it had been before the investigation. Two years following these arrests was the Mongols' clash with the Hells Angels at the annual Laughlin River Run. Soon after Laughlin, under the leadership of the now-deposed Doc Cavazos, the Mongols expanded once again.

At least two books have been written about the 2001–2002 investigation/infiltration of the Arizona Hells Angels. The first-person account of this investigation is Jay "Bird" Dobyns' story, *No Angel*. The second book, by former federal prosecutor now criminal defense attorney and author Kerrie Droban called *Running with the Devil*, is her account of the same investigation conducted by Jay Dobyns. Of the two books, Dobyns' is definitely the strongest, probably because it was written from an insider's perspective. Droban is a legitimate "true crime" author whose current day job is defending the alleged criminals she writes about at night.

Dobyns' story offers a chronology of how he successfully infiltrated the Hells Angels by fabricating membership in the legitimate Tijuana, Mexico-based Solo Angeles, a club established in 1959. It's amazing that Dobyns' cover wasn't blown by a cautious Hells Angel who could easily have gone to the Solo Angeles to check Dobyns' bona fides. But that didn't happen, and the investigation went forward.

After two years involvement with the HAMC, the ATF finally made their busts; most of the subsequent prosecutions fell apart. The majority of the charges levied against members were minor (possession of body armor, felons in possession of firearms, or firearm sales without a license) and several of them were dismissed with prejudice and cannot be re-filed. Two Hells Angels were convicted of drug trafficking and one turned state's evidence to avoid prosecution on a murder charge. He's alleged to currently be in the witness protection program. The member who vouched for Dobyns is no longer in the club. Two members were connected with a 2001 murder charge that occurred before Dobyns and his team gained momentum in their investigation. The first Hells Angel charged with this murder was Paul Eischeid who remained a fugitive for eight years until he was arrested in Argentina on February 3, 2011. The second, Kevin Augustiniak, went to court on murder charges and is currently listed on the Mesa, Arizona, HAMC chapter's website as being in jail.

☩

FICTION

Arobateau, Red Jordan. *The Black Biker*. Rosebud Books, 1998.

Ball, K.Randall. *Harbor Town Seduction*. 5-Ball Inc., 2010.

Barger, Ralph "Sonny". *Dead in 5 Heartbeats*. Harper-Torch, 2004.

Barger, Ralph "Sonny," Keith Zimmerman, and Kent Zimmerman. *Ridin' High, Livin' Free: Hell-Raising Motorcycle Stories*. Harper Paperbacks, 2003.

Danielsen, Dale. *The Seahorses: The Motorcycle Club*. Bookstand Publishing, 2009.

Gardner, Mary, *Salvation Run*. University Press of Mississippi September 7, 2005.

Jamiol, Paul. *Bikers Are Animals: A Children's Book on Motorcycling*. Dog Ear Publishing, 2009.

Jamiol, Paul. *Bikers Are Animals 2: The Rest of the Crew*. Dog Ear Publishing, 2010.

Langton, Jerry. *Biker: Inside the Notorious World of an Outlaw Motorcycle Gang*. Wiley, 2009.

Quinn, Peyton. *Dog Soldiers MC*. Outskirts Press, 2006.

Solari, J.J. *When Bikers Meet Humans*. Tapcab, 2007.

Winterhalder, Edward, and James Richard Larson. *The Mirror: A Biker's Story*. Blockhead City Press, 2010.

There are several titles in the fiction category by authors who've also published in non-fiction: Sonny Barger, Jerry Langton, and Edward Winterhalder.

If you're a serious student attempting to understand one percenter MCs, this category probably won't offer much value. If you're just looking for some light reading, you should at least take a look at Sonny's *Ridin' High and Livin' Free*. It contains a collection of short stories, all tales of bikes, rides, and riders.

The same goes for Keith Ball's *Harbor Town Seduction*. Keith is a Motorcycle Hall of Fame member and was Editor of *Easyriders* magazine for a couple of decades. While not exactly focused on motorcycle club activities, *Harbor Town Seduction* is kind of a Dave Mann biker-perfect portrait in words.

And maybe the most unique selections on all these lists are Paul Jamiol's children's books, the first two of the *Bikers Are Animals* series. These really *are* club-oriented, with a fuzzy cast of characters who are all a part of the Bears MC. The members make for an interesting take on the overworked old pejorative, "bikers are animals." These guys are indeed animals—real ones!—and they give kids a positive, healthy, and even didactic outlook on the biker culture.

✠

MISCELLANEOUS

Barbieri, Jay, and Michele Smith. *Biker's Handbook: Becoming Part of the Motorcycle Culture.* Motorbooks, 2007.

Gagan, Peter. *Antique Motorcycle Club: Fifty Years of Fun!* Turner Publishing Company, 2005.

Kennedy, Daniel. *Directory of Motorcycle Clubs and Associations 1989–90.* Whitehorse Press, 1989.

Mullins, Sasha. *Bikerlady: Living and Riding Free!* Citadel, 2003.

Osgerby, Bill. *Biker: Truth and Myth: How the Original Cowboy of the Road Became the Easy Rider of the Silver Screen.* The Lyons Press, 2005.

Peebles, Gypsy. *Chopper Bike Club—Motorcycle Gang (How to Form a Club).* (Out of Circulation).

Seate, Mike. *Two Wheels on Two Reels: A History of Biker Movies.* Whitehorse Press, 2001.

Smedman, Lisa. *From Boneshakers to Choppers: The Rip-Roaring History of Motorcycles.* Annick Press, 2007.

Yates, Brock. *Outlaw Machine: Harley-Davidson and the Search for the American Soul.* Broadway, 2000.

The above batch of books may not center on the one percenter culture *exactly*, but they do all touch it in various ways. With subjects that include the biker movies we've all seen, to a woman's perspective on things, to Brock Yates' nice survey of the lifestyle, there is plenty of info that may not be chock-full of revelations and secrets but for the most part, they are at least fun.

✠

WIKIPEDIA SUMMARIES

Books Group. *Gangs in Detroit, Michigan: Black Mafia Family, Chaldean mafia, Los Zetas, Outlaws Motorcycle Club, Mara Salvatrucha, Crip.* Books LLC, 2010.

LLC Books. *Athenian Democracy: Outlaw Motorcycle Club.* Books LLC.

LLC Books. *Fictional Gangs: Sons of Anarchy Motorcycle Club, List of Gangs in the Warriors, List of Fictional Gangs, Blood Syndicate.* Books LLC.

LLC Books. *Gangs by Type: Bicycle Gangs, Drug Cartels, Fictional Gangs, Historical Gangs, Organized Crime Gangs, Outlaw Gangs, Outlaw Motorcycle Clubs.* Books LLC.

LLC Books. *Gangs in Arizona: Bandidos, Hells Angels, Los Zetas, Mongols, Devils Diciples, Black P. Stones, Vagos Motorcycle Club, La Raza Nation.* Books LLC.

LLC Books. *Gangs in Arkansas: Bandidos, Outlaws Motorcycle Club, Crips, Bloods, Dixie Mafia, Black P. Stones, Almighty Vice Lord Nation, Black Disciples.* Books LLC.

LLC Books. *Gangs in Australia: Rocks Push, Bandidos, Hells Angels, Outlaws Motorcycle Club, Gypsy Joker Motorcycle Club, Bra Boys, Dlasthr.* Books LLC.

LLC Books. *Gangs in Belgium: Bandidos, Hells Angels, Outlaws Motorcycle Club, Nijvel Gang, Blue Angels Motorcycle Club, Sun Yee On.* Books LLC.

LLC Books. *Gangs in California: Aryan Brotherhood, Hells Angels, Los Zetas, Mexican Mafia, Sure os, Nuestra Familia, Gypsy Joker Motorcycle Club, Mongols.* Books LLC.

LLC Books. *Gangs in Canada: Bandidos, Hells Angels, Latin Kings, Outlaws Motorcycle Club, Crips, etas, Mongols, Aboriginal Based Organized Crime.* Books LLC.

LLC Books. *Gangs in Chicago, Illinois: Hells Angels, Latin Kings, Chicago Outfit, Outlaws Motorcycle Club, Los Zetas, North Side Gang, Almighty Saints.* Books LLC.

LLC Books. *Gangs in Colorado: Bandidos, Hells Angels, Outlaws Motorcycle Club, Mongols, Black P. Stones, Sons of Silence.* Books LLC.

LLC Books. *Gangs in England: Bandidos, Hells Angels, Gun Crime in South Manchester, Outlaws Motorcycle Club, Clerkenwell Crime Syndicate, Devils Diciples.* Books LLC.

LLC Books. *Gangs in Florida: Outlaws Motorcycle Club, Dominicans Don't Play, Mongols, Black P. Stones, Warlocks Motorcycle Club, Trafficante Crime Family.* Books LLC.

LLC Books. *Gangs in France: Bandidos, Bonnot Gang, Hells Angels, Outlaws Motorcycle Club, Gang Des Postiches, Unione Corse, Hammerskins, Sun Yee On.* Books LLC.

LLC Books. <*Gangs in Germany: Bandidos, Hells Angels, Outlaws Motorcycle Club, Gypsy Joker Motorcycle Club, Warlocks Motorcycle Club, 36 Boys.* Books LLC.

LLC Books. *Gangs in Illinois: Hells Angels, Latin Kings, Outlaws Motorcycle Club, Devils Diciples, Black P. Stones, Almighty Vice Lord Nation.* Books LLC.

LLC Books. *Gangs in Italy: Bandidos, Hells Angels, Outlaws Motorcycle Club, etas, Mongols, Hammerskins.* Books LLC.

LLC Books. *Gangs in Louisiana: Bandidos, New Orleans Crime Family, Dixie Mafia, Black P. Stones, Sons of Silence.* Books LLC.

LLC Books. *Gangs in Maryland: Hells Angels, Pagans Motorcycle Club, Black P. Stones, Iron Horsemen, Sex Money Murda, Dead Man Incorporated.* Books LLC.

LLC Books. *Gangs in Michigan: Outlaws Motorcycle Club, Devils Diciples, Almighty Vice Lord Nation, Highwaymen Motorcycle Club, Mickey Cobras.* Books LLC.

LLC Books. *Gangs in Nevada: Bandidos, Hells Angels, Mongols, 311 Boyz, Vagos Motorcycle Club.* Books LLC.

LLC Books. *Gangs in New Jersey: Hells Angels, Latin Kings, Decavalcante Crime Family, Outlaws Motorcycle Club, Dominicans Don't Play.* Books LLC.

LLC Books. *Gangs in New York: Hells Angels, Latin Kings, Outlaws Motorcycle Club, Pagans Motorcycle Club, Mongols, Black P. Stones.* Books LLC.

LLC Books. *Gangs in Norway: Bandidos, Hells Angels, Outlaws Motorcycle Club, Gypsy Joker Motorcycle Club, Original Gangsters.* Books LLC.

LLC Books. *Gangs in Ohio: Hells Angels, Outlaws Motorcycle Club, Pagans Motorcycle Club, Devils Diciples, Black P. Stones, Warlocks Motorcycle Club.* Books LLC.

LLC Books. *Gangs in Oklahoma: Bandidos, Outlaws Motorcycle Club, Wild Bunch, Mongols, Rufus Buck Gang.* Books LLC.

LLC Books. *Gangs in Oregon: Hells Angels, Gypsy Joker Motorcycle Club, Volksfront, Mongols, Vagos Motorcycle Club, Brother Speed, European Kindred.* Books LLC.

LLC Books. *Gangs in Philadelphia, Pennsylvania: Outlaws Motorcycle Club, Philadelphia Crime Family, Mara Salvatrucha, Black Mafia, Pagans Motorcycle Club.* Books LLC.

LLC Books. *Gangs in Scotland: Blue Angels Motorcycle Club, List of Gangs in Glasgow, Wo Shing Wo, Sun Yee On, Moss-Trooper, Tongland, Penny Mobs.* Books LLC.

LLC Books. *Gangs in the United Kingdom: Gangs in Scotland, Blue Angels Motorcycle Club, List of Gangs in Glasgow, Wo Shing Wo, Sun Yee On, Moss-Trooper.* Books LLC.

LLC Books. *Gangs in the United States: Bandidos, Hells Angels, Latin Kings, Chaldean Mafia, Outlaws Motorcycle Club, Dominicans Don't Play.* Books LLC.

LLC Books. *Gangs in Washington (U.S. State): Bandidos, Hells Angels, Gypsy Joker Motorcycle Club, Brother Speed, Free Souls Motorcycle Club.* Books LLC.

LLC Books. *Mongols (Motorcycle Club): Jesse Ventura, Mongols, William Queen, Ruben Cavazos, Under and Alone, Operation Black Rain, River Run Riot.* Books LLC.

LLC Books. *Motorcycle Clubs: South Bay Riders.* Books LLC.

LLC Books. *Motorcycling Subculture: Outlaw Motorcycle Club.* Books LLC.

LLC Books. *Outlaw Motorcycle Clubs: Bandidos, Hells Angels, Outlaw Motorcycle Club, Outlaws Motorcycle Club, Pagans Motorcycle Club.* Books LLC.

Timpledon, Lambert M., Miriam T. Markseken, and Susan F. Surhone. *Pagans Motorcycle Club,* Betascript Publishing, 2010.

The Wikipedia summaries are kind of a separate world unto themselves—certainly they are more reference material than compelling reading with brilliantly stimulating writing, but they are valuable. What they do is to excerpt material available through Wikipedia's online encyclopedia into book format.

These reviews take the drudgery out of compiling information from online searches, by providing summaries of street gangs, organized crime groups, and motorcycle clubs in various locations, state by state in the U.S., and by countries including Australia, Belgium, Canada, England, France, Germany, Italy, Norway, Scotland, and the United Kingdom. This category also contains entries for fictional gangs including the Sons of Anarchy, and a volume containing gangs by type including Bicycle Gangs, Drug Cartels, Organized Crime, and Outlaw Motorcycle Clubs.

Owning a complete set of these books might be valuable to someone—maybe law enforcement—but from my perspective, I think buying any of them would be a waste of money. Stick with the online version and realize that even what you're getting there is just *somebody's* basic background on each subject.

✠

SUMMARY

Recent years have seen a rise in the number of books that portray motorcycle club life with a balance that was a long time coming.

Autobiographical works from authors who lived the life and have the ability to effectively communicate their stories is what the majority of readers will be interested in reading in the future. *The One Percenter Encyclopedia* lists so many clubs that have so many members who *each* have stories yet to be told. The best of these stories will be the ones that convey a positive message about the brotherhood that motorcycle clubs offer to those committed to living their lives on two wheels.

SOURCE NOTES & ACKNOWLEDGEMENTS

A book like this isn't written; it's assembled like a complex machine. No one person is capable of fabricating each and every part, slow-grinding it to a fine tolerance, and then fastening it into its precise place.

This labor has required more than just a team and the biker lifestyle takes that team concept well into another level—the level of brotherhood. Everyone involved with this book has had to understand love, respect, and trust to a degree that the rest of society could learn from.

The information, thoughts, personal commentaries, facts, legends, anecdotes, and everything else in this book came from a shitload of sources. There were the basic dry utilitarian wells: websites, books, periodicals—stuff like that. But then there were the phone calls. The bikes rolling into the driveway. The knocks at the door. The random meetings somewhere (out comes the recorder!).

There were the friends of friends and the true brothers who were there to help—right now. *What do you need? No problem!*

There were the intercontinental emails and phone calls. There were translations. There was brotherhood with no borders.

But there were also the "no, thank yous." And the "we don't want to be in any books!"

All of that is part of this lifestyle, and this potent mix pours into a pretty strong taste of the one percent of things represented between these covers. And none of it could have been rolled together without the help of the following:

The editorial wizardry, love, and dedication of my talented teammate, Jennifer Thomas; and the ideas and patient push of Darwin Holmstrom.

The "I'm-right-there-when-I'm-needed" hands-on brotherhood help of Felicia Morgan, Gypsy Raoul, Spike (from the Hessians), Pit (from the Boozefighters Europe), and Skinz (from the Devils Diciples).

And to everyone else who contributed to The One Percenter Encyclopedia, with love and respect, my thanks: Charlie Brechtel (a true Renaissance Man!); Captain Ron (Viet Nam Vets MC); George Christie (Hells Angels MC, retired); Clay (Long March MC China); Dizzy, Uncle Jess, Knuckles, and all of the Vagos MC; Ruth Erickson; Rich "Weebles" Halmuth (Knights MC); Chris "Speed" Heaven; Hemi (Hells Angels MC Zurich); Holly (DDOL); "Hollywood" (Top Hatters MC); PJ Hyland (*Thunder Press* magazine and beyond!); John D. "Klanker"; Ken Karagozian (photographer extrodinaire!); Kevin (Boozefighters Tribute Group England); Jeff "EZJ" Kraus; Lenny (Freewheelers MC Ireland); Lil Jon (Devils Diciples MC); Lommel (Born to Be Wild MC Germany); Lompico Lyle and all of the Ghost Mountain Riders MC; Marcus7 (Gremium MC Germany); Marko (Boozefighters Europe); Bob McMillen (Yellow Jackets MC); Odd Job (Boozefighters MC Europe); Donny Petersen (Hells Angels MC Canada); Glen "Professor" Pine (Midnite Riders MC); Razor (Razorbacks MC Switzerland); Ringo (Viet Nam Vets MC); Doc Robinson (*Heavy Duty* magazine, Australia); Lindsey Robinson (a truly inspired photographer); Rogue and "Padre" Russell (The legendary Connecticut Huns MC); Ruby, James Meredith Miles, and all of the Hellbent MC; Billy Warlock (Warlocks MC); Randall Wilson (the best producer of biker documentaries there is!)

✠

Index

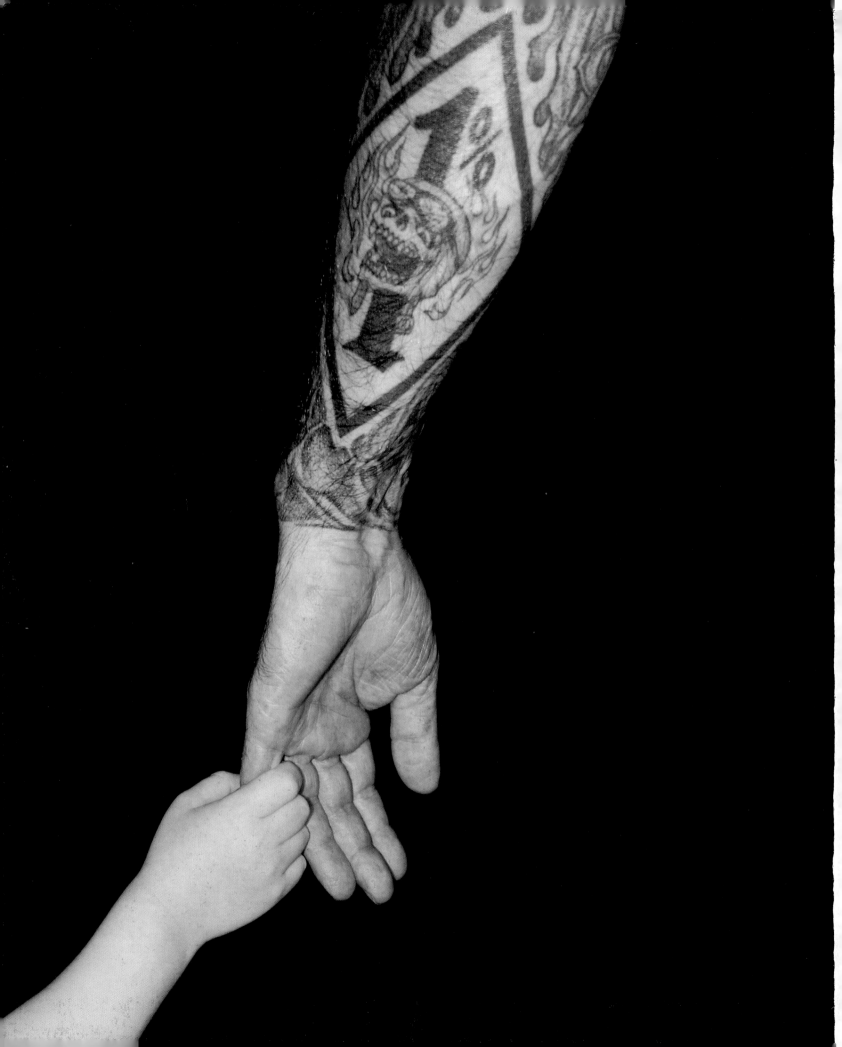